AQUINAS ON VIRTUE

AQUINAS ON VIRTUE

A CAUSAL READING

NICHOLAS AUSTIN

Georgetown University Press / Washington, DC

The publisher is not responsible for third-party websites or their content. URL links were active at time of publication.

Library of Congress Cataloging-in-Publication Data

Names: Austin, Nicholas, 1970– author.
   Title: Aquinas on Virtue : A Causal Reading / Nicholas Austin.
Description: Washington, D.C. : Georgetown University Press, 2017. | Includes
   bibliographical references and index.
Identifiers: LCCN 2016044707 (print) | LCCN 2017001329 (ebook) |
   ISBN 9781626164741 (ebook) | ISBN 9781626164727 (hc : alk. paper) |
   ISBN 9781626164734 (pb : alk. paper)
Subjects: LCSH: Thomas, Aquinas, Saint, 1225?-1274. | Virtue. | Christian ethics.
   Classification: LCC B765.T54 (ebook) | LCC B765.T54 A98 2017 (print) |
   DDC 179/.9092—dc23
LC record available at https://lccn.loc.gov/2016044707

♾ This book is printed on acid-free paper meeting the requirements of the American National Standard for Permanence in Paper for Printed Library Materials.

18 17   9 8 7 6 5 4 3 2   First printing

Printed in the United States of America
Cover design by Trudi Gershenov
Classic Image / Alamy Stock Photo

It is the sweetest note that man can singe
When grace in Vertews keye tunes natures stringe.

—Saint Robert Southwell, SJ (1561–95)

CONTENTS

ACKNOWLEDGMENTS

This project has been a long time in the making, and I am happy to have the opportunity to thank those who have made it possible.

The idea for the causal approach to virtue was born a good few years ago in my doctoral dissertation on temperance, distilled in the first chapter of this book. I owe most of all to James Keenan, whose contribution goes well beyond his wise and skillful supervision of that dissertation. Without his example, mentorship, and friendship, I would not be engaged in theological ethics today. I could not have wished for better readers and teachers than Stephen Pope and Jorge Garcia. A special thanks to Dominic Doyle and Edward Vacek for their help with my licentiate thesis on infused moral virtue, and all my teachers at Boston College, especially Lisa Cahill, Arthur Madigan, and David Hollenbach. Thanks also to my fellow doctoral students and friends: Monica, Greg and Kathryn, Amanda, Meghan, Tom and Erin, Richard and Catherine, Scott and Beth, Lila and Liz, Theodora, and many others. I am grateful to my communities of the last few years: the St. Mary's Jesuit community at Boston College, especially Mayflower House; the Jesuit community at Brixton, London; and my current community at Copleston House. The Sacred Heart community in Edinburgh were wonderful hosts during the summers as I worked on the book and took the occasional fishing trip! Many Jesuits have kept me going: Todd Kenny, Frank Clooney, Ross Romero, Tom Regan, Paul Harman, the late T. Frank Kennedy, Roger Dawson, Damian Howard, David Smolira, Michael Holman, Dermot Preston, and others. I am sad to have lost Lucas Chan, a brother Jesuit, a colleague, and a friend. Several others have kindly read drafts of parts of the book, and their feedback has strengthened the project: Gerry Hughes, Jim Keenan, Robert Deinhammer, and John Moffat. Thanks especially to Jack Mahoney for his welcome support and insights. I was blessed to work with Richard Brown from Georgetown University Press, whose patient attention to the project has greatly contributed to its final form. Ann Baker's skilled copyediting was much appreciated. Several anonymous reviewers helped me both with their encouragements and their constructive criticisms. Thanks to the members of the Association of Teachers of Moral Theology for excellent conversation. Heythrop College has been a wonderful place to teach and write theological ethics; thanks especially to Anna Abram, for her support and friendship, and to my students.

My greatest debt of gratitude is to my family. Thanks to Helen, Neil, and Paul. Lastly, thanks to my parents, Brian and Janice Austin. I can best offer my heartfelt thanks to them by repeating a favorite saying of the late Patrick Purnell, a much-loved novicemaster, to be found in the last sentence of the last chapter of this book.

NOTE ON SOURCES

Abbreviations are used for frequently cited works by Thomas Aquinas and three major interpreters of Aquinas's works. The first is Cardinal Cajetan (also known as Tommaso De Vio) (1468–1534), whose classic commentary on Aquinas's *Summa Theologiae* influenced all later interpreters, although recent Thomistic work on the virtues has yet to mine the riches of his work. The second is not an individual but a school: the Discalced Carmelites of Salamanca, Spain, whose impressive twenty-volume *Cursus Theologicus* was produced over the course of a number of decades (1631–1712). The third is John Poinsot (also known as John of St. Thomas) (1589–1644), who is currently the subject of renewed interest. I draw on both his *Cursus Philosophicus* and his incomplete *Cursus Theologicus*. See the selected bibliography for details of their works.

All translations are my own. For translations of Aquinas's works, I have checked my translations against others' when possible.

THOMAS AQUINAS

I have relied on *Corpus Thomisticum: Opera Omnia* and the Leonine edition of the *Summa Theologiae*. Citations to the *Summa Theologiae* and the *Disputed Questions on the Virtues* appear in the text; other works are referenced in the endnotes. References to the *Summa* denote part, question, article, and so on. For example, "(I.II 55.4c)" refers to the first part of the second part, question 55, article 4, body c ("corpus") of the article. "(I.II pr)" refers to the prologue to the first part of the second part. In the reference "(I.II 1.1 arg 3, ad 3)," "arg 3" refers to the third objection or *argumentum* and "ad 3" denotes the response to that objection.

Abbreviations for commonly used texts are as follows:

On the Virtues   *Questiones Disputatae on the Virtues*

Contra Gentiles   *Summa Contra Gentiles*

Comm. De Anima	*Sententia De anima*
Comm. Ethic.	*Sententia Libri Ethicorum*
Comm. Metaph.	*Sententia Libri Metaphysicae*
Comm. Physic.	*In Libros Physicorum*
De Veritate	*Questiones Disputate de Veritate*
Super Sent.	*Scriptum super libros Sententiarum*

Other Aquinas texts are noted by their full titles.

CAJETAN

References are to the Leonine edition of the *Summa Theologiae*, which includes Cajetan's commentary. For example, "(I.II 55.1 n.2)" denotes paragraph 2 of Cajetan's commentary on article I.II 55.1.

THE SALAMANCANS

References are to the *Cursus Theologicus* in the complete edition (Paris: Palme, 1870–83; originally published 1631–1712). For example, "*Cursus Theologicus,* Tract. 11, *De Bonitate et Malitia Humanorum Actuum*, Disp.1, Dub.2, n.16 (6:11)" denotes the work, book, book title, disputation, *dubium*, numbered paragraph, and volume and page number.

John Poinsot or *Joannes a Sancto Thoma* (John of St. Thomas)

References to the *Cursus Philosophicus* are to the Beato Reiser edition. For example, "*Cursus Philosophicus, Logica,* Question XVIII, *De Qualitate* (1:609–21)" denotes the work, book, question number, title, and volume and page numbers.

The excellent critical edition of the *Cursus Theologicus* by Dom Boissard of Solesmes Abbey (1931–1965) is used wherever possible. For example, "I.II, Disp.1, Art.1, n.12 (Solesmes 5:8)" denotes the first disputation on the *Prima secundae*, first article, paragraph 12, and the volume and page number. Unfortunately, as yet there is no critical edition of Disputation 13 on the *Prima secundae* and those following, including the important disputations on habits and virtues. A. Mathieu and H. Gagne (Québec: Presses universitaires Laval, 1952) did a valiant job but had to base their version on the corrupted text of the Ludovicus Vivès edition (Paris, 1886). Fortunately, there are various seventeenth-century versions now available that provide a more reliable witness to the text. I have relied especially on the two volumes edited by Diego de San Nicolás (Didacus of Alcalá), both of which were published in 1665, the year after Poinsot's death.

INTRODUCTION

Not every theological ethicist is comfortable with the oft-repeated claim that the best approach to the discipline is offered by virtue ethics. Theological ethics (moral theology, Christian ethics) can be thought of as the systematic attempt, through reasoned reflection on revelation, tradition, and human experience, to answer the question, "How should we live?" Moralists have been searching for a way to improve on the old morals manuals, too focused as they were on the freeze-frame of individual acts divorced from the narrative and relational context of human life. Catholic moral theologians see in virtue a corrective to this legalistic approach and a way to respond to the call of the Second Vatican Council for a greater focus on "the loftiness of the calling of the faithful in Christ and the obligation that is theirs of bearing fruit in charity for the life of the world."[1] In parallel, ethicists in the reform tradition argue that an "ethics of character" is necessary to account for the way a moral agent can be formed by and live out the Christian narrative. The turn to virtue therefore calls for more than an extra chapter or two in otherwise unchanged textbooks; rather, virtue has taken on "a major overhaul of the whole methodological apparatus of the discipline."[2]

The enrichment of theological ethics through virtue continues apace. Moral theologians see in virtue a way of centering the discipline on the discipleship of Jesus and of drawing out the ethical implications of scripture. Christian social ethics is now turning to virtue, both to elaborate the need for just persons and just social structures and to conceive of the ethics of institutions. Theological studies of specific virtues such as mercy, humility, and charity are enriching the conversation. And, by putting virtue to work in personal ethics, bioethics, and environmental ethics, theological ethicists have shown that virtue is not too vague to have normative implications. Above all, theological ethics has found in virtue a language that resonates deeply with human experience and with our best sense of what is worthwhile and meaningful in human life.

In the light of these advances, it is unsurprising that virtue ethics has been seen as the best approach to Christian moral reflection. The case has been put by Protestant, Catholic, and Orthodox theologians.[3] Yet many are wary of claims to have found "the" comprehensive account of morality.

Other perspectives—natural law, divine command, or relational-responsibility theories—have their own insights. To be fair to those who own the label "virtue ethicist," such inclusivity to other approaches often is intended; still, the term itself risks being misleadingly hegemonic.

We need a way to acknowledge virtue's significant contribution without overclaiming its significance. To this end, it helps to adopt from moral philosophy the distinction between "virtue ethics" and "virtue theory."[4] "Virtue ethics" is notoriously difficult to define, yet the phrase does suggest by its constituent terms an *ethics* in which virtue serves as the *basic idea* or *central focus*. Virtue ethics is most frequently presented as an alternative to deontology or consequentialism, and is therefore seen as a self-standing moral theory in which all important ideas are derived from one basic concept—namely, virtue. A virtue theory, in contrast to a virtue ethics, is an account of the nature, genesis, and role of virtue (and the virtues). It does not claim to be an autonomous ethics. The theory of virtue sits well within a more holistic and less hierarchical approach that is open to illuminating connections between virtue and other significant moral concepts, without claiming primacy for any one.

Theological ethics needs a place for virtue but also for commandments, covenant, happiness, law, and grace; it should not, then, advocate a virtue ethics. Yet, as the recent history of the discipline amply shows, a virtue theory is required as an integral and important part. This is one reason, among others, that it needs Thomas Aquinas.

WHY AQUINAS?

The philosopher Julia Annas has argued, and indeed has amply illustrated by her own work, that the classical accounts of virtue constitute our "best entry-point" into any discussion about virtue.[5] This applies to theology as well: there is no better point of entry into the theological exploration of virtue than through the accounts of Augustine, Aquinas, Erasmus, Jonathan Edwards, and other great patristic, scholastic, humanist, and reform theologians. While a healthy pluralism would not focus on Aquinas to the exclusion of others, the work of this great thirteenth-century Dominican theologian is especially influential and presents a systematic virtue theory of singular power.

At the heart of Thomas Aquinas's tripartite masterwork, the *Summa Theologiae*, lies the section he calls the *Treatise on Morals* (see I 82.3 ad 2). For the persevering reader who reaches the far shore of this oceanic theological ethics, Aquinas explains what the voyage has been all about: nothing less than "the investigation of the ultimate end of human life and of the virtues and vices" (III pr).[6] The direct treatment of the virtues and vices can be estimated at about seven-tenths of the whole of his ethics. There is no question, then, that the virtues play an important role in Aquinas's ethics.

Is virtue, then, the keystone? Not long ago, Aquinas's moral thought was counted as almost synonymous with natural law theory, for which it remains an important reference point. More recent interpretation has, however, highlighted other important aspects of Aquinas's thought. Some argue that Aquinas advocates a eudaimonistic ethic; others emphasize Aquinas's theological anthropology of grace; still others see Aquinas's ethics as act-focused in that it provides a way of determining the moral species of an action through its object, end, and circumstances.

One could go on. Emotion is said to be one of the "major organizing principles" of Aquinas's ethics.[7] A recent study reminds us that, for Aquinas, the primary rule of the human will, and therefore the fundamental standard of morality, is eternal law.[8] Others have argued for "the centrality of Christ in Aquinas's view of the moral life."[9]

There is yet more. Aquinas's ethics has been characterized as an "orthological ethics"—that is, an ethics of right reason.[10] And, as has been argued more recently, "the key for an understanding of Aquinas's moral thinking would be the human person as *imago Trinitatis*."[11]

What are we to make of this bewildering diversity of claims about what idea is central to or fundamental in interpreting Aquinas's ethics? Each is put forward by scholars closely acquainted with the texts, and yet they cannot all be true.

There once was a fashion for pinpointing the fundamental concept of Aquinas's metaphysical thought as the keystone on which all the others depend. Some believed it to be the distinction between essence and existence; others singled out the idea of analogy, or participation, or causation. Each reading made its contribution and opened new perspectives. Because of this history of divergent interpretations, however, it has sensibly been suggested that Aquinas's metaphysics is too complex for any one of these ideas to be singled out as *the* keystone. Each plays an important role. Similarly, what seems to emerge from a survey of the diverse readings of Aquinas's ethics is that the important concepts of his ethical thought are too interrelated to be reduced to a single principle. As Thomas Williams puts it, "Aquinas's moral theory is so systematically unified that no single discussion—whether of the human good, the natural law, the nature of responsible action, or the virtues—can claim pride of place."[12] The quest to find "the" keystone is futile.

It would be misleading to say that Aquinas is a virtue ethicist, if by that one means that virtue is the basis or central focus for his entire ethics. Aquinas is a holistic thinker and there is no basic idea or central focus in his ethics; none serves as the foundation for all the others. Rather, there is a nexus of interrelated ideas.

If Aquinas is not a virtue ethicist, does he offer a virtue theory? Because Aquinas sees ethics as practical rather than theoretical knowledge, some would argue it is wrong to see him as proposing a "theory" of virtue.[13] However, while we should not project modern presuppositions about theory onto Aquinas's ethics, there is no need to reject the term altogether. Aquinas speaks of the more abstract and theoretical part of medicine.[14] Likewise, his ethics includes some abstract and some theoretical sections despite being oriented to practice overall. A "virtue theory," as I shall employ the term, is an account of the nature, genesis, and role of virtue and the virtues in human life. Aquinas offers such an account in *Treatise on Virtue in General* in the *Summa Theologiae* (I.II 55–70).[15] The treatise begins with a definition of virtue in general (55) and then looks at the way virtue forms the capacity of the human soul for thought, desire, and passion (56). The next questions show how virtue can be divided into different kinds and thereby organized into a classificatory scheme (57–62). The question of how a person comes to be virtuous through practice and grace is examined (63). Then follows a discussion of the "properties" of virtue, such as the interconnection between virtues, their existing in the mean, their relative value, and their persistence into the next life (64–67). Aquinas concludes with a discussion of a special set of virtues—namely, the gifts of the Holy Spirit and their operations and effects (68–70). This "virtue theory" is later fleshed out in greater detail in the *Secunda secundae*, wherein the specific virtues are examined (II.II 1–170). Aquinas's rich and sophisticated account of virtue, moreover, does not pretend to be freestanding, since it is embedded in a dynamic and holistic vision of the Christian moral life. It is difficult to imagine a better starting point for an exploration of the central questions of a properly theological virtue theory.

A CAUSAL APPROACH

When I began work on Aquinas's ethics, I wanted to examine a specific virtue. I chose the cardinal virtue of temperance. It quickly became clear that Aquinas's treatment of temperance in the *Secunda secundae* does not stand alone. Rather, it presupposes many aspects of his ethics, especially his systematic account of virtue found in the *Treatise on Virtue in General* in the *Prima secundae*. Aquinas begins this treatise with the question, "What is virtue?" His answer is confusing and opaque and presents itself as an evaluation of the Augustinian definition of virtue as "a quality of the mind, by which we live rightly, which we cannot use badly, and which God works in us without us" (I.II 55.4).[16] But the article's title does not fully express what is being argued. Commentators have squabbled over whether Aquinas's understanding of virtue is Aristotelian or Augustinian. I suspect that they are missing the central point: in the article

Aquinas is doing something new not previously attempted by the Philosopher nor the Bishop of Hippo. Aquinas is offering a *causal* definition of virtue.

Aquinas inherits from Aristotle the understanding that there are four "causes"—namely, formal, final, material, and efficient. The identification of these four causes or modes of explanation leads to an important principle: the search for a full understanding of anything is a search for its causes. Aquinas applies this principle to understanding law, grace, habit, sin, and, most explicitly of all, virtue. As found in the first sentence of Aquinas's attempt to define virtue, "The complete rationale of anything is gathered from all its causes" (55.4c).[17] With this interpretive key in hand, I was able to approach temperance in a more systematic way: by investigating its causes.[18]

The causal analysis of virtue, however, is not merely a tool for defining virtues; it is also a more general methodological principle. Causes set an agenda for virtue theory: to examine the genesis (efficient cause), role (final cause), and nature (formal and material causes) of virtue and the virtues. Yet the causes also provide a dynamic method of investigation into the key issues: the distinction between intellectual, moral, and theological virtue; the principles and processes of moral development; the relation between virtue and happiness; and so on. The causal approach also provides an authentically theological mode of proceeding since the first cause of virtue is divine: God is virtue's prime agent, exemplar, and end. The unexpected result of my investigation into a single virtue was to learn that Aquinas provides a hermeneutical principle with which to read his entire virtue theory. Even so, a causal reading of Aquinas on virtue is not without its challenges.

THREE TENSIONS

While many take Aquinas as a source for theological ethics, few agree on how to read his works. A navigational tactic is needed so as not to fall between the hermeneutical cracks. The strategy I have chosen is an attempt to hold together various tensions, indicated by three pairs of opposites: the theological and the philosophical, the return to the source with attention to later tradition, and the historical and the systematic. The danger is to emphasize one pole to the diminishment of the other.

One tension concerns the relationship of theology and philosophy in the interpretation of Aquinas's ethical thought. "Aristotelian Thomism," of which Ralph McInerny is an important representative, emphasizes that Aquinas's theological ethics are based in Aristotle's work. McInerny sees Aquinas as "the greatest Aristotelian in the history of Western philosophy."[19] His motivating concern is to defend the legitimacy of a Thomist moral philosophy that can participate in the "philosophical marketplace" today. He therefore resists those who emphasize Aquinas's distinctiveness rather than his indebtedness to Aristotle. On the other side are those like Mark Jordan, who propose a strongly Augustinian, non-Aristotelian reading of Aquinas.[20]

The critique of Aristotelian Thomism, which calls us to acknowledge that Aquinas is first and last a theologian, does have the merit of shaking us out of the remarkably persistent temptation to read him through a reductively Aristotelian lens. Yet a resolutely non-Aristotelian reading can itself lead to interpretive distortions and close off important avenues of dialogue. We should surely welcome the fact that the atheist philosopher Philippa Foot, a leader in the renewal of virtue, can say, "It is possible to learn a great deal from Aquinas that one could not have got from Aristotle."[21] An either-or approach is to be avoided. It is precisely Aquinas's theological commitment to the goodness of creation, and hence to natural human reason, that makes his ethics accessible from a philosophical as well as a theological perspective. Aquinas's work is best read in its integrally theological context, where it finds its fullest meaning, with openness to philosophical argument.

A second contentious debate concerns the use of the classical commentaries and disputations on the *Summa Theologiae*. I do not hesitate to make reference to three of the most famous, those of Cajetan, John Poinsot, and the Salamancans (see Note on Sources). It should be noted that the legitimacy of reading Aquinas with the help of this tradition has been seriously out of favor since opposition to Cajetan, Poinsot, and the Salamancans was voiced by Étienne Gilson and Henri de Lubac.[22]

Certainly, it is important to avoid the "fantasy of progressive unanimity among commentators, of a monument built on and out of authoritative consensus," as Jordan has put it.[23] Leonine Thomism (of which Reginald Garrigou-Lagrange is the best-known twentieth-century representative) is, in my view, questionable in its claim to be *iuxta mentem Thomae* ("according to the mind of Thomas"). Yet, while there is no uniform commentarial tradition, there is a multivocal, conflictual, often problematic but at times brilliantly enlightening tradition. This is especially so of the golden age of Iberian scholasticism in the sixteenth and early seventeenth centuries (whose representatives should not be confused with the more homogenous manualists of succeeding eras). While the historian may legitimately raise questions about an uncritical acceptance of the commentators (or, better, the "disputants," for their primary concern is not exegesis but argument), my reason for attending to them carefully, albeit critically, is sound: the conversation is all the richer for including them. I hope to show a way of engaging with the great figures of the Thomist tradition that falls neither into slavish appeal to authority nor a denial of the genuine insights they provide on key questions. Once again, the better approach is one of balance: a historically informed respect for the original source combined with discerning attention to the best of the tradition that flows therefrom.

Finally, the greatest methodological challenge is to offer an exegetically illuminating account of Aquinas's theory of virtue while simultaneously considering what contributions it may have for contemporary discussions in theological ethics. Either task would be difficult enough, but to attempt both inevitably risks confusion.

One question here concerns the tension between history and relevance. Historical Thomism, as evidenced today by scholars such as Jean-Pierre Torrell, rightly insists that Aquinas must be understood in context. This approach has been fruitful in highlighting the diverse genres of Aquinas's works, the development of his thought, and the benefits of situating him in his own milieu.[24] A contrasting approach is found in the movement of "analytical Thomism." The term was introduced by philosopher John Haldane to denote the use of the methods and ideas of analytic philosophy to discern and develop what Aquinas has to say.[25]

The two schools are often suspicious of each other. While the historical approach fears that an (allegedly) ahistorical analytical approach misinterprets, the analytic approach is frustrated by what it sees as an ironic failure to engage argumentatively with a body of work that itself "consists almost entirely of arguments, one after another, page after page."[26] Since I am an ethicist, not a historian, my approach is primarily systematic; at the same time, I spend longer on the text itself than some in the analytical school may appreciate. The challenge is to offer a careful exposition and reconstruction of Aquinas's viewpoint while also critically examining what in his account may be true and helpful or, indeed, in need of revision.

The ideal I propose, then, is to keep these tensions together: to be theological yet open to philosophy, to be respectful of the need to "return to the source" while engaging seriously with the Thomistic tradition of commentary and disputation, and to be analytical without neglecting the text. Inevitably there will be compromises. Yet the endeavor is in its own way an effort to follow in the footsteps of Aquinas, who excels at uniting without confusing such apparent opposites.

THE JOURNEY AHEAD

This book has a twofold aim: to substantiate and elaborate a causal reading of Aquinas on virtue and to present, at least incipiently, a causal virtue theory robust enough to be worthy of a place in the theological and philosophical discussion. I am aware that I am asking of the reader a significant investment of energy, and indeed patience, so it is only reasonable to expect at this stage some indication of the value of taking this causal approach to virtue. First and foremost, the causal reading is not another study of this or that aspect of Aquinas's account of virtue. Rather, it offers a synoptic view of his virtue theory as a whole. Beyond interpretation, it also proposes and illustrates a way of defining specific virtues and of addressing key issues in a theological and philosophical virtue theory more broadly.

Part 1 addresses the question of how to define virtue. Chapter 1 serves as an overture to the book since it introduces the causal approach by applying it to the cardinal virtue of temperance. Chapters 2 through 4 examine Aquinas's question on the essence of virtue (I.II 55). Aquinas's understanding of virtue as a habit is seen to be rich in comparison to the more reductive modern psychological and philosophical versions of "habit." Virtue is a morally *good* habit, and Aquinas defines its goodness by its conformity to divine and human wisdom. The definition of virtue is shown to incorporate the idea of a morally good habit within a more-comprehensive causal perspective. Part 2 digs more deeply into Aquinas's understanding of causation and its role in his ethics, exploring key "causal" concepts such as object, exemplar, end, and agent. Part 3 offers a comprehensive (albeit not exhaustive) account of virtue in terms of all its causes—formal, material, final, and efficient—plus a causal analysis of the most contested question in contemporary theological virtue theory: the relation of grace and virtue. While the navigation of this complex and nuanced theory of virtue is challenging, Aquinas is a worthy conversation partner for anyone searching for a richer, more dynamic, and ultimately more attractive answer to the question, "How should we live?"

NOTES

1. *Optatam Totius: Decree on Priestly Training*, paragraph 16. References to Church documents are taken from the Vatican website, http://www.vatican.va.

2. David Cloutier and William C. Mattison III, "Review Essay: The Resurgence of Virtue in Recent Moral Theology," *Journal of Moral Theology* 3, no. 1 (January 2014): 228–59.

3. For a recent example see Michael G. Lawler and Todd A. Salzman, "Virtue Ethics: Natural and Christian," *Theological Studies* 74, no. 2 (2013): 442–73.

4. For the origin of this distinction see Julia Driver, "The Virtues and Human Nature," in *How Should One Live? Essays on the Virtues*, ed. Roger Crisp (Oxford: Oxford University Press, 1996), 111–29.

5. Julia Annas, "Virtue Ethics," in *The Oxford Handbook of Ethical Theory*, ed. David Copp (Oxford: Oxford University Press, 2006), 515.

6. III pr: "considerationem ultimi finis humanae vitae et virtutum ac vitiorum."

7. Nicholas E. Lombardo, *The Logic of Desire: Aquinas on Emotion* (Washington, DC: Catholic University of America Press, 2010), 198–99.

8. John Michael Rziha, *Perfecting Human Actions: St. Thomas Aquinas on Human Participation in Eternal Law* (Washington, DC: Catholic University of America Press, 2009).

9. Thomas P. Harmon, "The Sacramental Consummation of the Moral Life According to St. Thomas Aquinas," *New Blackfriars* 91, no. 1034 (2010): 475, 480.

10. Vernon Joseph Bourke, *Ethics: A Textbook in Moral Philosophy* (New York: Macmillan, 1966).

11. Brian J. Shanley, "Aquinas's Exemplar Ethics," *The Thomist* 72 (2008): 369.

12. Thomas Aquinas, *Disputed Questions on the Virtues*, ed. E. M. Atkins and Thomas Williams (Cambridge, UK: Cambridge University Press, 2005), xxix.

13. See Denis J. M. Bradley, *Aquinas on the Twofold Human Good: Reason and Human Happiness in Aquinas's Moral Science* (Washington, DC: Catholic University of America Press, 1997), 3–4, 266–72. Jacques Maritain's account of the "speculatively-practical" is still instructive. Maritain, *Distinguish to Unite, Or, The Degrees of Knowledge*, The Collected Works of Jacques Maritain, vol. 7 (Notre Dame, IN: University of Notre Dame Press, 1995), 481–89. For Maritain's defense against criticisms similar to Bradley's, see his *Science and Wisdom*, trans. Bernard Wall (London: Geroffrey Bles and Centenary Press, 1954), 138–45.

14. Super De Trinitate, pars 3 q. 5 a. 1 ad 3.

15. Especially relevant to his virtue theory are three other ethical texts: the *Commentary on the Sentences* III d.33; *Disputed Questions on the Virtues*; and *Commentary on the Nichomachean Ethics*.

16. I.II 55.4c: "virtus est bona qualitas mentis, qua recte vivitur, qua nullus male utitur, quam Deus in nobis sine nobis operatur."

17. 55.4c: "Perfecta enim ratio uniuscuiusque rei colligitur ex omnibus causis eius." Aquinas's term *ratio* is a multivalent one, which I translate as "rationale." See chapter 5 for discussion.

18. Nicholas Austin, "Thomas Aquinas on the Four Causes of Temperance," PhD dissertation, Boston College, 2010.

19. Thomas Aquinas, *Commentary on Aristotle's Nicomachean Ethics*, trans. Rev. C. I. Litzinger, (South Bend, IN: Dumb Ox, 1993), ix–x.

20. Mark D. Jordan, *Rewritten Theology: Aquinas after His Readers* (Oxford: Blackwell, 2005), 85.

21. Philippa Foot, *Virtues and Vices and Other Essays in Moral Philosophy* (New York: Clarendon, 2002), 2.

22. For a helpful discussion of this rejection see John Deely, "Quid Sit Postmodernismus?," in *Postmodernism and Christian Philosophy*, ed. Roman T Ciapalo (Mishawaka, IN: American Maritain Association, 1997), 68–96.

23. Jordan, *Rewritten Theology*, 5.

24. Thomas F. O'Meara, "Jean-Pierre Torrell's Research on Thomas Aquinas," *Theological Studies* 62, no. 4 (December 1, 2001): 787–801.

25. John Haldane, "Analytical Thomism: How We Got Here, Why It Is Worth Remaining, and Where We May Go Next," afterword to *Analytical Thomism: Traditions in Dialogue*, ed. Craig Paterson and Matthew S. Pugh (Aldershot, UK: Ashgate, 2006), 303–10.

26. Robert Pasnau, "Review of *The Ethics of Aquinas*," ed. Stephen J. Pope, *Notre Dame Philosophical Reviews* (January 2003). To be fair to the authors, the aim of the book is primarily exegetical, and their other works exhibit a strong critical engagement.

PART I

Defining Virtue

CHAPTER 1

Defining Temperance Causally

Suggested reading: *Summa Theologiae* I.II 61.2;
II.II 141, 143, 155, 166

Let us begin with an analysis of temperance. The purpose is to construct a causal account of temperance that begins from the one found in the *Summa Theologiae*. The interpretation of Aquinas to be built on later is not argued in depth here but is left for later chapters, when the more controversial claims will be justified. The reader is therefore asked temporarily to take on trust what is yet to be established, especially the claim that causal virtue theory analyzes each virtue into seven elements (matter, mode, target, subject, overall end, agent, and exemplar) and relates them in certain characteristic ways. How might this causal framework, in dialogue with contemporary accounts, enable the analysis of a specific virtue?

The choice of temperance may puzzle. Many associate temperance with a moralistic puritanism. A survey of over a million people interested in character development found that of the six "core virtues" recognized by positive psychology (wisdom, courage, humanity, justice, temperance, and transcendence), the least endorsed is temperance.[1] Is it plausible still to see temperance as a cardinal virtue, or even as a virtue at all?

The classical argument for temperance's cardinality or principality rests on perennial features of human nature, such as the need to limit superficial or momentary attractions for deeper and more-enduring goods.[2] While this rationale retains its original force, today there are other equally compelling arguments. Psychological research indicates that good self-control is positively correlated with better interpersonal relationships, better adjustment, and even better grades.[3] In a consumerist society, temperance is needed to moderate the impulse toward consumption.[4] Understood as "moderation for the sake of eco-justice," it has an important place in an environmental virtue ethic.[5] High rates of addiction and compulsion in relation to drugs, food, and digital media, as

well as the hectic pace of modern life, all signal the urgent need for the simpli-
fying and balancing influence of temperance. What, then, may a causal analysis
contribute to the burgeoning discussion of this perennial yet timely virtue?

MODE

A natural place to begin the analysis of a virtue is its name. This is where Aquinas begins (II.II 141.1c). He holds that the name of a virtue expresses its *mode*
(I.II 61.4). The mode of a virtue is its characteristic manner of achieving the
good at stake in some specific field of human life. It is the most formal element
of any moral virtue and therefore its primary defining feature, which is precisely
why it is normally expressed by the virtue's name. Does the name "temperance,"
then, indicate the virtue's mode? Immediately we run into difficulties.

"Temperance" has a lot of baggage. As Louke van Wensveen says, the term
is "riddled with negative connotations, such as small-mindedness, prudish-
ness, preachiness, missionary zeal, and especially lack of joy."[6] One reason
for this unhappy set of associations is the enduring legacy of the temperance
movement of the nineteenth and early twentieth centuries, which advocated
enforced abstinence from alcohol. Temperance, therefore, tends to convey an
outmoded, repressive ideal.

However, ethicists are increasingly aware of how virtue terms, detached
from the ancient ethical traditions in which they were forged, today are often
mere shadows of their former selves. Temperance is not unique: prudence, magnanimity, humility, and, above all, charity, have similarly "dwindled miserably,"
to use Josef Pieper's apt description.[7] These terms once had richer meanings.

Is etymology, or the original meaning, a surer guide than current usage? Not
always. Sometimes a virtue has been badly named. The original Greek word
for what we call temperance is *sophrosyne,* which in its root meaning conveys
a positive soundness of mind. The Stoics employed various Latin translations
that have migrated into English as "sobriety," "chastity," "moderation," "continence," and "temperance." What is striking is that, in contrast to the affirming
Greek word, they all "imply restriction or denial."[8]

Aquinas similarly characterizes the mode of temperance in negative terms,
such as "moderation," "retraction," or "restraint." Moderation sounds the least
restrictive, yet Aquinas adds that the moderation of temperance is achieved
precisely through restraint (II.II 141.2). As he explains, "Temperance is a certain disposition of the soul that imposes the limit on any passions or operations, lest they be carried beyond what is due" (I.II 61.4).[9] In his accounting of
temperance's mode as restraint, has Aquinas been misled by a virtue vocabulary saddled with a Stoic suspicion of passion?

When he discusses the virtue of studiousness (*studiositas*) as the well-ordered desire for knowledge, Aquinas does recognize the fallibility of arguing directly from a virtue's name to its mode (II.II 166). He insists that studiousness is related to temperance, which suggests to him that its mode is restraint. But Aquinas also notes that its name suggests a positive mode that is contrary to the mode of restraint since the "studious" person is eager to know (166.2 arg 3). Aquinas's solution is to distinguish a twofold mode in studiousness: a strengthening of the purpose to learn (that is, a conquering of sluggishness) and restraint (curbing vain curiosity). The latter mode, he claims, is more essential to studiousness than the former (ad 3). Aquinas here concedes, then, that an argument from a virtue's name, at least to its primary mode, does not work in all cases. He also acknowledges that a virtue associated with temperance may possess a more complex and more positive mode than restraint. Why not, therefore, apply a similar twofold mode for the specific virtue of temperance itself, of rightly ordered intensification as well as restraint?

Concern about the negativity of restraint and restriction has led today's advocates of temperance to reinterpret what we are calling the "mode" of temperance not as restraint but as integration. Mark Carr argues that the "work of temperance" is the inclusion of emotion in the moral life.[10] Van Wensveen submits that temperance involves not "militaristic mastery" of our appetites but rather "creative channeling," or "the inventive redirection and transformation of ordinary desires."[11] She advocates an ethic of "*formed* spontaneity" rather than one founded on restraint.[12] This strategy of redefinition is attractive in that it avoids canonizing a repressive moral ideal; however, at the same time something may be lost because the definition of the cardinal virtue of temperance then seems to shirk what has always been seen as its primary work—namely, voluntary self-limitation. Defining a virtue is a complex business. How do we adjudicate these issues?

The Mode Fits the Matter

Aquinas has a second, more-compelling method for establishing a virtue's mode that is not so reliant on semantics. A crucial principle is that the mode of a virtue is congruent with its "matter," or the interior and exterior acts (and, by extension, their objects) with which that virtue is especially concerned. A virtue's mode is what, when applied to the matter, makes it virtuous and reasonable. Just as a craftsman works in a different manner when using the diverse matters of wax, wood, or clay, and just as the methods of the sciences differ according to their specific subject-matters, so the mode of each virtue differs according to its proper matter.

Aquinas employs this principle of mode-matter correlation when determining the mode of temperance, as contrasted with the mode of fortitude:

> For it is necessary to place the order of reason in the matter of passions due to their resistance to reason, which is twofold. First, insofar as passion impels to something contrary to reason, and thus it is necessary that passion be restrained, and from this is named temperance. Second, insofar as passion withdraws from that which reason dictates, just as fear of dangers or of toils, and thus it is necessary that man be strengthened in that which is of reason, lest he recede [from it]; and from this is named fortitude. (I.II 61.2; see also 62.3–4; II.II 141.3)[13]

The argument employs analogies from physical motion. The primary mode of temperance is a *restraint from attraction*, whereas the primary mode of fortitude is an *impulse against a retraction*. Different passions have characteristic ways of becoming disordered and distracting from what is reasonable and good. Passions of sensible attraction, when not correctly moderated, tend to seduce one toward something against the good of reason, such as adultery or drunkenness. Passions of retraction in the face of danger or hardship have a contrasting tendency to move a person into evading what is reasonable. Whereas a mode of restraint is necessary to resist the magnetic pull of the emotionally attractive, in contrast, a mode of strengthening is needed to overcome the tendency to avoid the emotionally repulsive.

It could be objected that excess is not the only way attraction can go wrong. All moral virtues (with the possible exception of justice) lie in the mean between a vice of excess and a vice of deficiency. The vice of deficiency opposed to the virtue of temperance is "insensibility," which fails to take a healthy pleasure in things (II.II 142.1). Yet the desires for food and sex are biologically based impulses that exhibit extraordinary power and tend to overrun their bounds. People tend to go wrong by intemperance rather than by insensibility, so the primary mode of temperance must be one of restraint.

Here the doubts about whether temperance is a virtue, or whether its mode involves restraint, should surely be laid to rest. It is a true good to cultivate a simplicity in our desires for material goods, food, drink, sex, entertainment, and so on. Insatiable, excessive, or misdirected appetite is disordered, as manifested in the many prevalent self- and other-destructive addictions and compulsions; virtue places limits on these desires in order to preserve certain lasting goods.

How do we resolve the worry that restraint is a negative and repressive ideal? Aquinas is once more of help. The question is not whether we need restraint, but what kind of restraint we need. First, temperate restraint is *positive* in that it involves only meaningful limitation: a "no" for a greater "yes." Aquinas notes, "Pure negation is not the act of any virtue, but only that which is done for a reasonable purpose" (147.1 ad 3).[14] Paradoxically, it could be argued that temperate desire is, in the long term, more passionate and more pleasurable than the continually indulged appetite that becomes apathy and disaffection. Temperance preserves and channels the vital energies of the human person. Pieper offers a compelling image: The "boundaries" recognized by temperance are like a river's banks, which do not merely defend against dissipation and the destructive flood but also channel the stream with force to its destination.[15]

Second, even if at times an element of suspicion of passion characterizes Aquinas's mind-set, he cannot fairly be accused of operating solely out of a paradigm of domination in his account of the restraint and self-mastery involved in temperance. Aquinas does not advocate the elimination of passion, only its right ordering. Temperate restraint, then, is *nonrepressive* and informs desire rather than extinguishing it (155.4c, ad 3).

Third, Aquinas distinguishes strongly between the restraint of temperance and that of continence or self-control (155.4 ad 1). The mode of self-control is to restrain by *resisting* desires; the mode of temperance is to restrain by *moderating* desires. The restraint embodied in temperance is therefore primarily *nonagonistic* in that it does not strain against disordered desire, since in the temperate person this does not arise, at least for the most part.

While this positive, nonrepressive, and nonagonistic restraint does characterize temperance, the mode of temperance cannot consist *solely* in restraint. The argument is quite simple: since temperance is a virtue, one cannot be too temperate, but one can be too restrained (as Aquinas admits by talking of the vice of "insensibility"). Therefore temperance cannot consist only in restraint. Just as fortitude strengthens the mind against fear and also moderates daring so that it does not lead to rashness, the cardinal virtue of temperance limits passionate attractions and also encourages a healthy appetite and delight in pleasant things. Carr and Van Wensveen are right to point out that one of the challenges posed by temperance is the positive integration and right ordering of our appetites and desires, something with which Aquinas himself would heartily agree (155.4c). The mode of temperance, therefore, operates in the mean between two poles: between restraint/limitation and positive redirection/ integration.

Should we exchange the word "temperance," with its negative connotations, for a more satisfactory term, as some suggest? In his most considered analysis, Aquinas goes back to the word's etymology. As he says, *temperantia* "in its very name implies a certain moderation or proper mixture [*temperies*]" (141.1).[16] Moderation is the keynote of temperance, achieved by "mixing" the appetite with reason so that one's desires become reasonable.[17] If "moderation" is thought to be still too negative, an alternative English term that preserves the core Latin etymology is "modulation." Modulation, as the *Oxford English Dictionary* defines it, is "the action of treating, regulating, or varying something so as to achieve due measure and proportion." The definition also mentions that modulation can refer to "the action or process of passing from one key to another in the course of a piece of music." The musical metaphor is helpful: even the ancients associated temperance with musical harmony. The mode of temperance, then, is *the harmonious modulation of attraction* that is accomplished sometimes by restraint and sometimes by the positive redirection and integration of desire.

Aquinas oversimplifies temperance's mode, at times identifying it too exclusively with its more negative pole. Yet the argument has been a confirmation of his causal method. Form is correlative to matter, and so the mode of a virtue is what is proportionate to its sphere of concern. Since temperance is the virtue that concerns the powerful attractions of the human psyche that tend to overrun their bounds, the mode of temperance lies in a modulation by which these desires are simplified, limited, and integrated positively into the moral life. While Aquinas's conclusion concerning the mode of temperance may fall short, his method does not.

MATTER

To inquire into the matter of temperance is to ask: What field or sphere of life does temperance concern? Any answer must face the difficulty of reconciling wide applicability with rich content. It is a logical principle that the greater a term's scope, the less is its content. Temperance is needed in any domain of life in which we experience strong emotional attractions with the potential to distract from, or undermine, the human good. This is a wide field indeed. Aquinas recognizes that temperance has been applied to the matters of food, drink, sex, wealth, clothing, curiosity, anger, and even play (II.II 143). Advocates of temperance are therefore faced with a dilemma. Either one limits the scope of temperance to the spheres of food, drink, and sex (following Aristotle), or one talks about temperance in almost any sphere of life whatsoever. Either temperance is specific and "thick," lacking relevance beyond a narrow sphere, or it has wide applicability and becomes abstract, vague, and "thin."[18]

Aquinas's principle of matter-mode correlation offers an elegant solution. If we define temperance's matter generically as powerful emotional attraction, then its mode is also to be defined generically as the modulation of that attraction. In this case temperance is what Aquinas terms a "general virtue," one that is not restricted to any narrow domain but is required in every morally virtuous act (I.II 61.3). However, if we specify the matter more closely, then a more specific mode will be required as well, one that is congruent to this more determinate matter. In this case temperance is not one, but many virtues. Temperate drinking, for example, differs from temperate eating, since drink and food present different challenges to the good of reason and therefore need to be modulated differently. Thus temperance refers not so much to a single specific virtue as to a set of related virtues.

The analysis of temperance into matter and form (mode), then, reconciles wide applicability with rich content. On the one hand temperance does indeed apply to numerous different matters; on the other it does not dissolve in intolerable vagueness, because the particular difficulties of achieving the respective good in each of these matters will give rise to distinctively specific modes.

Are all temperances equal? Aquinas distinguishes between temperance as a "principal" or "cardinal" virtue and the other "secondary" virtues associated with it (II.II 143). The former is the archetypal temperance: it concerns the matter that it is most necessary and most difficult to modulate—namely, the bodily appetites and pleasures of touch. "Touch" (*tactus*) for Aquinas refers not just to contact with the skin but more generally to how the body feels. Touch is therefore involved in the feelings of hunger and thirst, warmth and cold, pleasure and pain, the sense of bodily movement, and so on.[19] In this way it makes sense to say that temperance is about the craving for the pleasures of touch, especially the pleasures of food, intoxicating substances, and sex: wanting to feel good in one's body.

The cardinal virtue of temperance for Aquinas is divided into four species: abstinence (regarding food), sobriety (regarding drink), chastity (regarding sex), and *puditia*, or what today we would call modesty (regarding the touches, hugs, kisses, and so on, that can have a sexual tendency) (II.II 143). While the modern ear may recoil at the decidedly negative ring of these traditional virtue terms, it remains that the virtues themselves, whose task it is to strike the right balance in these spheres, are themselves necessary.

Aquinas offers two arguments for thinking bodily appetites require a principal virtue for their modulation. First, these appetites have the greatest power to undermine good of reason, due to the way they can possess a person (141.3–5). Second, we share these appetites with nonrational animals, which suggests that they are the kind of appetite furthest from reason and therefore the most difficult to modulate rationally (141.7 arg 1, ad 1). This is not to say that there is not a specifically human way of desiring and enjoying food, drink, or sex that "mixes" reason with appetite, only that the task of finding a human way of desiring, enjoying, and refraining from these pleasures in a manner fitting for a rational animal is all the more challenging.[20] Hence this set of appetites and pleasures constitutes the sphere of the *principal* virtue of temperance.

Aquinas improves on Aristotle because, drawing on Cicero and other later sources, he is able to acknowledge a number of other temperances. Aquinas calls the latter the "potential parts" of temperance since they share in the potency of the principal temperance: they observe the same generic mode that principal temperance imposes, but they are applied specifically to other matters that have less difficulty (II.II 143). Aquinas lists here virtues such as gentleness (which modulates anger), clemency (which moderates strictness), and an ancient virtue named modesty (*modestia*). Under the latter Aquinas includes the virtues of humility and studiousness as well as other intriguing virtues such as simplicity in material requirements and appropriate playfulness.

Aquinas's classificatory scheme of principal and secondary temperances succeeds in providing a structure within which to place these virtues. At the same time, there are loose ends. For example, it is questionable whether the key Christian virtue of humility should be seen as secondary to temperance; it is also unclear whether it should be conceived primarily as a kind of modulation (e.g., of the desire to excel). Aquinas seems aware of these difficulties and acknowledges that, at least in some respects, humility is more important even than the cardinal virtue of temperance since it disposes a person to receive other gifts from God (including growth in the virtues) (161.4–5). Furthermore, he recognizes that humility is about more than modulation of an appetite to excel. For example, he notes that humility originates in reverence for God and is measured by a realistic self-knowledge (161.6). Humility, then, is not merely a kind of secondary temperance.

As with any classificatory scheme, anomalies exist. The basic insight, however, remains helpful: there are analogical resemblances between different kinds of temperance because all share the generic mode of modulation, although each specifies this mode differently in regard to its respective matter. Within this family grouping the cardinal virtue of temperance remains archetypal and applies modulation where it is needed most.

SUBJECT

Temperance often appears unattractive because it is seen as suppressing or repressing natural desires, or a kind of quashing of the spontaneity of a wholesome human life. Aquinas offers an attractive alternative to this kill-joy temperance that avoids repressive rationalism without swinging to the other extreme of indiscriminate acceptance of appetite. The key is the contrast between temperance and the semi-virtue of continence or self-control.

Temperance versus Continence

Self-control, or continence (*continentia*), etymologically has to do with self-containment or self-possession. Continence "contains" disordered appetites that otherwise would spill out and lead to disordered actions. Continence is therefore "that through which someone resists disordered concupiscences, which in him are vehement" (155.2 arg 2).[21] It follows that continence is not a virtue in the strict sense but rather is "something mixed" (*quaedam mixta*) (152.2c). Just as a teacher who successfully controls a rowdy class is not yet the kind of teacher whose class is not rowdy in the first place, so continence participates in virtue in strengthening reason against the distracting power of the passions but falls short of the kind of temperance that is not subject to vehement disordered passion.

How, then, does a causal analysis distinguish self-control from the full-blown virtue of temperance? Aquinas says that continence "agrees with temperance both in matter, because it is about pleasures of touch; and in mode, because it lies in a certain restraint" (143 ad 1).[22] One key difference between temperance and continence, however, lies in the *subject* of these two habits. A virtue's subject (*subiectum*) in Aquinas's terminology is the capacity that virtue perfects. The intellect is the subject of intellectual virtues, as it is disposed to making true and well-reasoned judgments through intellectual virtues; justice orients a person to desire the good of others, so its subject is the will. What, then, are the respective subjects of temperance and continence? Since temperance rectifies the passions of sensible attraction, its subject must be the "concupiscible appetite," or the power of the soul in which these passions reside. However, continence has a different subject since it controls vehement, disordered concupiscences, which simply do not arise in the temperate person (155.3). Rather, the subject of continence must be the will, since that is how the continent and the incontinent (the weak-willed) differ: the former choose not to follow the vehement evil desires they suffer, whereas the latter, overcome by their appetites, choose to do so.

It follows that temperance and continence differ in mode as well as in their respective subjects, despite Aquinas's initial statement to the contrary (143 ad 1): "Continence has as matter the concupiscences of the pleasures of touch, not as that which it moderates, which belongs to temperance, which is in the concupiscible, but it is about them as resisting them" (155.2 ad 1).[23] In other words, the mode of temperance is to restrain *by moderating* concupiscences; the mode of continence is to restrain *by resisting* concupiscences.

There exists, therefore, a clear contrast between temperance and continence in the way they order the "sensitive appetite," which is the locus of the passions in the soul: "The rational good flourishes more in the temperate one, in whom even the sensitive appetite itself is subject to reason and, as it were, tamed by reason, than in the one who is containing himself, in whom the sensitive appetite strongly resists reason by its crooked desires" (155.4c).[24] Continence restrains strong disordered appetites. As a kind of *imperfect* temperance (156.4), continence is marked by effort rather than by the ease and delight that characterizes the exercise of true virtue.[25] The restraint of temperance is, in contrast, not the resistance of desire but rather an interior ordering of desire itself. In the temperate person there is a concord of passion and reason that is lacking in the internally conflicted, continent person. As Paul Van Tongeren puts it, "Virtue is not a force opposed to an evil, dangerous and guilty desire; virtue is simply well formed desire itself."[26] Temperance is nothing other than well-ordered *eros*.

Temperance and Control

While he distinguishes the continence that contains unruly desires from the temperance that modulates them, Aquinas does not say that temperance involves no form of control at all. In his view the passions become virtuous when they are "obedient" to the rule of reason (I.II 56.4). To claim that the passions should be made subordinate to reason is likely to be seen as the reflection of an outmoded medieval hierarchical mind-set. This impression is reinforced by various patriarchal metaphors and similes Aquinas uses to express how the sensitive appetite should be subordinated to reason. For example, he claims that just as a boy needs to be disciplined by the rod, so the appetites need to be curbed by reason (II.II 142.2c).

Other strands of Aquinas's thought support a more positive interpretation. Aquinas says that reason rules over the passions with a "political" rather than "despotic" authority, so that the passions are like freemen who have in some respects their own will (I 81.3 ad 2). Reason, we might say, should be "authoritative" rather than "authoritarian" in relation to the passions. Indeed, in this view a tyrannical control of the passions would be a form of over-control that suppresses the legitimate role of passion in the moral life. The function of moral virtue is not to render the sensitive appetite otiose or idle but rather to dispose it to exercise its proper acts well (I.II 59.5c).

Aquinas's distinction between political and tyrannical authority offers a helpful way of understanding the control involved in temperance. The hierarchy of a parent to a child, a teacher to a student, or reason to passion, is not a bad thing. What matters is the *kind* of hierarchy. The aim of reason's political authority over the passions is not to eliminate them; it is to enable them to play their proper role in virtuous human action. For Aquinas this is possible because the passions possess a participative rationality. Passion is potentially intelligent and therefore potentially virtuous.

The solution to an excessively controlling concept of temperance is not to fall into the opposite extreme by taking the advocacy of unfettered passion too far. A romanticism that elevates passion without acknowledging its destructive potential is as undesirable as a rationalism that suppresses passion. The ideal of self-mastery associated with temperance remains legitimate as long as this mastery is purified of its excessively paternalistic connotations. However, to reject such authority as irretrievably repressive is to pave the way for a different kind of tyrannical domination, that of bodily and emotional cravings over the mind and the will. Those who act purely on untutored emotion are not true agents. They are driven by something half-alien and do not act themselves but are acted on by something "other" (*non agunt seipsas, sed ab aliis aguntur*) (cf. I.II 93.5c).

Is there evidence that the political authority of reason over passion ascribed to temperance is possible? Rosalind Hursthouse points to the cultural variations in what is enjoyable and disgusting, even in regard to the appetites for food or sex.[27] This indicates that our appetites are not merely given but are somewhat plastic and capable of being formed by judgments about what is good and right and honorable versus what is bad and wrong and shameful. For the temperate person, when an initially attractive object is *seen as* falling under a certain description, such as "consumer product negatively impacting the environment," the desire for it vanishes.[28] Reason can inform the passions.

The harmony between reason and passion in temperance helps explain why one of the marks of temperance is a kind of inner peace. However, Aquinas does not advocate a "no friction" view of temperance, as though a temperate person would never have to struggle to overcome certain attractions. It is true that *violent* disordered passions are absent from the life of moral virtue (*On the Virtues* 1.10 ad 14). However, due to the origin of many of our appetites in the body, and because of our fallen nature, even the virtuous will experience a certain degree of chaos in her passions. Sometimes, then, temperance, like continence, will have to put up some resistance, for "there always remains the struggle of the flesh against the spirit, even after moral virtue" (*On the Virtues* 1.10 ad 14).[29] The temperate person keeps "a firmness of mind against the force of pleasures" (I.II 61.4 ad 1).[30]

Aquinas gets the balance just right. He is realistic in acknowledging that even the temperate person at times will have to exert effort to not give in to irrational passions. Yet the primary work of temperance is not containment and is still less suppression; it is the integration and right ordering of the desires of attraction rooted in the human body and capacity for emotion. Temperance is indeed a "formed spontaneity."

TARGET AND END

What is the end of temperance? The common view, that the point of being temperate is to preserve physical health, is highly reductionist. To habitually eat, drink, or have sex purely according to health reasons is not a sign of virtue but of a disordered attachment to health. To interpret temperance merely as the body's servant is to fail to respect the human and spiritual dimensions of temperance.

Also problematic is the tendency to see temperance as a purely self-regarding virtue. Aquinas falls into this trap sometimes, as when he says that temperance "ordains to the proper good of the agent" (I.II 56.6 ad 1; cf. ad 3).[31] He divides moral virtues into self-regarding virtues about passions (including temperance and fortitude) and other-regarding virtues about exterior operations (justice and its allied virtues) (60.2). Underlying this division is the questionable premise that passion, unlike the will, is necessarily oriented toward one's own perceived good rather than the good of others. This assumption is subverted by Aquinas's own understanding that passion can listen to and participate in reason. It is also undermined by his acknowledgment that some of the passion-modifying virtues do concern the other's good. For instance, liberality (or generosity with wealth) can moderate a person's emotional attachment to money (II.II 117.3 ad 3). Yet this virtue "is [directed] principally towards another, like justice" (117.5c).[32] Mercy, which is certainly about the passions (30.3 ad 4), is also other-regarding: "Mercy is compassion for another's distress, and so properly mercy is [directed] towards another" (30.1 ad 2).[33] Why, then, cannot temperance have a relational, other-directed aspect?

Jean Porter repeats Aquinas's unfortunate dichotomy between relational justice and self-regarding fortitude and temperance. But she makes a qualification: temperance "is characterized by desiring what is good *for oneself* in the way of food, drink, and (to some degree) sexual pleasure."[34] The hesitation is significant. While sexual intercourse can be beneficial or harmful for the agent, such activity also concerns the good or harm of the sexual partner and also potential offspring. Temperance therefore concerns a moral matter that asks to be directed to another's good as well as to one's own. What is more, when we notice that eating and drinking together are near-universal practices of human family and friendship, we are compelled to acknowledge that virtue regarding food and drink is not purely self-regarding either. The mistake is to forget that while we share with nonrational animals the impulses to food, drink, or sex, in humans these same impulses take on a specifically human and relational form. The goods at stake in the matter of *human* eating, drinking, sexual activity, and so on are not purely those of the agent.

If it is implausible to see temperance as nonrelational or, even worse, as serving only the temperate person's physical health, how are we to articulate a fuller understanding of this virtue's end? Fortunately, other strands of Aquinas's thought undermine the idea that any virtue, even as fleshy a virtue as temperance, can be purely concerned with servicing bodily need.

Aquinas distinguishes two ends of a moral virtue such as temperance. To clarify this he compares the virtue of temperance with a builder (II.II 141.6 ad 1). The builder's intention in building a house is to gain the money with which he can support himself and his family; the purpose of the activity of building, however, is to produce a house. So we need to distinguish the agent's *overall end* from the action's proximate end or *target*. Obviously the two are linked: the builder cannot attain his living unless prepared to put in the hard work of building the house. By analogy, Aquinas suggests that temperance has both an overall end and a more proximate target in its use of pleasant things.

Aquinas states, "The end and rule of temperance itself is beatitude, but the end and rule of what it uses is the need of human life" (141.6c and ad 1).[35] As a virtue of the soul, temperance is concerned with something higher than purely physical well-being. It shares with all the moral virtues beatitude as the overall end; its more proximate target, which is specific to temperance, is *what we need to live*.

This view of the target of temperance may seem unduly ascetic, bodily, and self-regarding. Is nothing enjoyable allowed beyond strict bodily necessity? Aquinas is aware of the objection, and he replies by defining the "need of life" generously (141.6 arg 2, ad 2). There is a difference, he explains, between the absolute need an organism has for what enables it to survive and its relative need for that without which it cannot live *fittingly*. Only the latter is the measure of temperance. Note, however, that while Aquinas repudiates excessive asceticism, he does propose an asceticism: necessity, albeit interpreted generously, is the rule—need, not want (141.6).

What, then, is needed to live a fitting human life? What we need certainly goes beyond the bare necessities of physical survival and health. One may take things, Aquinas argues, that are not necessary for the body, so long as they are not impediments to health or fitness and they are used in the right way. Indeed, the temperate person uses these harmless pleasures "moderately, according to place and time and what is fitting towards those with whom one associates" (ad 2).[36] So here Aquinas recognizes a social aspect to temperance. As he also puts it in *Commentary on the Ethics*, the temperate person delights in things "as is required for health and fitness of the body *and for appropriate interaction with others*" (emphasis added).[37] The need of life is to be understood in terms of the general requirements of morality: "As we have said, temperance pays attention to need as regards what is fitting for life. This is understood not only according to what is fitting for the body, but also according to what is fitting with regard to exterior things, for example, riches and duties; and even more according to what fits with honesty [*honestas*]" (ad 3).[38] Thus the target of temperance, the relative need this virtue aims at, is multidimensional. It incorporates what someone needs for bodily health, what becomes one's status and office, and what she needs in order to live the "honest"—that is, the morally good life.[39]

In the end, then, Aquinas proposes a fuller and more moral understanding of temperance's end than some of his more schematic comments might suggest. Robert C. Roberts points out that for the temperate person, even the bodily appetites have been formed by "moral concerns" such as friendship, justice, and personal dignity, and not merely by considerations of personal health. It would therefore *not* be temperate to eat what is optimally healthy, for example, for a parent of many children during the scarcity of wartime.[40] One might add that there is no need to appeal to such extreme circumstances for illustration: in today's globalized world, considerations of justice and ecological concern will inform the temperate person's eating and other "consumer choices," so it would be intemperate to focus purely on personal health and well-being.

This more-moral conception of temperance's target does not exclude relevant concern for personal health; it does imply, however, that personal health cannot be the only consideration. In the early text of *Commentary on the Sentences*, Aquinas says, "The good of the body can be the end of virtue, as a certain terminus or effect of virtuous operation, but not as something in which the intention of virtue stands."[41] He suggests that the target of virtue is a bodily good, although its overall end is beatitude. As we have seen, in his mature work of the *Treatise on Temperance* in the *Summa Theologiae*, Aquinas offers a fuller understanding of the target of temperance as "the need of this life," where "need" is interpreted to include whatever is required to live a fitting human, social, and moral life. In the matters of food, drink, sex, and the many other matters with which temperance is concerned, there are many other goods at stake that therefore help to constitute the proximate aim or target of temperance. Whatever its immediate aim, temperance will always choose with a view to the overall human end: the truly blessed life.

AGENT

Aquinas also examines the agent of virtue: What brings about virtue such that we become virtuous, stay virtuous, and even increase in a virtue like temperance? Aquinas recognizes that the human is an agent of growth in virtue. He advances the principle that a virtue is acquired and increased through virtuous acts. Just as a student of the violin could hardly become a proficient player without playing and practicing well, so a temperate person cannot become temperate without performing the acts of temperance. The basic principle is that like acts produce like habits (*similes actus similes habitus causant*) (I.II 52.3c).

How does this apply to temperance? By temperate acts Aquinas means primarily temperate *desire* rather than temperate *behavior*. "Exterior acts proceed from interior passions of the soul. And therefore their moderation depends on the moderation of interior passions" (II.II 141.3 ad 3).[42] An illustration can be drawn by consideration of gluttony, a vice directly opposed to temperance. Aquinas thinks of gluttony primarily as a disordered desire to eat; for example, craving excessively sumptuous or gourmet foods, desiring too much food, being too eager to eat, or desiring to eat too early (148.4 arg 1). For Aquinas the correct strategy is to go on a kind of *interior* diet: to learn to moderate one's cravings.

While the focus is on the interior, Aquinas does not imagine that the modulation of appetite can be achieved without bodily practices. He claims that fasting is the paradigmatic act of "abstinence," the virtue of temperance as applied to food (147.1). Fasting from food, therefore, is not only the act in which abstinence is primarily displayed but also the practice by which temperance is acquired (147.1, 3). Aquinas claims that fasting is not merely a precept of positive Church law. Rather, it is a requirement of human nature, albeit one that needs to be adapted to times, places, and circumstances (147.3). It is impossible to find the "virtuous mean" in the sphere of temperance, in his view, without a regular practice of fasting.

Is fasting an outdated practice? Aquinas's view of the value of fasting is confirmed by the current interest in "intermittent fasting" as a way of achieving a healthier pattern of food consumption, especially in a society that finds it difficult to attain the virtuous mean due to the availability of sugar-rich processed foods, the breakdown of social rituals of eating, and a host of other factors. One could argue that "fasting" from other forms of consumption is equally necessary. Digital technologies are one example: though helpful in many ways, when they are used without measure they threaten our ability to attend deeply to something without distraction and to develop relationships of authentic intimacy.[43] What is required is not a moralistic denunciation of the Internet or smart phones but rather the wisdom of temperate use that knows when and how to use them and when to put them down. We are unlikely to find the virtuous mean for digital technology use without digital asceticism.

Fasting may be seen as an application of Aristotle's prescription: when we find ourselves tending to one extreme we should aim for the opposite in order to arrive at the mean, just as by bending a crooked piece of wood we can make it straight. Aquinas, however, makes an enlightening observation: "[Aristotle's] way of acquiring the virtues is the most efficacious, namely, that someone leans to the contrary of that to which he is inclined either by nature or custom; however, the way taught by the Stoics is easier, namely, that someone recedes little by little from what he is inclined to, as Cicero explains" (*Tusculan Disputations*: Bk. IV, C. 31–35, nn. 65–76*).*[44] This practical piece of wisdom recognizes that in many cases it is better to proceed by small acts of voluntary self-limitation rather than sudden or extreme acts of wholesale abstinence. A continual process of incremental change has a greater chance of being woven into the fabric of one's life, thus making the change more permanent and avoiding the danger faced by anyone who makes drastic changes to eating or other patterns of consumption— that is, backsliding into the opposite extreme. At the same time, there may be occasions when the more radical Aristotelian approach is indicated.

Laura Hartman proposes two "attitudes" as normative for Christians with regard to the ethics of consumption, whether of food or of other goods. The first is one of renunciation and censure, which opposes the tendency toward personal and social sin in consumption. This attitude is a corrective to greed, gluttony, and participation in unjust social structures.[45] The second is one of "acceptance and response," or an acknowledgement of the goodness of created desires and goods. The appropriate response to human hungers and appetites can often be joyful fulfillment with grateful recognition of the gifts of God.[46] If a twofold mode of restraint and positive enjoyment is constitutive of temperance, then there will be practices that correspond to both poles: we need virtuous practices of feasting as well as of fasting, of Easter and of Lent, so that we may acquire and grow in this virtue.

Aquinas attempts to synthesize the Aristotelian account of virtue-acquisition by habituation with the Augustinian claim that virtue is infused by God (I.II 63.3–4). In his discussion of humility, which for him is a "potential part" or kind of temperance, Aquinas says: "A human arrives at humility by two paths. In the very first place, and principally, by the gift of grace. And in this respect, interior [dispositions] precede externals. The other path, however, is human discipline, by which a human first restrains exterior things, and afterwards manages to uproot the interior root [of pride]" (II.II 161.6 ad 2).[47] In Aquinas's theology, grace and human effort are not in competition; rather, they cooperate. Temperance is a matter of both discipline and grace. Yet grace works from the interior in a way that human effort cannot. We become temperate "in the very first place, and principally, by the gift of grace."

EXEMPLAR

Aquinas understands a human virtue to exist in an exemplary and originative way in God: "It is necessary that the exemplar of human virtue preexist in God, just as the rationales of all things also pre-exist in him" (I.II 61.5c).[48] While God is seen as wise, just, and merciful, there is a special problem in saying that

God is temperate: the immediate sphere of temperance—namely, the bodily and emotional passion of attraction—is not to be found in the divine being. Nevertheless, in an analogous way Aquinas believes there to be a divine temperance, a "conversion of the divine intention to himself, just as in us temperance is that whereby the concupiscible appetite is conformed to reason" (ibid.).[49] Aquinas also holds that the exemplar virtues are brought within human reach, so to speak, by the Incarnation, and especially in the cross, where all the divine virtues are manifested in human form. "For whomsoever desires to live perfectly should do nothing other than despise what Christ despised on the cross, and desire what he desired."[50] Christian temperance lives out the incarnation, death, and resurrection of Christ by appreciating and valuing the goodness of the bodily and emotional attractions we experience in our humanity, by putting to death disordered desires through practices of mortification, and by beginning to participate in the risen life even in our bodies and attractions. A properly Christian temperance will be Christoform.

A CAUSAL ACCOUNT OF TEMPERANCE

The above account of temperance suggests the following causal definition:

> The virtue of temperance is nothing other than the habit that (i) harmoniously modulates (ii) the passions of attraction and their corresponding actions, sometimes (ia) by restraint, sometimes (ib) by positive channeling; orders (iii) the concupiscible appetite in order to meet (iv) what is needed to live a fitting bodily, relational, and moral life (v) with a view to the overall end of human life; and which (vi) comes about through virtuous practices of fasting and feasting and through grace, (vii) thereby following, dying, and rising with Christ.

This definition illustrates how a specific virtue can be analyzed in terms of the seven elements: (i) mode, (ii) matter, (iii) subject, (iv) target, (v) overall end, (vi) agent, and (vii) exemplar. These are all "causes" in Aquinas's causal account of virtue, and together they offer a powerful way to address the difficult question of interpreting this virtue and provide a comprehensive account of its nature, origin, and role.

NOTES

1. Ryan M. Niemiec and Jeremy Clyman, "Temperance: The Quiet Virtue Finds a Home," *PsychCritiques* 54 (November 18, 2009).

2. For contemporary restatements of this argument see Jean Porter, "Perennial and Timely Virtues," in *Changing Values and Virtues*, ed. Dietmar Mieth and Jacques Marie Pohier (Edinburgh: T&T Clark, 1987), 60–68; and David S. Oderberg, "On the Cardinality of the Cardinal Virtues," *International Journal of Philosophical Studies* 7, no. 3 (1999): 305–22.

3. June P. Tangney, Roy F. Baumeister, and Angie Luzio Boone, "High Self-Control Predicts Good Adjustment, Less Pathology, Better Grades, and Interpersonal Success," *Journal of Personality* 72, no. 2 (2004): 271–324.

4. Peter Wenz, "Synergistic Environmental Virtues: Consumerism and Human Flourishing," in *Environmental Virtue Ethics*, ed. Ronald D. Sandler and Philip Cafaro (Oxford: Rowman and Littlefield, 2005), 208.

5. Louke Van Wensveen, "Attunement: An Ecological Spin on the Virtue of Temperance," *Philosophy in the Contemporary World* 8, no. 2 (2001): 67–78.

6. Ibid., 71.

7. Josef Pieper, *The Four Cardinal Virtues: Prudence, Justice, Fortitude, Temperance* (Notre Dame, IN: University of Notre Dame Press, 1966), 145.

8. Helen North, *Sophrosyne: Self-Knowledge and Self-Restraint in Greek Literature* (Ithaca, NY: Cornell University Press, 1966), 267.

9. I.II 61.4: "temperantia vero sit quaedam dispositio animi quae modum quibuscumque passionibus vel operationibus imponit, ne ultra debitum efferantur."

10. Mark F. Carr, *Passionate Deliberation: Emotion, Temperance, and the Care Ethic in Clinical Moral Deliberation* (Boston: Kluwer Academic, 2001), vii, 53, 159.

11. Van Wensveen, "Attunement" 71, 73.

12. Van Wensveen, "Attunement," 72. Italics in the original.

13. I.II 61.2: "Ordinem enim rationis necesse est ponere circa passiones, considerata repugnantia ipsarum ad rationem. Quae quidem potest esse dupliciter. Uno modo secundum quod passio impellit ad aliquid contrarium rationi, et sic necesse est quod passio reprimatur, et ab hoc denominatur temperantia. Alio modo, secundum quod passio retrahit ab eo quod ratio dictat, sicut timor periculorum vel laborum, et sic necesse est quod homo firmetur in eo quod est rationis, ne recedat; et ab hoc denominatur fortitudo."

14. Van Wensveen, "Attunement," 72.

15. Pieper, *Four Cardinal Virtues*, 175.

16. 141.1: "[Temperantia] in ipso eius nomine importatur quaedam moderatio seu temperies." On temperance as "proper mixture," see North, *Sophrosyne*, 262, and Carr, *Passionate Deliberation*, 29–33.

17. Robert C. Roberts, "Temperance," in *Virtues and Their Vices*, ed. Kevin Timpe and Craig A. Boyd (Oxford: Oxford University Press, 2014), 93.

18. I owe this idea to a comment by Eric Kraemer.

19. Thomas Gilby, *St. Thomas Aquinas: Summa Theologiae, Temperance*, vol. 43 (2a2ae. 141–54) (Cambridge: Cambridge University Press, 2006), 16–17.

20. Roberts, "Temperance," 100–106.

21. 155.2 arg 2: "per quam aliquis resistit concupiscentiis pravis, quae in eo vehementes existunt."

22. 143 ad 1: "Convenit tamen cum temperantia et in materia, quia est circa delectationes tactus; et in modo, quia in quadam refrenatione consistit."

23. 155.2 ad 1: "continentia habet materiam concupiscentias delectationum tactus, non sicut quas moderetur, quod pertinet ad temperantiam, quae est in concupiscibili, sed est circa eas quasi eis resistens."

24. 155.4c: "Plus autem viget bonum rationis in eo qui est temperatus, in quo etiam ipse appetitus sensitivus est subiectus rationi et quasi a ratione edomitus, quam in eo qui est continens, in quo appetitus sensitivus vehementer resistit rationi per concupiscentias pravas."

25. *De Veritate* 14.5.

26. Paul Van Tongeren, "Temperance and Environmental Concerns," *Ethical Perspectives* 10, no. 2 (2005): 123.

27. Rosalind Hursthouse, *On Virtue Ethics* (Oxford: Oxford University Press, 1999), 245–46.

28. Ibid., 249.

29. *On the Virtues* 1.10 ad 14: "semper remanet colluctatio carnis contra spiritum, etiam post moralem virtutem."

30. I.II 61.4 ad 1: "animi firmitatem contra impetus delectationum."

31. I.II 56.6 ad 1: "ordinat ad bonum proprium ipsius volentis."

32. 117.5c: "Liberalitas . . . principaliter est ad alterum, sicut et iustitia."

33. 30.1 ad 2: "Quia misericordia est compassio miseriae alterius, proprie misericordia est ad alterum."

34. Jean Porter, *The Recovery of Virtue: The Relevance of Aquinas for Christian Ethics* (Louisville, KY: Westminster John Knox, 1990), 117. Italics in the original.

35. 141.6c and ad 1: "temperantiae ipsius finis et regula est beatitudo, sed eius rei qua utitur, finis et regula est necessitas humanae vitae, infra quam est id quod in usum vitae venit."

36. 141.6 arg 2 ad 2: "his moderate utitur, pro loco et tempore et congruentia eorum quibus convivit."

37. *Comm. Ethic.*, lib. 3 l. 21 n.5: "idest quam requiratur ad sanitatem et bonam habitudinem corporis et ad decentem conversationem cum aliis."

38. 141.6 arg 2 ad 3: "sicut dictum est, temperantia respicit necessitatem quantum ad convenientiam vitae. Quae quidem attenditur non solum secundum convenientiam corporis, sed etiam secundum convenientiam exteriorum rerum, puta divitiarum et officiorum; et multo magis secundum convenientiam honestatis."

39. Aquinas divides the good into the useful, the delightful, and the honest (I.5.6). In the broad sense, then, the honest is anything that is good in itself and therefore can be desired for its own sake. In a more specific sense, the honest is the moral good, so coincides with the virtuous. See II.II 145, especially the first article.

40. Roberts, "Temperance," 99.

41. *Super Sent.*, lib. 4 d. 49 q. 1 a. 1 qc. 1 ad 4: "Bonum ergo corporis potest esse finis virtutis, quasi quidam terminus vel effectus virtuosae operationis; non autem sicut in quo stet virtutis intentio."

42. II.II 141.3 ad 3: "exteriores actus procedunt ab interioribus animae passionibus. Et ideo moderatio eorum dependet a moderatione interiorum passionum."

43. Sherry Turkle, *Alone Together: Why We Expect More from Technology and Less from Each Other* (New York: Basic, 2011).

44. *Comm. Ethic.*, lib. 2 l. 11 n.8.

45. Laura Marie Hartman, "An Ethics of Consumption: Christianity, Economy, and Ecology" (PhD dissertation, University of Virginia, 2008), 94.

46. Ibid., 74–113.

47. II.II 161.6 ad 2: "homo ad humilitatem pervenit per duo. Primo quidem et principaliter, per gratiae donum. Et quantum ad hoc, interiora praecedunt exteriora. Aliud autem est humanum studium, per quod homo prius exteriora cohibet, et postmodum pertingit ad extirpandum interiorem radicem. Et secundum hunc ordinem assignantur hic humilitatis gradus."

48. I.II 61.5c: "Oportet igitur quod exemplar humanae virtutis in Deo praeexistat, sicut et in eo praeexistunt omnium rerum rationes."

49. I.II 61.5c: "conversio divinae intentionis ad seipsum, sicut in nobis temperantia dicitur per hoc quod concupiscibilis conformatur rationi."

50. Symbolum Apostolorum, a. 4: "Quicumque enim vult perfecte vivere, nihil aliud faciat nisi quod contemnat quae Christus in cruce contempsit, et appetat quae Christus appetiit."

CHAPTER 2

Virtue as a Habit

Suggested reading: *Summa Theologiae* I.II 49.1–4,
55.1–2; *On the Virtues* 1.1

Thomas Aquinas prefaces his causal definition of virtue by characterizing virtue as a good operative habit: "Human virtue, which is an operative habit, is a good habit, and operative of the good" (I.II 55.3c).[1] In answer to the question, "What kind of thing is a virtue?" Aquinas, in effect, replies, "a habit."

The concept of habit may seem commonplace and hardly mysterious. Yet the history of reflection on this idea, from Aristotle to the social theorist Pierre Bourdieu, is a complex and rich one. For theological ethics its importance lies in the fact that the good Christian life has to comprise more than a series of discrete actions; it must involve the formation and even transformation of the human agent. By habit our moral character is constituted. For Aquinas, the habitual formation of desire toward the good is of nothing less than ultimate importance; it is, he says, "necessary for the end of human life" (50.5 ad 1).[2]

What is a habit? Aquinas uses the Latin word *habitus*, from *habere*: to have or possess. While this term is often translated as "habit," it will quickly become apparent that there is a great difference between our contemporary idea of habit and Aquinas's *habitus*. For virtue theory this difference is not insignificant.

THE PROBLEM WITH MODERN HABITS

There is an acute danger of misinterpreting Aquinas's virtue theory as we read his understanding of habit through modern eyes. Even scholars who recognize some differences between modern and medieval accounts of habit are often unaware of how wide the gap really is. To simply substitute the modern idea of habit for Aquinas's *habitus* would be a significant failure of exegetical accuracy and, more important, would obscure the riches of Aquinas's helpful account.

We find the modern idea of habit expressed in the classic treatment by the philosopher and psychologist William James (1842–1910). James sees habits as potentially positive: virtues and vices are both habits. We are a "mass of habits," and whichever habits we possess determines our well-being or otherwise.[3] Due to the "plasticity" of our nature we are capable of voluntarily forming habits in ourselves by repeated action in order to diminish the effort and fatigue required to attain certain goals.[4] James advises that the one who has carefully cultivated the right habits in life "will stand like a tower when everything rocks around him, and his softer fellow-mortals are winnowed like chaff in the blast."[5]

Aquinas would likely agree, at least thus far. But we also find in James a strong emphasis on the "automatic" nature of habits. By his account, habit *"diminishes the conscious attention with which our acts are performed."*[6] Contemporary psychological treatments of habit carry on from where James began, analyzing habits into a "cue," a "behavior," and a "reward." Once a habit is established, if given a particular trigger the behavior is automatic: "Contexts activate habitual responses directly, without the mediation of goal states."[7] Indeed, contemporary psychological studies take *automaticity* as a key indicator of when a habit has been formed. Yet the more something is done automatically, the less it is done consciously and voluntarily. The modern concept of habit therefore picks out a mechanistic pattern of response, generated by multiple repetitions of identical actions. Habits, therefore, lead to unthinking and nonvoluntary action. As James puts it, habitual actions, like dressing, eating, or greeting friends, "are things of a type so fixed by repetition as almost to be classed as reflex actions. To each sort of impression we have an automatic, ready-made response."[8] There are even hints of a neuro-physical determinism in James's account, such as when he refers to habits being "grooved out" in the brain.[9]

It is easy to see why there is a modern ambivalence about habits, even "good" ones. Even if we agree with James about the need to develop good routines, a purely habitual life seems lacking in spontaneity. As one student of modern habits concedes, "As automaticity increases, our experience of being in the moment recedes; we feel less alive, fail to notice the world around us, and become disconnected from our experience."[10] Indeed, habits can take control of us and "lock us into the same boring grooves."[11] In the modern view, habits are a form of automatic pilot in which our free conscious agency is diminished or even nearly eliminated.

This concept of habit leads to problems in virtue theory. A virtue, following Aristotle and Aquinas, is both a habit and a principle of rational operation, in that it incorporates practical reasoning about how to act. Yet how can a habit of unthinking, nonvoluntary response also be rational?

Bill Pollard attempts to square the circle by offering an account of rational action that makes room for automaticity. He argues that an action can be rational even though free from deliberation. How could this be possible? Pollard claims that, insofar as someone can *construct* an account of how her action makes sense rationally, her action can be considered rational.[12] He therefore takes the rationality of virtuous action out of the action itself and sees it merely as something the agent devises to makes sense of what she does habitually. Post hoc rationalization substitutes for action that flows from a deliberative process. With this dubious move Pollard saves the idea that virtuous action can be habitual, but this move comes at a cost: virtuous action is no longer deliberate. That Pollard does not question the idea that habitual action is automatic—a more promising way of reconciling virtuous and habitual actions—shows the grip that the modern idea of habit has.

In the psychological literature there is an awareness that modern models of habit may need to be revised. Wendy Wood and David T. Neale offer the following definition: "Habits are learned dispositions to repeat past responses."[13] By their account, contexts have the power to "trigger" habitual responses without any behavioral goal guiding performance. They rightly worry, therefore, that habitual action falls outside of the sphere of responsibility: "'I can't help it, it's just a habit,' is an excuse that people might offer for such cued behaviors as bad habits (e.g., chronic overeating) and action slips (e.g., accidentally driving to work when intending to go to the store). By offering such accounts, people perhaps are acknowledging that their responses are cued by performance contexts independently of what they intended to accomplish."[14] To reintroduce some degree of intentionality into habit, Wood and Neale propose that "habits interface with goals." For example, goals can motivate repetition and lead to the intentional formation of habits that serve one's goals. In other words, while habitual action as such is unintentional, there can be a kind of voluntariness in choosing which habits to cultivate in oneself.

While this is some progress in trying to reconcile intention and action, the solution remains within a largely mechanistic understanding of habit as a reflex response to a cue or trigger. The only acknowledged intentionality in habits is the extrinsic one of choosing which habits to cultivate; there is no sense that the exercise of habit itself could be intrinsically voluntary. Once again, virtuous and habitual action seem incompatible. Does Aquinas offer a way forward?

HUMAN AGENCY

In the prologue to the *Treatise of Habits*, Aquinas begins: "After considering acts and passions, we now consider the principles of human acts" (I.II 49 pr).[15]

A habit, for Aquinas, is the principle of a human act. This is why ethics needs to look at habits: it is interested in the good human acts that lead us toward beatitude and the bad ones that lead us away; it needs also to look at habits (that is, virtues and vices) as their intrinsic principles (ibid.; I.II 6 pr). If a habit is an intrinsic principle of a human act, what is a human act?

Aquinas's ethics takes human acts seriously. In the prologue to the *Treatise on Morals* Aquinas transitions from the first part of the *Summa Theologiae*, about God and what proceeds from God, to the image of God: "We now must consider God's image, that is, the human being, insofar as he also is the principle of his works, as having freewill and power over his works" (I.II pr).[16] Aquinas's ethics begins with the human agent.

Aquinas lays out a way of understanding human action in the three articles immediately following. His definition proceeds by means of a famous contrast: the distinction between a human act, *actus humanus,* and the act of a human, *actus hominis* (I.II 1).[17] A human act, as the term implies, is an act that is proper to a human insofar as she is human; a human being, as he has just stated, is a being with intellect and free will and therefore having control over her own acts. He concludes, therefore, that strictly so-called human actions are those that proceed from a will that has been disposed and directed by practical reason through a process of deliberation: "Those actions properly termed 'human' are those that proceed from a deliberate will" (1.1c).[18] These *human actions* are distinguished from mere *actions of a human*, such as moving a hand or foot while intent on something else, or absentmindedly scratching one's beard (cf. I.II 1 arg 2). As David M. Gallagher puts it, blinking (an act of a human) is different from winking (a human act).[19]

Human action is the action proper, not to an *intellectual* but a *rational* nature (1.2). As Aquinas explains, "The intellect knows by a simple intuition, whereas reason [knows] by a process of discourse from one thing to another" (I 59.1 ad 1).[20] Human beings are not angels: they arrive at the truth by a discursive process rather than through direct apprehension. Since in ethics we are in the realm of the practical rather than the speculative, arriving at the truth is in particular the process of counsel, judgment, and decision that is being singled out as characteristically human: human action is deliberate action.

John Poinsot notices a problem with this equation of "human" and "deliberate."[21] Some uniquely human acts are not deliberate, and some deliberate acts are not uniquely human. For example, only humans cry, laugh, are overcome by wonder, recognize that the whole is greater than any part, and sing and shout drunkenly. But all these uniquely human acts are usually indeliberate. Moreover, humans also perform many actions from deliberation that are not uniquely human, such as running and eating.

Poinsot clarifies, then, that the equation of human with deliberate action is not intended to identify a set of actions that humans, and only humans, perform; rather, it identifies the manner of acting that is proper to humans.[22] Indeliberate actions, such as crying and laughing, being overcome by wonder, and so on are unique to humans, but they are not done in a human way: they happen by impulse rather than through reasoned choice. As Poinsot puts it, the *substance* of these indeliberate actions is human since they depend on human intelligence, but since they are not done from deliberation, their *manner of agency* is not. Similarly, what can make running and eating properly human is not that they are done only by humans but rather that they are done in a human way—that is, deliberately. A properly human action is one that is performed in a manner proper to or characteristic of humans and proceeding from reason and will.

THE DEFINITION OF HABIT

Having looked at human action, we are ready to turn to Aquinas's concept of habit as a *principle* of human action.[23] How may one go about defining habit? One could consider including various elements in the definition. Habits are often acquired by *repetition*, are more or less *stable*, are *disposed* toward some object or act, are *good or bad*, and add *facility* to operation. Different definitions emphasize different elements. For example, contemporary psychology defines habits as "learned dispositions to repeat past responses," showing an emphasis on their repetitive nature.

One element conspicuously lacking in Aquinas's account of the essence of habit is acquisition by repetition. Why this lacuna? Theologically, Aquinas recognizes that some habits are "infused" by God; that is, they come as divine gifts rather than by human achievement (51.4). A definition that includes "generation by repetition" would therefore fail by being too narrow in extension and apply to only some habits.[24]

There is a more fundamental reason for the omission. Aquinas does recognize, following Aristotle, that repeated action may generate a habit. Just as one becomes a good or bad builder by customarily building well or building badly, so by acting well or acting badly one becomes just or unjust. "Generally, as one may put it in a word, like habits come about from like operations."[25] Yet this important principle identifies at best the efficient, not the formal cause of habits; that is, it explains what brings them into *existence* rather than saying anything about their *essence* (I.II 51–53). It is notable, then, that Aquinas's questions on the efficient cause of habits (51–53) come after his treatment of the habit's "substance" or essence (49). Before one looks at *how* habits come about, one must say *what* a habit is. What, then, does Aquinas say?

Quality, Disposition, Habit

Aquinas's theory of habit is a causal one. He offers an account of the nature of habits from its four causes: formal (I.II 49.1–2), final (49.3–4), material (50), and efficient (51–53).[26] Here we will focus mainly on the formal cause since of all the causes this is the most definitional; the others will be considered when we examine virtue.

To characterize habit, Aquinas initially follows the method of definition from Aristotelian logic. The first step is to identify habit's "category," or its most general kind (*summum genus*). A habit, Aquinas argues, is neither a substance nor a relation nor a quantity but only a *quality* (49.1). This is hardly surprising. A habit must be a quality since when we acquire or lose a habit such as wisdom, beauty, or knowledge, a real change takes place within us. Furthermore, when we describe a person as wise or beautiful or knowledgeable, we are genuinely describing what they are like. Habits are not essential qualities; rather, they are accidental qualities that come genuinely to modify and qualify the subject.

A habit is a quality: that is its "category." The next step is to determine the specific kind of quality a habit is. According to Aristotle's *Categories*, there are four species of quality, each of which is denominated by a binary pair: disposition and habit, potency and impotency, passion and passible quality, and form and figure. Thus "habit" falls into the first species of quality, alongside "disposition."

A terminological nicety needs to be noted. The word "Holland" can be used generically to refer to the whole of the Netherlands or specifically to a particular region of that country. Similarly, for Aquinas "disposition" is ambiguous and lies somewhere between a generic sense that names the first species of quality and a specific sense that names a particular kind of this species (and which is contradistinguished from habit). A habit is a disposition when "disposition" is taken in its generic sense; it is not disposition when "disposition" is taken in its more specific sense.

As Aquinas gleans from Aristotle's *Metaphysics*, "a disposition is an order of that which has parts" (49.1 arg 3).[27] This is what disposition refers to in its general sense. Admittedly, when we refer to a habit as a kind of disposition, we do not mean it is a physical arrangement of a thing's parts. Nevertheless, by a kind of analogy from the physical ordering of parts, a habit reduces complexity to unity and orders a power or capacity of the soul to a single act, object, or end; by itself a power is indifferent to many different acts and objects (49.1 arg 3, c. and ad 3).

Thus a habit is a kind of disposition, where "disposition" is taken in its generic sense to refer to a quality that focuses human capacities to operate in a specific way, like the software of a computer that enables the hardware to perform some specific task. At the same time, a habit is *contrasted* with a disposition, if "disposition" is taken in its more specific and proper sense. We can call the former a "generic" disposition and the latter a "mere" disposition since for Aquinas it does not possess the stability that characterizes habit (49.2 ad 3). A mere disposition is a tenuous version of the more firmly rooted habit. Given that a habit is a quality, and more specifically a disposition (although not a mere disposition), what is the feature that ultimately defines habit as habit?

Four Candidates for the Defining Feature

There are four candidates for the specifying difference that makes a disposition into a habit. A habit, Aquinas claims, is a quality or disposition that is *stable, operative, valent,* and *nature-directed.* First, a habit is a *stable* quality or disposition (I.II 49.2). Aquinas's preferred term is *difficile mobilis*: changeable with difficulty. A habit is not an easy-come, easy-go kind of quality, since then it would not be a *habitus* or something truly *had* or possessed. (*Habitus* derives from *habere*: to have or possess.) In some instances I may temporarily be inclined to kindness, and even on occasion act kindly, but that does not make me a kind person; only a more stable disposition can do that. A habit is not a "transient quality," like the blush of someone who has become embarrassed, but is an "immanent quality" of its bearer.[28]

Second, a habit is an *operative* quality. Habits are disposed toward acts or operations (49.3). Indeed, since habits are not directly observable, they can be known only through the acts to which they dispose their bearer (II.II 4.1). A habit, then, is neither the pure potentiality of some subject nor its complete realization in operation; it is something intermediate between the two. "A habit lies midway between potentiality and actualization" (I.II 73.1c).[29] Before learning to play the piano a child has the capacity to do so; yet if she presses random keys, only noise emerges. After years of practice the child becomes a musician and has acquired a quality: a habit that enables her to play the works of Chopin and Liszt when she chooses. This habit is something actual that goes beyond the bare capacity (*potentia nuda*) that the child initially possessed; yet it is still a potential of some sort since it is actualized only on those occasions when the musician sits at the piano and plays (II.II 171.2 ad 1). The habit of piano playing is already actual in relation to the potential she possessed by nature, but it is merely potential in relation to the act of performing.[30] A habit is what Aquinas calls the "first actuality" of a capacity, in that it does begin to perfect a potential. But it is not itself the "second actuality," or its full completion in operation (I.II 49.3 ad 1). Habit, then, is "halfway between pure potentiality and the complete act" (50.4).[31] Habits are operative because they are principles of operation.

Third, a habit has a *valent* quality—that is, one that it is either good or bad. For Aquinas, a habit is never value-neutral. Indeed, as he tells us, a habit is "a disposition according to which something is disposed well or badly" (49.2c).[32] Being good or bad belongs to the very concept of habit (ibid.). Compare the word "habit" with that of "state." If we ask about the state of a violin, say, we are not merely interested in just any of its characteristics, such as shape, size, and so on, but whether it is in *good* or *bad* condition. The state of a violin is a good or bad state; it is never a value-neutral one. It is the same with habit: to dispose well or badly belongs to habit's rationale (49.2 ad 1). For Aquinas, a habit is by definition a good or bad state to be in; that is, it is a *valent* quality.

So far we are moving toward a definition of habit as a quality or, more precisely, a disposition that is *stable, operative,* and *valent.* Finally, Aquinas claims that habits are qualities that are *nature-directed.* Summarizing, he states: "As has been said, habit implies a certain disposition in order to a being's nature, and to its operation or end, according to which [disposition] it is well or badly disposed to this [nature and operation]" (49.4).[33] This characterization includes both valence and being operative, although it leaves out stability. And an additional element is included: habit is a disposition *in order to a being's nature.* All qualities, Aquinas says, are "modes" or "determinations" of a subject; a habit is that specific kind of quality that modifies or determines its subject "in order to the nature of a thing" (49.2c).[34]

This final of the four marks of habit is the most opaque yet the most fundamental. Aquinas does not simply identify a conglomeration of properties; rather, he attempts to identify the essential core from which the others flow. It is *because* habit is a nature-directed disposition that it is also stable, operative, and valent.

It is not necessary to see the link immediately: the derivation of the other characteristics from this one will be left to the next chapter. For the moment, armed with Aquinas's understanding of habit as a disposition that is stable, operative, valent, and nature-directed, we return to our current question: Does it make sense to see virtue as a habit, as Aquinas does?

VIRTUE AS A HABIT

Defining a virtue as a kind of habit is problematic. In the modern view, habits are marked by automaticity because they are reflex responses that bypass the rational and volitional faculties. If virtuous action is voluntary and rational, and habitual action is not, it is difficult to see virtue as a habit.

In contrast to this dominant modern view, for Aquinas the relationship between habit and deliberate agency is not one of competition. Merely to state the noncontradiction of the habitual and the voluntary does not remotely get to the heart of the matter: for Aquinas, habits, far from undermining voluntariness, actually perfect it. Let us examine this in more depth.

Is Virtue a Habit?

Aquinas's *habitus* is derived from the reflexive use of the Latin verb *habere*: to have or to possess (49.1c). For example, a person with an earache might say in Latin, "*Male se habet auris mea!*" literally, "My ear has itself badly!" This makes little sense in English, so such a phrase might be translated as "My ear is in a bad state!" But the Latin is informative: it links *habitus* to the reflexive verb *habere se* and therefore to the idea of self-possession.

To possess something is to have dominion over it and to be able to use it when one wants. Aquinas makes the connection with habit: "A habit is compared to a possession, insofar as we have the thing possessed at our fingertips."[35] Aquinas never tires of repeating a thesis derived from "the Commentator" Averroes (Ibn Rushd): "A habit is that by which someone acts when he wills" (I.II 5).[36] Similarly, he likes to quote Saint Augustine: "A habit is that by which we act when there is need" (49.3sc).[37] Something akin to this idea survives in contemporary English usage, as when we admire the "self-possession" of a person who does not behave in a reactive manner but is calm, confident, and in control of her feelings and actions. Aquinas's *habitus* is something one possesses, or even a form of self-possession, in contrast to a modern habit, which is something that possesses me.

It may sensibly be objected that if a habit is that by which we act whenever we want, like a possession we can use at will, then a virtue can hardly be habit. A virtuous person is not inclined to be virtuous only when she chooses, but all the time.

This objection misses the way that moral habits, for Aquinas, are unique: they form desire itself, by perfecting the will (50.3 ad 3; 4): "It is necessary to posit some habit in the will, by which it is well disposed to its act. For, from the very rationale of habit, it appears that it has a certain principal order to the will, insofar as a habit is that which one uses when one wills" (50.5c).[38] Whereas modern habit is a substitute for conscious agency, putting a person on cruise control, Thomistic moral habits engage rather than bypass the human will. The moral virtues are dispositions to *choose* to act in certain ways: moral virtue is a habit that chooses, an elective habit (58.1 ad 2). Habits, rather than bypassing human agency, are perfective of it.

For this reason Aquinas denies that animals can possess habits in the full and proper sense. One may train a dog, for example, to do certain things from custom, by using punishments and treats. However, these are not fully habitual: "The rationale of a habit [in animals] is lacking as regards the use of the will, because they do not have dominion of using or not using, which seems to belong to the rationale of habit" (50.3 ad 2).[39] Note the difference between modern habit and Aquinas's *habitus*: where modern habit is antithetical to will, Aquinas's *habitus* requires it. Where modern habit is a principle of an act of a human (*actus hominis*), a *habitus* is a principle of a human act (*actus humanus*).

This enables Aquinas to argue that virtue is a habit: "Virtue names a certain perfection of a power" (55.1c).[40] A power is perfected by being determined to its end. Nothing can fulfill this role except a habit, which, as we have seen, focuses the rational powers on a specific object: "Rational powers, those that are properly human, are not determinate to one [*ad unum*], but stand indeterminately to many things [*ad multa*]. However, they may be determined to act by habits, as is evident from what has been said [49.4]. And therefore human virtues are habits" (55.1c).[41] Again, a virtue is like a piece of software that builds on a computer's basic but indiscriminate capacity and enables it to accomplish definite tasks.

How does this resolve the paradox of virtuous action being habitual action? The key is the idea that the habit of virtue is a perfection of a power (*perfectio potentiae*). Virtuous habits do not diminish but improve our capacity to act from reason and will. A virtue cannot be a modern habit, since the more something is done from modern habit the less it is done from reason and will; it must be a *habitus* since virtue, as a principle of a *human* act, is nothing other than a perfection of the rational powers of agency.

Habit versus Habitus

Is there any truth in the modern understanding of habit? Psychological enquiry into habit is informative but often concerns something different from Aquinas's *habitus*. It is true that we can program ourselves to react to certain triggers in predictable ways. This is morally relevant information because just as we need to be wary of acquiring bad habits, there are advantages to cultivating good ones.[42] Habits can be relatively banal, such as brushing teeth in the morning, or morally significant, such as sitting in prayer once one's teeth have been brushed. Yet while it is valuable to acquire a habitual time, place, and method of prayer, it is crucial that the practice does not remain on the level of the "habitual" (in the modern sense). It should be exercised with one's full heart and mind. Modern habits are useful, but limited.

There is nothing to prevent psychological inquiry being motivated by a richer concept of habit. As Julia Annas points out, a responsible empirical study of virtue "would require close cooperation of philosophers and psychologists, since it is crucial that virtue be understood properly, and not in terms of routine or automaticity."[43] Before that day comes, modern habit must be seen as a pale imitation of its ancient and medieval ancestor. First, there is a remnant of earlier accounts in the idea of that there is a *uniformity* to habitual action (*On the Virtues* 1.1c). Habits simplify and dispose the complex subject to one thing (*ad unum*) (49.4c). However, although a virtuous person reliably acts justly and temperately, this reliability is not a matter of rote repetition of materially identical actions, since what it means to be just or temperate will differ from situation to situation (*On the Virtues* 1.6c).[44] Virtue can never be a "ready-made response."

Second, there is, from a Thomistic perspective, some truth in the idea that habits are *automatic*. Aquinas claims that habits are characterized by facility (*facilitas*)—namely, the ability to exercise a capacity with promptness and without inner resistance.[45] There is a difference between *facility* and *automaticity*: facility is akin not so much to the unthinking automaticity of lighting up a cigarette as to the full engagement of an athlete or musician. To observe the snooker player Ding Junhui secure a clearance with apparent effortlessness is to see someone who is focused, thinking, and fully invested—not someone on automatic pilot, no matter how much his skill derives from repetitive practice. Automaticity diminishes conscious agency; facility increases it.

Finally, there is a grain of truth in the thought that habitual actions happen unthinkingly. Aquinas notes that one reason we need habits is "so that we may perform perfect operation promptly. For unless the rational power is in some way inclined to one [act or object] by habit, it would be necessary always to perform some inquiry about operation before operating, as happens in the case of those who want to act virtuously, but lack the habit of virtue" (*On the Virtues* 1.1c).[46] However, promptness in deciding is not the same as not deciding. Moral habits may bypass the need for inquiry; they do not eliminate the need for choice. While morally virtuous action can happen without *forethought*, it does not happen without *thought*.

What accounts for the contemporary demoralized conception of habit? Consider this hypothesis: the dominant mechanistic, impersonal model of causation bequeathed to us by the modern natural philosophers leaves little room for intentional human agency. When the reductionistic acid of naturalism is applied to the rich moral concept of *habitus,* it is no wonder that all that remains is the empty shell of a Pavlovian automaticity. The exploration of habit is the first major sign that the virtue theorist does well to consider a richer account of causation and agency. Virtue is a habit, not because it generates automatic reactions but because it is a stable quality that perfects our capacity for rational agency and disposes us to deliberate, intentional, human action.

NOTES

1. I.II 55.3c: "virtus humana, quae est habitus operativus, est bonus habitus, et boni operativus."
2. 50.5 ad 1: "necessarium est ad finem humanae vitae."
3. William James, *Talks to Teachers on Psychology, and to Students on Some of Life's Ideals* (Rockville, MD: Arc Manor, 2008), 42.
4. William James, *The Principles of Psychology*, vol. 1 (New York: Cosimo, 2007), 105, 112–14.
5. James, *Talks to Teachers*, 47.
6. *Principles of Psychology*, 1:114. Italics in the original.
7. Wendy Wood and David T. Neal, "A New Look at Habits and the Habit-Goal Interface," *Psychological Review* 114, no. 4 (2007): 843.
8. James, *Talks to Teachers*, 66.
9. James, *Principles of Psychology*, 126.
10. Jeremy Dean, *Making Habits, Breaking Habits: Why We Do Things, Why We Don't, and How to Make Any Change Stick* (Philadelphia: Da Capo, 2013), 225.
11. Ibid., 228.
12. Bill Pollard, "Can Virtuous Actions Be Both Habitual and Rational?," *Ethical Theory and Moral Practice* 6, no. 4 (2003): 411–25; and Julia Peters, "On Automaticity as a Constituent of Virtue," *Ethical Theory and Moral Practice* 18, no. 1 (February 2015): 165–75.
13. Wood and Neal, "New Look," 843.
14. Ibid., 844.
15. I.II 49 pr: "Post actus et passiones, considerandum est de principiis humanorum actuum."
16. I.II pr: "restat ut consideremus de eius imagine, idest de homine, secundum quod et ipse est suorum operum principium, quasi liberum arbitrium habens et suorum operum potestatem."
17. I.II 1.1; cf. III 19.2; *On the Virtues* 1.4c; and *Comm. Ethic.*, lib. 1 l. 1 n.3.
18. 1.1c: "Illae ergo actiones proprie humanae dicuntur, quae ex voluntate deliberata procedunt."

19. David M. Gallagher, *Thomas Aquinas and His Legacy* (Washington, DC: Catholic University of America Press, 1994), 47.

20. I 59.1 ad 1: "intellectus cognoscit simplici intuitu, ratio vero discurrendo de uno in aliud."

21. *Cursus Theologicus*, in I.II, Disp.1, *De fine morali et ultimo*, nn.57–65 (Solesmes 5:18–19).

22. Ibid., paragraphs 66–81 (Solesmes 5:20–24).

23. As well as the *Treatise on Habits* in the *Summa Theologiae* (I.II 49–54), Aquinas also deals with habits in III Sent. dist 23, q.1, a.1–3; in V Metaphy. Lect. 16, 20; in *On the Virtues* 1.1; and in *De Veritate*, q.22, a.2. John Poinsot discusses the nature of habit in two places: *Cursus Philosophicus, Ars Logica (Secunda Pars)*, Q.23, (1:609–21) and *Cursus Theologicus,* Disp.13, Art.1–3. Jacobus Ramírez's two-volume treatise on habits is the most thorough Thomistic treatment. Also worth consulting is G. P. Klubertanz, *Habits and Virtues* (Appleton-Century-Crofts, 1965).

24. Bonnie Kent, "Habits and Virtues (Ia IIae, qq.49–70)," in *The Ethics of Aquinas*, ed. Stephen J. Pope, Moral Traditions Series (Washington, DC: Georgetown University Press, 2002), 117.

25. *Comm. Ethic.*, lib. 2 l. 1 n.9: "Et universaliter, ut uno sermone dicatur, ex similibus operationibus fiunt similes habitus."

26. Aquinas also adds a final question on how, given this account of habit, one may distinguish different habits into those that are good or bad (54).

27. 49.1 arg 3: "dispositio est ordo habentis partes."

28. *Super Sent.*, lib. 3 d. 23 q. 1 a. 1c; *De Veritate*, q. 20 a. 2c.

29. I.II 73.1c: "habitus medio modo se habet inter potentiam et actum."

30. See *Comm. De Anima*, lib. 2 l. 11 n.4; I.II 49.3 ad 1. See also Robert Pasnau, *Thomas Aquinas on Human Nature: A Philosophical Study of Summa Theologiae 1a, 75–89* (Cambridge, UK: Cambridge University Press, 2002), 426.

31. 50.4: "medius inter puram potentiam et actum perfectum."

32. 49.2c: "Unde in V Metaphys. philosophus definit habitum, quod est dispositio secundum quam aliquis disponitur bene vel male."

33. 49.4: "sicut supra dictum est, habitus importat dispositionem quandam in ordine ad naturam rei, et ad operationem vel finem eius, secundum quam bene vel male aliquid ad hoc disponitur."

34. 49.2c: "modus et determinatio subiecti in ordine ad naturam rei, pertinet ad primam speciem qualitatis, quae est habitus et dispositio."

35. *Super Sent.*, lib. 3 d. 23 q. 1 a. 1c: "habitus possessioni comparatur in 1 Ethic. secundum quam res possessa ad nutum habetur."

36. I.II 5: "habitus est quo quis agit cum voluerit."

37. 49.3sc: "habitus est quo aliquid agitur cum opus est."

38. 50.5c: "oportet in voluntate aliquem habitum ponere, quo bene disponatur ad suum actum. Ex ipsa etiam ratione habitus apparet quod habet quendam principalem ordinem ad voluntatem, prout habitus est quo quis utitur cum voluerit."

39. 50.3 ad 2: "Deficit tamen ratio habitus quantum ad usum voluntatis, quia non habent dominium utendi vel non utendi, quod videtur ad rationem habitus pertinere."

40. 55.1c: "virtus nominat quandam potentiae perfectionem."

41. 55.1c: "Potentiae autem rationales, quae sunt propriae hominis, non sunt determinatae ad unum, sed se habent indeterminate ad multa, determinantur autem ad actus per habitus, sicut ex supradictis patet. Et ideo virtutes humanae habitus sunt."

42. Charles Duhigg, *The Power of Habit: Why We Do What We Do in Life and Business* (London: William Heinemann, 2012).

43. Julia Annas, *Intelligent Virtue* (Oxford: Oxford University Press, 2011), 175.

44. Compare Servais Pinckaers, "Virtue Is Not a Habit," *Cross Currents* 12 (1962): 77–79.

45. *Super Sent.*, lib. 3 d. 23 q. 1 a. 1 ad 4.

46. *On the Virtues* 1.1c: "ut operatio perfecta in promptu habeatur. Nisi enim potentia rationalis per habitum aliquo modo inclinetur ad unum, oportebit semper, cum necesse fuerit operari, praecedere inquisitionem de operatione; sicut patet de eo qui vult considerare nondum habens scientiae habitum, et qui vult secundum virtutem agere habitu virtutis carens."

CHAPTER 3

Virtue as a Good Habit

Suggested reading: *Summa Theologiae* I 5.1,
22.1; I.II 19.4, 49.2–3, 54.3, 55.3, 71.2,
71.6, 91.1; *On the Virtues* 1.13

"Human virtue, which is an operative habit, is a good habit, and operative of the good" (I.II 55.3).[1] A virtue is a habit. To say that it is a *good* habit may seem to border on the tautological. Yet Aquinas is aware that there is need for some account of what makes a habit good (in the constitutive or formal sense of "makes"). What distinguishes good habits from bad ones, or virtues from vices?

WHAT MAKES A HABIT GOOD?

In answering this question, Aquinas lays down the basic principle as follows: "A good habit is said to be one that disposes to an act fitting to the nature of the agent, whereas a bad habit is said to be one that disposes to an act not fitting to nature" (I.II 54.3c).[2] Thus "nature" is what provides the basis to distinguish between virtue and vice. To see why, it is necessary to return to a question left hanging in the last chapter—namely, how exactly to define a habit.

Poinsot versus Suárez

We have seen that a habit is a particular kind of quality or disposition: it is stable, operative, valent, and nature-directed. Yet Aquinas does not define an essence by listing a set of characteristics; rather, he identifies the core element from which the others follow as properties. To understand how Aquinas establishes that being *nature-directed* explains a habit's other marks, especially the

37

one we are most interested in here (i.e., its *valence*, or it being either good or bad), it will help to refer to a disagreement between John Poinsot (1589–1644) and Francisco Suárez (1548–1617).

Suárez offers the following definition of habit: "A habit . . . is a certain permanent quality, and of itself stable in its subject, in itself and in the first place ordered to operation, not providing the first capacity for operation, but helping and facilitating it."[3] "Suárezian habits," then, are simply stable inclinations that perfect our capacities for operation. They add *facility* to a pure *capacity*. As Suárez says, a habit is "a certain species of quality proximately ordered to helping a power in its operation."[4] The foundational characteristic of a habit, then, is that it is operation-directed. He conveys this by using the technical terminology of Aristotelian logic: habits are *primo* and *per se*, in the first place and of themselves, ordered toward operation. A predicate belongs to the subject *primo* and *per se* when it belongs to its essence or quiddity; it is not merely a property flowing from that essence. Suárez *defines* a habit as an operative quality.

John Poinsot recognizes that Suárez is close to Aquinas here. Yet he notices a difference: Aquinas would agree that habits are operative but, unlike Suárez, he declines to define habit as an operative quality.[5] Aquinas says, "Habit, in the first place and of itself, implies a relatedness to the nature of the thing" (49.3c).[6] For Aquinas, then, it is not order to operation but order to nature that *per se et primo*, of itself and in the first place, is what makes a quality or disposition to be a habit. Poinsot draws our attention to the fact that, whereas for Suárez the core essential element of habit is *being operative*, for Aquinas it is *being nature-directed*.[7] What is the significance of this subtle difference?

Nature and Habit

"Nature" is a notoriously multifaceted concept in all of Aquinas's work. For example, he recounts a list of six different senses of "nature" derived from Aristotle's *Metaphysics*.[8] Without going into excessive exegetical detail, a central point for Aquinas is that nature is dynamic, not static. A thing's nature is what that thing is: "Generally speaking, the essence of anything, what its definition signifies, is called a nature" (I.II 29.1 ad 4).[9] However, "essence" and "nature," although the same in reference, differ in sense. "Essence" signifies what a thing is, as it can be defined and grasped by the human mind; "nature" adds a telic note: "Nature . . . seems to signify the essence of a thing insofar as it has an order to the proper operation of a thing, since no thing is without its characteristic operation."[10] Aquinas holds a teleological concept of nature: created beings, because of their natures, are oriented to their own end (or *telos,* to use the Greek word for "end"), which consists in nothing other than their proper activity or function.

Aquinas therefore adopts Aristotle's teleological maxim, "Nature acts for an end."[11] This is not meant to be an esoteric principle but something observable from everyday occurrence. Some of Aquinas's examples: teeth are sharp, swallows build nests, plants grow roots that draw up nourishment from the earth, spiders spin webs, and ants coordinate in such a way that some have wondered whether they are intelligent (although, he adds, clearly they are not).[12] The simple inference is that all of these processes and realities must be for the sake of some end: teeth are sharp to cut food and nourish the body, swallows build nests to rear young and protect them from danger, and so on. (As will be argued later, despite claims that Darwinian evolution has eliminated teleology from the scientific worldview, biologists continue to employ such teleological language to describe plant and animal behavior.) What, then, explains this end-oriented activity? Aquinas recognizes that these beings do not direct themselves through rational deliberation or art. Nor, in his view, do their activities happen by chance. Aquinas also discounts the idea that God is the immediate cause of all these activities. Rather, in his view the principle of these final-causal processes is something intrinsic to these things and by which they are moved toward their intended operations and ends. This principle is called "nature."

The teleological understanding of nature is significant for Aquinas's ethics. Humans, like other natural beings, have their own proper operation and natural *finis* or end. Just as a flourishing oak tree is being and doing what an oak tree is "meant," as it were, to be and do, so for us. As Aquinas puts it, "The nature of a thing, which is the end of generation, is also further ordered to some end, which is either an operation or some object of operation (to which someone attains through operation)" (49.3c).[13]

Aquinas's conception of habit is embedded in this final-causal understanding of human nature. He states, "It is of the rationale of the habit that it implies a certain relation in order to the nature of the thing" (49.3).[14] How should we understand this?

Human nature, for Aquinas, entails certain rational powers or capacities oriented to act. Yet these powers in and of themselves are incomplete and indeterminate. Human nature alone is not an adequate principle of a human being's characteristic operation and flourishing. Rather, these natural powers need to be completed by dispositions that complete and perfect them (55.2c). Just as a pianist cannot hope to fulfill the end of piano playing without acquiring certain musical habits and dispositions, so too a human being can reach the human end only through acquiring and exercising human habits. For that is what human habits are: realizations of a human's incomplete natural powers. Habits are nature-directed dispositions.

The Core Defining Feature of Habit

Why, then, does Aquinas take *being nature-directed* to be the core and essential feature of habits, the one that explains why habits are dispositions that are also stable, operative, and valent? Aquinas argues, first, that the nature-directedness of habits explains their stability: "We observe . . . *stability* in the first species of quality, inasmuch as a certain nature is the end of generation and motion" (49.3c).[15] Think of a young sapling that grows to become a flourishing oak tree: its maturity is the end and terminus of its development. Similarly, humans reach maturity and full development, the end point of growth, through their habits. Having acquired habits, we become less plastic and changeable. A habit, because it is directed toward nature as an end, is more or less fixed. Aquinas has explained one of the properties of habit—its *stability*—in terms of its nature-directedness.

What about the second property of habit, its being *operative*? Aquinas states: "Habits not only imply order to the very nature of a thing, but even, consequently, to operation, insofar as [operation] is the end of nature, or something leading to the end" (49.3c).[16] Habits are necessary for Aquinas because human nature, of itself, has an unfinished quality that can only find completion in two steps: the completion of its powers in habits and the realization of these perfected powers in action, like a computer that needs software to be installed and then to be run before it completes any tasks. Habit achieves the completion of human nature both by its formal causality (qualifying and completing the powers of the soul) and by its efficient causality, inclining a human being to operation (which further perfects and realizes human nature).[17]

It is because habits are nature-directed, therefore, that they are also *operative*—that is, principles of human action. All habits are operative, even a bodily habit such as health, since by conserving and perfecting a being's bodily nature it thereby enables bodily activities to be performed well. However, some habits are especially operative in that they perfect the soul's powers or capacities for operation (49.3c). Aquinas calls these "operative" habits and explains them as follows: "The nature and rationale of a power is that it be the principle of an act. And so every habit that belongs to some power as its subject *principally* implies order to act" (49.3c).[18] In these especially operative habits the two offices of a habit—of perfecting nature and its characteristic operation—are almost indistinguishable: nature is perfected precisely by its operative power being perfected.

Poinsot offers an image that helps us to understand what these operative habits are. Sharpness would be a good operative habit for a knife, if knives had habits, since sharpness directly disposes a knife to perform well its characteristic operation of cutting. Similarly, a virtue is a good operative habit because it is the "sharpness or the cutting edge of a power."[19] It is through good operative habits, or virtues, that this naked potential of a human person to act becomes, as it were, sharpened.

So it is because habits are nature-directed that they are both stable and operative. Finally, and most important of all, it is because habits are nature-directed that they are also valent—that is, either good or bad. Aquinas infers the valence of habits from their nature-directedness via the principle that nature is itself an end—that is, that for the sake of which something comes to be. "And because the form and nature of the thing is the end and that for the sake of which something comes to be, as Aristotle says (*Physics*, Bk II), therefore we find good and bad in the first species [of quality]" (49.2c).[20] A habit that helps to perfect a nature and its operation will be a good habit; a bad habit realizes nature in a distorted way and twists a being's proper operation.

The valence of a habit, therefore, is grounded in the fact that habits are nature-directed. "It is of the rationale of *habit* that it implies a certain relation in order to a thing's nature, to which it is either consonant or dissonant" (49.3c).[21] "When there is a modification consonant to the nature of the subject, then it has the rationale of good; but when it is not consonant, then it has the rationale of bad" (49.2c).[22] Habits, then, are either good or bad (54.3).

Good Habits

John Poinsot was right to highlight for us the difference between Aquinas and Suárez in their respective definitions of habit. Suárezian habits, which prefigure modern conceptions of habit, do not have any essential connection to the nature of the subject in which they inhere. Suárez risks having to shoehorn goodness into habits we describe as virtues and badness into vices; there is nothing in his definition that provides a basis for the valence of habits. In contrast, Aquinas's operative habits, *primo et per se*, in the first place and of themselves, are related to the nature of the powers in which they inhere, serving their full realization in operation. As J. M. Ramírez comments, the union between a habit and the subject or power in which it inheres is much more intimate in Aquinas than Suárez; it is like a branch growing from a root rather than an exterior piece of clothing.[23]

Nature as the fundamental criterion of the distinction between good and bad habits or virtues and vices is therefore written into the very concept of habit as Aquinas defines it. In Aristotelian terminology, the definition enables an "essential division" into the two species of good and bad habits. A habit either succeeds in realizing nature well through its proper operation, or it doesn't; in the former case it will be a good habit, in the latter a bad one. The valence of habits, for Aquinas, is rooted in human nature.

THE GOODNESS OF VIRTUE

If virtue is a "good" habit, what, then, is the content of this "good"? That is our question. The basic principle has been established: "A good habit is one that disposes to an act fitting to the nature of the agent" (54.3c).[24] But we still have more to explore before we get to the full riches of Aquinas's account.

Drawing on his familiar premise that a human being is by nature a rational animal, Aquinas takes his account of virtue's goodness one step further:

> The virtue of anything consists in its being well fittingly disposed to its nature. . . .
> But we must consider that the nature of anything is especially the form from which
> it derives its species. Now a human being derives its species from its rational soul.
> Therefore, that which is against the order of reason is properly against the nature
> of a human being insofar as he is a human being; on the other hand, what is in
> accordance with reason is in accordance with the nature of a human being insofar
> as he is a human being. . . . So human virtue, which makes a human being good,
> and his work good, is in accordance with the nature of a human being, in as much
> as it agrees with reason, whereas vice is against the nature of a human being, inso-
> far as it is against the order of reason. (54.3c)[25]

A virtue, a good habit, is one fitting to a being's nature; a human's nature is to be rational; so what ultimately makes a human habit to be a good habit, and therefore a virtue, is this: conformity to reason. As Aquinas puts it, "A moral habit has the rationale of human virtue, insofar as it is conformed to reason" (58.2).[26] This is the account of virtue's goodness as conformity to "reason" that we need to explore.

Goodness as Conformity to a Rule

The standard approach of Thomists today is to attempt to ground Aquinas's account of moral goodness, and hence virtue's goodness, on a metaphysics of goodness. Eleonore Stump, for example, notes that Aquinas's most import-ant treatment of goodness comes early on in the *Summa Theologiae*, where he deals with "goodness in general." Central to his account is the claim that "good and being are the same according to the thing, but differ only according to rationale" (I 5.1c).[27] "Goodness," unlike "being," connotes "desirability."

Thus, in Stump's paraphrase, "being" and "goodness" are the same in reference but differ only in sense. For her, this is Aquinas's "central meta-ethical thesis."[28] When this thesis is combined with an account of human nature as rational, she claims, it generates an account of moral goodness, or the natural goodness specific to humans, as rational operation. For Stump, then, it is possible to go from meta-ethics (the metaphysics of goodness) to normative ethics via an understanding of human nature as rational: "Aquinas's central meta-ethical thesis, worked out in the context of his general metaphysics, provides a sophisticated metaphysical grounding for his virtue-based ethics."[29]

While this approach is not without value, one problem is that Aquinas often seems to distinguish between the good that is interchangeable with being and the moral good. For example, in the causal definition of virtue, Aquinas points out: "The 'good' that is placed in the definition of virtue is not the general good, which is interchangeable with being, and extends further than quality, but is the good of reason, which fits with what [Pseudo-]Dionysius says, 'the good of the soul is to be according to reason' (*Divine Names*, ch. 4)" (55.4 ad 2).[30] The moral or rational good, then, is not the metaphysical good.[31] Indeed, Aquinas seems to distinguish the metaphysical and moral good of a human action (1.3 ad 3; 18.4c). The claim that "good" and "being" are interchangeable is not a "meta-ethical thesis"; it is a metaphysical one.

In defining virtue Aquinas says that "the good that is convertible with being is not posited here in virtue's definition, but the good that is determined to a moral act" (*On the Virtues* 1.2 ad 2).[32] What we need is a clearer understanding of how general or metaphysical good gets "determined" or specified to moral goodness, so as to define virtue's goodness. I suggest we turn to a second important claim in Aquinas's theory of goodness: its conformity to a rule or measure. "The good of anything having a rule and measure consists in this, that it is equalized to its rule or measure" (*On the Virtues* 1.13c; cf. I.II 64.1c).[33] The key to virtue's goodness, then, lies in the rule and measure of human actions and habits. What is this rule?

For Aquinas, it is "reason," or "the mode of reason," or "the order of reason" that is the rule of human action, and by implication the rule of human virtue: "Good in human passions and operations is that it attains the mode of reason, which is the measure and rule of all human passions and operations" (*On the Virtues* 1.13c).[34] Moral goodness, then, is the conformity of a human act to reason. What applies to human actions will apply to their principles—namely, good and bad habits: "A moral habit has the rationale of human virtue, insofar as it is conformed to reason" (I.II 58.2).[35] Human actions and human habits are good when they are rational.

It may seem that this definition of moral goodness in terms of rationality is confused. Being rational is not only a characteristic of morally good action; it also is characteristic of morally bad action. Rationality, after all, is a *prerequisite* for any action being assessed in moral terms since if an action is performed without any attending thought, then this is an action of a human, not a human action. Aquinas seems to be making an illicit jump from "is" to "ought," from the way human actions are to how they should be.

This objection misses an important distinction. Consider the following argument:

> In regard to human acts, good and bad, is predicated by *a comparison to reason.* For, as [Pseudo-]Dionysisus says [Div. Nom. IV], "The good of a human is being according to reason," bad however is being "against reason." For the good of each thing is what suits it according to its form, and the bad is what is outside the order of its form. [. . .] However, certain actions are called human, or moral, insofar as they are *from reason.* And so it is manifest that good and evil diversify species in moral acts. (18.5c, emphasis added)[36]

In Aquinas's view, for a human act to be *from* reason (*a ratione*) and *according to* reason (*secundum rationem*) are two different things. For an action to be from reason it must be, as we might say, *originatively rational*, or deriving from a process of deliberation. For an action to be according to reason it must be *normatively rational*, or conforming to reason as to a rule or standard. Aquinas, then, does not make an illicit jump from "is" to "ought." Rather, there is a valid argument: all originatively rational actions must be either normatively rational (morally good) or normatively irrational (morally bad). "The good of each thing is what suits it according to its form": if an action derives from rational deliberation, it can be assessed according to the standards of rationality.

If moral goodness is a human action's or habit's conformity to reason, we need some account of what "reason" is in this normative sense, or the rule by conformity to which an action or habit is made morally good.

Duplex Regula

Aquinas claims, "The rule of the human will is twofold: one [rule] is proximate and homogenous, namely, human reason itself; the other [rule], however, is the first rule, namely, the eternal law, which is as it were the reason of God" (I.II 71.6c).[37] This idea of the *duplex regula,* or the double-sided rule of the human will, is of singular importance in Aquinas's ethics.

Aquinas asserts that the eternal law is the first rule (*prima regula*) of the human will, or the primary standard of all human action. It is by conformity to this rule or measure that a human action is judged morally good or bad. As Aquinas puts it, "The goodness of the human will depends on the eternal law much more than on human reason" (19.4c).[38] Given this position, it is no surprise that when Aquinas comes to define a sin, he defines it, as Augustine did, as a human action *against* this rule: "a word or deed or desire against the eternal law"[39] (71.6). The eternal law is the primary standard for distinguishing morally good from sinful actions, or moral virtue from vice.

Why is the eternal law the first rule? Aquinas states that it must be the first rule because it is the basis for the entire moral order: "In all ordered causes, the effect depends more on the first cause than on the secondary cause, for the secondary cause does not act unless in virtue of the first cause" (19.4c).[40] Since morality concerns the ordering of all actions to the overall end of human life (21.2 ad 2), the first rule of this ordering will be the first rule of morality. As the Salamancans put it: "Morality in human acts is understood by order to the ultimate end of human life. Therefore, whatever turns out to be the first rationale of this order will be the first rule of morality. This cannot be other than reason existing in God, which is called his eternal law, just as no other than God himself can be the first one directing into this end."[41] The first and indefectible "rule" or "standard" of morality—the directedness of all human things to the good—can be found only in God's reason, which draws all things to their end in Him.

Aquinas claims that while the first rule of morality is the eternal law, human reason is the *proximate* and *homogenous* rule. Eternal law, which is divine reason, is not manifested to human creatures except through the mediation of the judgment and directives of human reason:

> It is from the eternal law, which is the divine reason, that human reason is the rule of the human will, measuring its goodness. Hence it is written (Psalm 4), "Many say, who shows us good things? The light of your face, O Lord, is signed upon us," as if to say, "the light of reason in us can show good things and regulate our will to the extent that it is the light of your face, that is, derived from your face." (19.4c)[42]

By its participation in the first rule (divine reason), human reason is the proximate rule of the human will.

The idea that the goodness of virtue lies in its conformity to reason, and especially its conformity to the eternal law, is problematic to many. One of the advances of the renewal of virtue has been the recognition that virtue cannot be reduced to conformity to some set of rules or laws. Is Aquinas offering a law-based conception of virtue? Another concern might be the threat posed to human autonomy by divine heteronomy. Aquinas states: "In what is done through will, the proximate rule is human reason, but the supreme rule is the eternal law" (21.1c).[43] Is the conception of morality that is being proposed an authoritarian one?

One danger here is to fall into modern dichotomies between law and virtue, or between divine and human freedom, oppositions that are not present in Aquinas's holistic theological ethics. Some accounts of Aquinas's ethics claim that propositional principles hold priority over the virtues.[44] Others assert the reverse and advocate the primacy of virtue over natural law.[45] The better approach is to find a balance between law and virtue, drawing out the connections and interrelations between them and reuniting what was never separate in Aquinas's original account.[46]

Still, Thomists often tend in the direction of an excessively legal interpretation of his ethics. David M. Gallagher helpfully notes that when Aquinas talks of the rule of actions, "rule should not be understood only as something which is written or spoken, such as a law or a set of instructions, nor is it even necessarily something grasped intellectually." However, Gallagher quickly follows this insight with the misleading statement, "In the case of rational beings the rule takes the form of law."[47] Aquinas is more careful in his language: law is *quaedam regula*, a certain or particular kind of rule, and it is such because it is something pertaining to reason, which is "the rule and measure of human acts" (90.1c).[48] Law is one manifestation of practical reason. Even the eternal law, while certainly a "law," should not be interpreted using a too-univocal comparison with human law. Doing so invites a mistaken reading of Aquinas's ethics as relentlessly deontological.

We should avoid the use of unhelpful dichotomies between natural law ethics and virtue ethics. When Aquinas claims that a moral habit is a virtue insofar as it is conformed to reason, it is more helpful to understand "reason" here primarily in terms of a virtue, not of a law—namely, in terms of prudence.

THE MEASURE OF HUMAN ACTS

It is worth briefly noting some central features of Aquinas's idea of prudence.[49] Aquinas distinguishes *scientia, ars,* and *prudentia: scientia* consists in the scientific knowledge of what is necessarily true; *ars* is a more practical form of knowledge about how to attain particular ends according to set rules; *prudentia* is a practical knowledge that rectifies human action (57.4c). Prudence therefore differs from art in that it concerns living well overall (*bene vivere totum*) rather than in some particular sphere of life (II.II 47.2 ad 1). Prudence's sphere of operation is the contingent and uncertain realm of the particular in which there is no fixed way of attaining the end (47.2 ad 3; 5c). There is therefore an investigative process in prudential reasoning, from deliberation to judgment to "command"—that is, applying what has been considered to what is done (II.II 47.8). While prudence is a kind of rationality, it is not an elitist virtue: even a simple person can be prudent (I.II 58.4 ad 2). Finally, prudence is not a "cold" rationality. Rather, it depends radically on a kind of affective knowledge since it presupposes a correct perception of the ends of human action, which arises when the subject is well-disposed through the moral virtues (58.5). What are the prospects for reading the twofold rule of morality in terms of the virtue of prudence?

Divine and Human Prudence

Crucially, Aquinas conceives of the role of prudence teleologically. As he puts it, "Prudence counsels us well about what pertains to the whole life of a human, and to the ultimate end of human life" (57.4 ad 3; cf. 21.2 ad 2).[50] Aquinas's accounts of prudence and the eternal law therefore overlap. As he describes the latter's office or function, "the eternal law primarily and principally ordains the human being to the end, but consequently makes the human being well disposed concerning what is towards the end" (71.6 ad 3).[51]

A similar teleology is evident in eternal law's definition. The eternal law, Aquinas says, is "the rationale of the governance of things" (*ratio gubernationis rerum*) (91.1c). *Gubernatio* refers literally to the art of navigating or steering a ship to its destination, but it is used by extension to refer to governance of any kind.[52] "To govern is to move certain things to a due end, just as a sailor navigates a ship" (II.II 102.2c).[53] The eternal law, then, is the underlying rationale of the governance or navigation by which God steers each creature to its ultimate end. It is not a set of universal formulas or laws.

Does God, then, have the virtue of prudence? Aquinas considers this question himself (I 22.1). He distinguishes the self-regarding and the other-regarding roles of prudence: "It is proper to prudence, according to the Philosopher [*Nichomachean Ethics* VI.12], to order other things to the end, whether in respect of one's own self, as a human is said to be prudent because he orders well his own acts to the end of his life, or in respect of others subject to him, in the family, or city, or kingdom" (ibid).[54] God has no need to direct His own life to the ultimate end, since He is the ultimate end of all things; yet He can nevertheless be said to have the virtue of prudence in that He does so direct other creatures. The virtue of prudence as it exists in God provides for others and guides them to their good, and is therefore called "providence": "Therefore the very rationale of the ordering of things into the end in God is named providence" (ibid.).[55]

It is clear, then, that there is very little difference between the eternal law, as Aquinas conceives it, and God's prudence, or providence, since both concern the guidance of the creature to its proper end. But there is a difference nevertheless: "The eternal law in God is not providence itself, but as it were the principle of providence."[56] As we have seen, the eternal law is not the very act of prudentially governing or directing things but the plan or idea on the basis of which God governs (I.II 91.1c).

If the first rule is best interpreted as the basis of divine prudence, how do we understand the proximate rule—namely, human reason? Aquinas states: "A human being attains to right reason by prudence, which is right reason about what is to be done" (*On the Virtues* 5.2c).[57] It is the virtue of prudence that is the proximate rule of human morality. The basic principles of natural law on their own are not, by themselves, a sufficient standard of moral goodness. As the Salamancans explain, "The universal principles of practical reason, of which *synderesis* is the judge, does not cause the goodness of operation, nor directs the operation itself, unless by the judgement of the prudent one attending to what is occurring here and now, and unless they are determined and applied to such an operation."[58] General principles of morality need to be applied wisely to a situation; by themselves they are not the rule. Only the virtue of prudence, which takes these general principles from *synderesis* and applies them here and now, can serve as the proximate rule of morality.[59]

Prudential versus Legalistic Rationality

How does this prudential reading of the *duplex regula* help to reply to concerns about Aquinas's account of virtue as being legalistic and leaving little room for human freedom? The emphasis on prudence addresses the worry about rationalistic legalism. Aquinas believes that ethics should offer normative direction.[60] Yet he insists that ethics can never be a substitute for the morally virtuous and practically wise judgment of a particular person "in the field": "And since the discussion of morals even in general is uncertain and variable, it becomes yet more uncertain if someone were to want to descend [to particulars] further, offering teaching about singulars in particular. For this does not fall under art, nor under any narration, because cases of singular actions vary in infinite ways. And so the judgment about particular is left to the prudence of each" (*Comm. Ethic.*, lib. 2 l. 2 n.5).[61] Only the wise agent in situ can determine what is to be done here and now; there is no way of knowing this in advance, except in broad outlines. As Cajetan puts it, regarding what is to be done here and now "*non est scibile, quia contingens,*" there is no scientific knowledge about the concrete moral requirements of the moment, because of its contingency (in I.II 58.5 n.9). Only a virtue, not a scientific application of a set of principles, can determine what is to be done here and now.

This is something recognized by contemporary virtue theorists, who question the modern assumption that an ethical theory should offer a "decision procedure"—that is, a set of instructions that tell us what to do and are applicable in the same way in all situations.[62] Rosalind Hursthouse points out, for example, that "knowledge of what one should do in a particular hard case is not knowledge that we expect adolescents, however clever, and however well-armed with a normative ethics they have been given in a book, to have."[63] It would be unwise to seek moral advice from a clever teenager who has mastered a book on ethical theory since she would lack the experience necessary for prudence. There is no way of "short-circuiting" the need for personal, prudential judgment, no matter how good the normative theory.

At the same time, it would be wrong to reduce Aquinas to a "situationist" or a "particularist." No act can be morally good if it is discordant with the dictates of *synderesis*, or the understanding of the basic principles of practical reason; *synderesis* "moves" prudence (II.II 47.6 ad 3). Rather, Aquinas's account of prudence steers a happy medium between particularism and rationalism: prudence mediates between the general and the particular (47.3). As the Salamancans observe, "Since moral operations are singular, and depend upon singular circumstances, *universal knowledge*, even if it be practical, cannot influence them, or regulate them, unless as applied to the here and now by *particular knowledge*, which, having inspected everything, judges about the existence of such operations: which is the office of prudence."[64] The formal, proximate rule of morality is therefore the concrete dictate of prudential reason, which nevertheless applies the general principles of morality in a situationally sensitive way. While this is not situationism, neither is it a legalistic, rationalistic conception of moral rationality.

Divine Heteronomy and Human Autonomy

The second concern about Aquinas's understanding of reason as the rule of morality is that it makes God's command the ultimate standard of morality, thereby appearing to subvert human autonomy. Aquinas, however, does not assert divine heteronomy at the expense of human autonomy, nor vice versa.[65] There is not one rule for morality, nor are there two; rather, there is one twofold rule, a *duplex regula*. Aquinas insists that morality consists in harmony or disharmony with human reason (its proximate rule) and *at the same time* consists in conformity or disconformity to divine reason, its first and indefectible rule.[66] In this moral vision the eternal law is far from substituting for human autonomy; it is what guarantees it. Once again the metaphor of seafaring navigation is germane: "Just as a ship is entrusted to the captain to direct its course, so a human being is entrusted to his will and reason. As it is said, 'God established the human being from the beginning, and left him in the hand of his own counsel' (Ecclesiasticus 15:14)" (I.II 2.5c).[67] The word Aquinas uses, here translated as "captain," is *gubernator*. So just as God is the Supreme Captain or Navigator directing all things to Himself, so has He made human beings captains or navigators of their own lives.

It is possible to understand Aquinas's reconciliation of human autonomy and divine heteronomy only in the context of his overarching cosmological vision. God provides for the telic orientation of humans to their ultimate end differently than He does for nonrational creatures, whose participation in the eternal law is entirely passive since they have no choice whether or not to follow the natural inclinations instilled into their natures. It is different for humans: "Among other creatures, the rational creature is subject to providence in a more excellent way, insofar as he also becomes a participant of providence, provident for himself and for others" (I.II 91.2).[68] Humans participate in the eternal law both passively (in that they are directed to their end by natural and supernatural inclination toward the good) and actively (by the exercise of deliberation about how best to achieve their natural and supernatural end). This delegated autonomy is not an arbitrary liberty to do whatever one happens to want to do, nor is it merely a following of the diktats of a divine micromanager. Rather, human autonomy is self-rule through the virtue of prudence; it is a specifically human, active participation in the eminent practical reason or navigation by which God directs all beings to their ultimate ends.

MEASURED GOODNESS

How does the idea of the *duplex regula* help to address the question with which we began—namely, how to understand virtue's goodness? Aquinas gives the answer as follows: "Human acts have goodness insofar as they are regulated by a due rule and measure, and therefore human virtue, which is the principle of all a human's good acts, consists in attaining the rule of human acts, which is twofold, as we have said, namely, human reason, and God himself" (II.II 23.3c).[69] The goodness of human virtue lies in its conformity to human and especially divine reason.

Note that this thesis has restricted application. The good of virtue is always conformity to some rule or measure, but it takes on different forms for the three genera of virtue—intellectual, moral, and theological—since each of these has its own distinctive rule or measure. As we have seen, the measure and rule of *moral* or *human* virtue is prudential reason. Thus, "A moral habit has the rationale of human virtue, insofar as it is conformed to reason" (I.II 58.2; cf. 59.4).[70] The measure and rule of speculative intellectual virtue, in contrast, is in things themselves, "for by the fact that a thing is or is not, there is truth in what we think and say" (64.3c).[71] What about the theological virtues? The goodness of faith, hope, and love is something more than determining the best path to an end through conformity to reason (as with moral virtue); the three virtues are good through their conformity to the end itself—namely, God, in His truth, power, love, and goodness. As Aquinas puts it, "The measure and rule of theological virtue is God himself" (ibid.).[72]

Identifying the correct measure and rule is most difficult in regard to the virtue of prudence. Here we meet two problems at once. Prudence is itself the measure and rule of moral virtue. But Aquinas makes the puzzling claim that, whereas speculative truth lies in conformity to reality, practical truth lies in conformity to right appetite (58.5 ad 3). We seem to have a vicious circularity: prudence is the measure of moral virtue, and moral virtue, which consists in right appetite, is the measure of prudence.[73]

To add to the confusion, Aquinas says, "The true of practical intellectual virtue, related indeed to reality, has the rationale of something measured" (64.3c).[74] How consistent is this: the measure of prudence is both right appetite and reality itself?

The problems arise because Aquinas recognizes that the relation between intellect and will, and consequently between prudence and moral virtue, is one of mutual interdependence (65.1 ad 3). He says, "These two powers, namely, intellect and will, revolve around each other" (*On the Virtues* 1.7c).[75] One way in which prudence depends on moral virtue is that it starts from a right perception of the end, which happens only through moral virtue:

> For a human to be rightly disposed concerning the particular principles of action, which are the ends, it is necessary that he be perfected by certain habits by which it becomes in some way connatural to judge rightly of the end. And this happens through moral virtue, for the virtuous one rightly judges of the end of virtue, because "such as each one is, so does the end seem to him" [*Nichomachean Ethics* II.5]. And so, right reason about what is to be done, which is prudence, requires that a human have moral virtue. (58.5)[76]

It is only the morally virtuous person who perceives what is truly good and which ends to pursue, and so is able to reason well about what is to be done here and now. Prudence needs moral virtue.

There is no self-defeating circularity in saying that prudence finds its measure in right appetite but right appetite finds its measure in reason. Aquinas explains: "Reason [*synderesis*] insofar as it apprehends the end, precedes the appetite for the end, but the appetite for the end precedes reason reasoning to choose what is for the end, which pertains to prudence" (I.II 58.5 ad 1).[77] Prudence finds its measure in right appetite for the end, and right appetite for the end finds its measure in *synderesis*, which is the habit containing the general understanding of moral principles (II.II 47.6 ad 1).

What about the idea that the measure of the practical intellect lies in reality itself? Cajetan notes that the practical intellect agrees with the speculative intellect in its act of understanding but differs in that it also directs action (in I.II 58.5 n.2). He infers that practical truth concerns both reality and desire, in different respects: "The true of the practical intellect in itself depends on reality, as regards understanding; on our part, however, [it depends] on right appetite, which makes the end appear to us according to the disposition of the appetite" (in 64.4 n.3). Prudential reasoning, as directive of action, is based on both a correct perception of the end (which happens through moral and indeed theological virtue) and a correct perception of the singulars that form the context for action (II.II 47.3c). Thus prudence finds its measure both in right appetite for the end and in reality itself. This helps to ward off the danger of infinite regress of virtues: the measure of moral virtue is intellectual virtue; the measure of intellectual virtue is reality. For, "It is not necessary to proceed into infinity in virtues, because the measure and rule of intellectual virtue is not some other genus of virtue, but reality itself" (I.II 64.3 ad 2).[78]

In general, a virtue's goodness lies in its conformity to its rule, and the rule will vary according to the kind of virtue. Yet it remains that the *duplex regula* is the primary rule for virtue. Virtue, in the unqualified sense, which directs a person to the overall end of human life, can be said to find its measure in the twofold rule of the human will: divine and human reason. Aquinas terms conformity to this rule of reason "the moral good" (*bonum moris*). It is therefore either the rational good (*bonum rationis*) or the moral good (*bonum moris*) that is included in the definition of virtue as a good habit (*On the Virtues* 1.2 ad 2, ad 6; I.II 55.4 ad 2). Poinsot, in his insightful summary of the *Summa Theologiae*, is correct to state, "'Morally good' is the difference ultimately constitutive of virtue."[79]

NOTES

1. I.II 55.3: "virtus humana, quae est habitus operativus, est bonus habitus, et boni operativus."

2. I.II 54.3c: "habitus bonus dicitur qui disponit ad actum convenientem naturae agentis; habitus autem malus dicitur qui disponit ad actum non convenientem naturae."

3. "Habitus . . . est enim qualitas quaedam permanens, et de se stabilis in subiecto, per se primo ordinata ad operationem, non tribuens primam facultatem operandi, sed adiuvans et facilitans illum." Francisco Suárez, *Disputationes Metaphysicae*, ed. Carolus Berton, Opera Omnia, vol. 26 (Paris: Vives, 1886), Disp.44:1, n.6 (664).

4. Ibid.

5. John Poinsot, *Cursus Theologicus,* in I.II, Disp.13, *De Habitibus in Communi,* Art.1, 23.

6. 49.3c: "habitus primo et per se importat habitudinem ad naturam rei."

7. Bernard Ryosuke Inagaki, who refers approvingly to Poinsot, also states: "No other thinker [than Aquinas] has ever developed a theory of habit in connection with human nature in such a systematic manner." "Habitus and Natura in Aquinas," in *Studies in Medieval Philosophy*, ed. John F. Wippel (Baltimore, MD: Catholic University of America Press, 1987), 159.

8. *Comm. Metaph.*, lib. 5 l. 5; and *Super Sent.*, lib. 3 d. 5 q. 1 a. 2c.

9. I.II 29.1 ad 4: "communiter essentia uniuscuiusque rei, quam significat eius definitio, vocatur natura."

10. De ente et essentia, cap. 1: "nomen naturae . . . videtur significare essentiam rei, secundum quod habet ordinem ad propriam operationem rei, cum nulla res propria operatione destituatur."

11. *Comm. Physic.*, lib. 2 l. 15 n.1.

12. *Comm. Physic.*, lib. 2 l. 13–14.

13. 49.3c: "Sed natura rei, quae est finis generationis, ulterius etiam ordinatur ad alium finem, qui vel est operatio, vel aliquod operatum, ad quod quis pervenit per operationem."

14. 49.3: "Est enim de ratione habitus ut importet habitudinem quandam in ordine ad naturam rei."

15. 49.3c: "in prima specie consideratur . . . facile et difficile mobile, secundum quod aliqua natura est finis generationis et motus."

16. 49.3c: "habitus non solum importat ordinem ad ipsam naturam rei, sed etiam consequenter ad operationem, inquantum est finis naturae, vel perducens ad finem."

17. On the efficient causality of habits, see Michał Głowala, "What Kind of Power Is a Virtue? John of St. Thomas OP on Causality of Virtues and Vices," *Studia Neoaristotelica* 9, no. 1 (2012): 25–27.

18. 49.3c: "natura et ratio potentiae est ut sit principium actus. Unde omnis habitus qui est alicuius potentiae ut subiecti, principaliter importat ordinem ad actum."

19. *Cursus Theologicus*, Disp.13, *De Habitibus in Communi*, Art. 4, 24.

20. 49.2c: "Et quia ipsa forma et natura rei est finis et cuius causa fit aliquid, ut dicitur in II Physic. ideo in prima specie consideratur et bonum et malum."

21. 49.3c: "Est enim de ratione habitus ut importet habitudinem quandam in ordine ad naturam rei, secundum quod convenit vel non convenit."

22. 49.2c: "Quando enim est modus conveniens naturae rei, tunc habet rationem boni, quando autem non convenit, tunc habet rationem mali."

23. Jacobus M. Ramírez, *De Habitibus in Communi: In I–II Summae Theologiae Divi Thomae Expositio (QQ. XLIX–LIV)*, ed. Victorinus Rodriguez (Madrid: Luis Vives, 1973), 1:106.

24. 54.3c: "habitus bonus dicitur qui disponit ad actum convenientem naturae agentis."

25. 54.3c: "Virtus autem uniuscuiusque rei consistit in hoc quod sit bene disposita secundum convenientiam suae naturae. . . . Sed considerandum est quod natura uniuscuiusque rei potissime est forma secundum quam res speciem sortitur. Homo autem in specie constituitur per animam rationalem. Et ideo id quod est contra ordinem rationis, proprie est contra naturam hominis inquantum est homo; quod autem est secundum rationem, est secundum naturam hominis inquantum est homo. . . . Unde virtus humana, quae hominem facit bonum, et opus ipsius bonum reddit, intantum est secundum naturam hominis, inquantum convenit rationi, vitium autem intantum est contra naturam hominis, inquantum est contra ordinem rationis."

26. 58.2: "habitus moralis habet rationem virtutis humanae, inquantum rationi conformatur."

27. I 5.1c: "bonum et ens sunt idem secundum rem, sed differunt secundum rationem tantum."

28. Eleonore Stump, *Aquinas* (London: Routledge, 2003), 60–91.

29. Ibid., 90.

30. 55.4 ad 2: "bonum quod ponitur in definitione virtutis, non est bonum commune, quod convertitur cum ente, et est in plus quam qualitas, sed est bonum rationis, secundum quod Dionysius dicit, in IV cap. de Div. Nom., quod bonum animae est secundum rationem esse."

31. See also *On the Virtues* 1.2 ad 2, ad 6; I.II 54.3 ad 2.

32. *On the Virtues* 1.2 ad 2: "bonum quod convertitur cum ente, non ponitur hic in definitione virtutis; sed bonum quod determinatur ad actum moralem."

33. *On the Virtues* 1.13c: "cuiuslibet habentis regulam et mensuram bonum consistit in hoc quod est adaequari suae regulae vel mensurae."

34. *On the Virtues* 1.13c: "bonum in passionibus et operationibus humanis est quod attingatur modus rationis, qui est mensura et regula omnium passionum et operationum humanarum."

35. I.II 58.2: "habitus moralis habet rationem virtutis humanae, inquantum rationi conformatur."

36. 18.5c: "In actibus autem humanis bonum et malum dicitur per comparationem ad rationem, quia, ut Dionysius dicit, IV cap. de Div. Nom. bonum hominis est secundum rationem esse, malum autem quod est praeterrationem. Unicuique enim rei est bonum quod convenit ei secundum suam formam; et malum quod est ei praeter ordinem suae formae. . . . Dicuntur autem aliqui actus humani, vel morales, secundum quod sunt a ratione. Unde manifestum est quod bonum et malum diversificant speciem in actibus moralibus."

37. I.II 71.6c: "Regula autem voluntatis humanae est duplex, una propinqua et homogenea, scilicet ipsa humana ratio; alia vero est prima regula, scilicet lex aeterna, quae est quasi ratio Dei."

38. 19.4c: "multo magis dependet bonitas voluntatis humanae a lege aeterna, quam a ratione humana."

39. 71.6c: *"dictum vel factum vel concupitum contra legem aeternam."*

40. 19.4c: "in omnibus causis ordinatis, effectus plus dependet a causa prima quam a causa secunda, quia causa secunda non agit nisi in virtute primae causae."

41. *Cursus Theologicus,* Tract. 11, *De Bonitate et Malitia Humanorum Actuum,* Disp.1, Dub.5, n.66 (6:35).

42. 19.4c: "Quod autem ratio humana sit regula voluntatis humanae, ex qua eius bonitas mensuretur, habet ex lege aeterna, quae est ratio divina. Unde in Psalmo IV, dicitur, *multi dicunt, quis ostendit nobis bona? Signatum est super nos lumen vultus tui, domine,* quasi diceret, lumen rationis quod in nobis est, intantum potest nobis ostendere bona, et nostram voluntatem regulare, inquantum est lumen vultus tui, idest a vultu tuo derivatum."

43. 21.1c: "In his vero quae aguntur per voluntatem, regula proxima est ratio humana; regula autem suprema est lex aeterna."

44. The New Natural Law theorists emphasize natural law in both their interpretation of Aquinas and in their contemporary rethinking of his ethical theory. John Finnis concedes that Aquinas arranges his exposition of morals in terms of the virtues, but Finnis insists that "principles, propositional practical truths, are more fundamental than virtues." Finnis, *Aquinas: Moral, Political, and Legal Theory* (Oxford: Oxford University Press, 1998), 124.

45. Daniel Mark Nelson argues that the perception of Aquinas as a natural law ethicist is "mistaken"; natural law is an overall theological framework for understanding the universality of morality, but it is the virtues that are action-guiding. Nelson, *The Priority of Prudence* (University Park: Pennsylvania State University Press, 1992).

46. Thus Pamela Hall appreciates Nelson's rejection of "conventional legalistic interpretations of Aquinas" but argues that Nelson unduly downplays natural law. Pamela M. Hall, *Narrative and the Natural Law: An Interpretation of Thomistic Ethics* (Notre Dame, IN: University of Notre Dame Press, 1994), 19–22.

47. David M. Gallagher, "Aquinas on Goodness and Moral Goodness," in *Thomas Aquinas and His Legacy* (Washington, DC: Catholic University of America Press, 1994), 51.

48. 90.1c: "Regula autem et mensura humanorum actuum est ratio."

49. For a helpful account see W. Jay Wood, "Prudence," in *Virtues and Their Vices,* ed. Kevin Timpe and Craig A. Boyd (Oxford: Oxford University Press, 2014), 37–58.

50. 57.4 ad 3: "prudentia est bene consiliativa de his quae pertinent ad totam vitam hominis, et ad ultimum finem vitae humanae."

51. 71.6 ad 3: "lex aeterna primo et principaliter ordinat hominem ad finem, consequenter autem facit hominem bene se habere circa ea quae sunt ad finem."

52. Roy J. Deferrari, *A Lexicon of Saint Thomas Aquinas* (Baltimore, MD: Catholic University of America Press, 1948), 482; T. C. O'Brien, *Summa Theologiae: Volume 14, (Ia.103–109) Divine Government* (Cambridge: Cambridge University Press, 2006), 2–3.

53. II.II 102.2c: "gubenare autem est movere aliquos in debitum finem; sicut nauta gubernat navem."

54. II.II 102.2c: "Prudentiae autem proprium est, secundum philosophum in VI Ethic., ordinare alia in finem; sive respectu sui ipsius, sicut dicitur homo prudens, qui bene ordinat actus suos ad finem vitae suae; sive respectu aliorum sibi subiectorum in familia vel civitate vel regno."

55. II.II 102.2c: "Ipsa igitur ratio ordinis rerum in finem, providentia in Deo nominatur."

56. *De Veritate* 5.1 ad 6: "in Deo lex aeterna non est ipsa providentia, sed providentiae quasi principium."

57. *On the Virtues* 5.2c: "Ad rationem autem rectam attingit homo per prudentiam, quae est recta ratio agibilium."

58. *Cursus Theologicus*, Tract. 11, *De Bonitate et Malitia Humanorum Actuum*, Disp.1, Dub.4, n.69 (6:36).

59. On *synderesis* and virtue see Angela McKay Knobel, "Synderesis, Law, and Virtue," in *The Normativity of the Natural: Human Goods, Human Virtues, and Human Flourishing*, ed. Mark J. Cherry (Austin, TX: Springer, 2009), 33–44.

60. *Comm. Ethic.*, lib. 2 l. 2 n.2: "Non enim in hac scientia scrutamur quid est virtus ad hoc solum ut sciamus huius rei veritatem; sed ad hoc, quod acquirentes virtutem, boni efficiamur"; see Super De Trinitate, pars 3 q. 5 a. 1 ad 3. On the "hybrid character of *scientia* or sacred doctrine, partly practical, partly speculative," see I.1.4 and Rudi A. te Velde, *Aquinas on God* (Aldershot, UK: Ashgate, 2006), 21–22.

61. *Comm. Ethic.*, lib. 2 l. 2 n.5: "Et cum sermo moralium etiam in universalibus sit incertus et variabilis, adhuc magis incertus est si quis velit ulterius descendere tradendo doctrinam de singulis in speciali. Hoc enim non cadit neque sub arte, neque sub aliqua narratione, quia casus singularium operabilium variantur infinitis modis. Unde iudicium de singulis relinquitur prudentiae uniuscuiusque."

62. Julia Annas, "Being Virtuous and Doing the Right Thing," *Proceedings and Addresses of the American Philosophical Association* 78, no. 2 (November 1, 2004): 63.

63. Rosalind Hursthouse, *On Virtue Ethics* (Oxford: Oxford University Press, 1999), 61.

64. *Cursus Theologicus*, Tract. 11, *De Bonitate et Malitia Humanorum Actuum*, Disp.1, Dub.5, n.69 (6:37).

65. Louis Roy, "Does Christian Faith Rule Out Human Autonomy?," *Heythrop Journal* 53, no. 4 (2012): 606–23.

66. For example, I.II 19.4c, 23.6c, 71.6c 2 De Malo 4; *On the Virtues* 5.4; and Super Iob, cap. 23.

67. I.II 2.5c: "Sicut autem navis committitur gubernatori ad dirigendum, ita homo est suae voluntati et rationi commissus; secundum illud quod dicitur Eccli. XV, *Deus ab initio constituit hominem, et reliquit eum in manu consilii sui.*"

68. I.II 91.2: "Inter cetera autem rationalis creatura excellentiori quodam modo divinae providentiae subiacet, inquantum et ipsa fit providentiae particeps, sibi ipsi et aliis providens."

69. II.II 23.3c: "humani actus bonitatem habent secundum quod regulantur debita regula et mensura, et ideo humana virtus, quae est principium omnium bonorum actuum hominis, consistit in attingendo regulam humanorum actuum. Quae quidem est duplex, ut supra dictum est, scilicet humana ratio, et ipse Deus."

70. I.II 58.2: "habitus moralis habet rationem virtutis humanae, inquantum rationi conformatur."

71. 64.3c: "ex eo enim quod res est vel non est, veritas est in opinione et in oratione."

72. 64.3c: "mensura et regula virtutis theologicae est ipse Deus, fides enim nostra regulatur secundum veritatem divinam, caritas autem secundum bonitatem eius, spes autem secundum magnitudinem omnipotentiae et pietatis eius."

73. *Comm. Ethic.*, lib. 6 l. 2 n.8.

74. 64.3c: "Verum autem virtutis intellectualis practicae, comparatum quidem ad rem, habet rationem mensurati."

75. *On the Virtues* 1.7c: "istae duae potentiae, scilicet intellectus et voluntas, se invicem circumeunt."

76. 58.5: "ad hoc quod recte se habeat circa principia particularia agibilium, quae sunt fines, oportet quod perficiatur per aliquos habitus secundum quos fiat quodammodo homini connaturale recte iudicare de fine. Et hoc fit per virtutem moralem, virtuosus enim recte iudicat de fine virtutis, quia qualis unusquisque est, talis finis videtur ei, ut dicitur in III Ethic. Et ideo ad rectam rationem agibilium, quae est prudentia, requiritur quod homo habeat virtutem moralem."

77. I.II 58.5 ad 1: "ratio, secundum quod est apprehensiva finis, praecedit appetitum finis, sed appetitus finis praecedit rationem ratiocinantem ad eligendum ea quae sunt ad finem, quod pertinet ad prudentiam."

78. 64.3 ad 2: "non est necesse in infinitum procedere in virtutibus, quia mensura et regula intellectualis virtutis non est aliquod aliud genus virtutis, sed ipsa res."

79. *Isagogue ad D. Thomae Theologiam* (Solesmes 1:170).

CHAPTER 4

Virtue's Definition

Suggested reading: *Summa Theologiae* I.II 55.4;
On the Virtues 1.2

A hologram has the surprising property that each of its constituent parts encodes information about the entire three-dimensional image. Even were only a fragment to remain, all would not be lost: when a single piece is illumined with a laser light, astonishingly, the full image unfolds.

If the recent history of interpretation of Aquinas's ethical thought suggests anything, it is that the image of a building constructed on a foundation is a misleading one. There is no basic or central idea, not even the concept of virtue. A more-promising metaphor would be the hologram. As Carlo Leget comments, "The greater one's acquaintance with Aquinas' theology, the more one discovers how, in the *Summa*, every article has the nature of a hologram in which the rest of the work is reflected."[1] As with a hologram, the whole is latent within each fragment.

On what, though, should a holographic reading of Aquinas's virtue theory focus? Having examined Aquinas's argument that virtue is a good operative habit (I.II 55.1–3), we are now in a position to look at the culminating article regarding the essence of virtue (55.4). If the focused light of sustained attention illumines that single article, does an image of Aquinas's virtue theory as a whole emerge?

THE DEFINITION OF VIRTUE

The article defining virtue, I.II 55.4, is a puzzling one. Aquinas presents himself as defending the formula found in Peter Lombard's *Sentences*, a theological compilation written around the mid-twelfth century. This work was considered a reader in theology and the first point of reference for medieval scholastic theologians. In a chapter titled "On Virtue: What It Is, and What Its Act Is," the master offers his definition: "Virtue, as Augustine said, is a good quality of the mind, by which we live rightly, and which no one uses badly, which God alone works in a human being."[2] This is not a direct quotation from Augustine but a patchwork gathered from various of his works, especially *On Free Choice of the Will* and *Retractions*. With the Bishop of Hippo's unrivaled authority behind it, and its presence in the primary scholastic textbook, this definition became the received formula for centuries.

Aquinas's early theological masterwork was a commentary on Lombard's *Sentences*, so it is unremarkable that there he defends the definition.[3] Even in his late writings on virtue, in both *On the Virtues* (1.2) and indeed in *Summa Theologiae* (I.II 55.4), when Aquinas is no longer constrained by the text of the *Sentences*, he again strongly endorses it.

The first puzzle about the choice of definition in the *Summa* is why Aquinas thinks it is necessary, given that he has already apparently provided one. In strict Aristotelian fashion, Aquinas has identified virtue's genus (habit), its more general difference (*operative* habit), and the specific difference that ultimately constitutes virtue as virtue (*good* operative habit).

A second puzzle is why Aquinas indicates a preference for Lombard's definition, since he has clearly memorized a number of worthy alternatives, notably those found in Aristotle and Cicero. A virtue is described as "a habit in the mode of nature, in harmony with reason," "what makes its possessor good and its possessor's work good," "the limit of a power," and "a disposition of the perfect to the best, but I call 'perfect' what is disposed according to nature." Moral virtue, in particular, is described by Aristotle as "an elective habit, lying in the mean relative to us, determined by reason insofar as the prudent one determines it."[4] Given these alternatives, why does Aquinas prefer to follow Lombard?

Aristotle or Augustine?

Consider how contemporary interpreters would solve this puzzle. Martin Rhonheimer's approach is to dismiss the significance of the article: "Thomas Aquinas bases his doctrine of virtues—against the trend of his time—not on the Augustinian definition but on the Aristotelian."[5] For Rhonheimer, Lombard's definition "contains almost no relevant ethical or action-theoretical elements."[6] He even refers to Aquinas's "rejection" of this formula.

If Rhonheimer is right, Aquinas has found a strange way to reject the Augustinian definition by constructing an argument in its defense. Admittedly, Aquinas does amend the definition. Yet Aquinas also states, "This definition completely embraces the whole rationale of virtue" (55.4c).[7] Rhonheimer's

Aristotelian approach to Aquinas's ethics offers no explanation of the weight Aquinas gives to it.

This thought lends support to the diametrically opposed reading provided by theologian Mark Jordan and others. Jordan suggests that Aquinas is motivated by the search for a properly theological definition that applies strictly only to the "infused" virtues that come to us as a gift from God and direct us to eternal life: virtues such as faith, hope, and charity. On Jordan's reading of Aquinas, "virtue" is an analogous term that applies to some virtues in a fuller sense than it does to others. Since infused virtue is "the first and clearest member of the analogy," this definition is given for that.[8] Similarly for Eleonore Stump, the Augustinian definition adopted by Aquinas is "manifestly an un-Aristotelian definition" since it refers only to virtues that are infused.[9]

Yet if Aristotelian Thomism is an interpretive risk, anti-Aristotelian Thomism can be an overcorrection. Jordan's reading has the merit of taking the final article on virtue's essence seriously; the explanation of why Aquinas opts for Lombard's definition is not persuasive. Aquinas comments that by omitting the final clause, "which God works in us without us," the definition will apply to all the virtues, both infused and acquired.[10] So Aquinas sees the final clause as something that needs to be excised to serve the purpose of the article—that is, the provision of a definition of virtue in general that extends to all virtues, whether infused or not. As Bonnie Kent observes, "Thomas wants his definition to cover both the human virtues acquired through our own natural resources and the superhuman virtues Christians have through God's grace."[11] Aquinas adopts Lombard's definition not because, but *despite* the fact that it strictly applies only to infused virtue. As Matthew O'Brien warns, a "rhetorical commitment" to the "non-Aristotelian" nature of Aquinas's ethics leads to its own hermeneutical distortions.[12]

If the Aristotelian approach eclipses the Augustinian definition because it does not fit its interpretive presuppositions, the Augustinian approach misuses the definition for its own overcorrective agenda. Neither approach allows the most important text in Aquinas's account of virtue, the one that defines virtue, to speak for itself.

The Search for a Comprehensive Definition

There is an alternative explanation provided by Aquinas himself. In the *Commentary on the Sentences*, Aquinas defends Lombard's definition against its rivals on the following basis: "If, by a definition of something, we mean one that embraces its whole being, insofar as it is constituted from all its causes, that is, a complete definition, then there can only be one definition for one thing.

The aforementioned definition [namely, Lombard's] of virtue embraces all its causes."[13] Aquinas notes that competing definitions express different causes of virtue without encompassing them all. For example, Aristotle's description of virtue, as "a disposition of the perfect to the best," expresses the final cause alone. While it is accurate, it is incomplete. Lombard's definition is preferable because it alone, of all the contenders, offers an account of all the causes of virtue.

This explanation, offered by the early Aquinas, remains valid for the *Summa Theologiae*. Aquinas begins the body of the article with a methodological principle: "The complete rationale of anything is gathered from all its causes" (55.4c).[14] We find the principle in the commentaries on Aristotle's *Posterior Analytics, Metaphysics,* and *Physics*: "Sometimes many definitions are assigned to one thing according to diverse causes; but the complete definition is gathered from all the causes."[15] There is, then, an alternative to the standard definitional procedure of identifying genus and difference—that is, using a "causal" method that gathers the formal, material, final, and efficient causes of what is to be defined. Only a definition in terms of all four causes will be all-embracing.

Aquinas does not forget this principle in his theology. For example, Robert Pasnau shows that *The Treatise on Human Nature* (I.II 75–89) is structured according to the four causes.[16] As Clifford G. Kossel notes, it is by "causal analysis" that Aquinas arrives at his comprehensive definition of law.[17] Jacobus Ramírez notes that the *Treatise on Habits* (49–54) is largely divided according to the schema of the four causes.[18]

On this basis it is necessary to turn on its head the standard reading of the article defining virtue. Aquinas's concern is not merely to defend a definition already given but rather to offer a four-causal account that is more comprehensive than a definition in genus and difference (which only gives the formal cause). In the body of the article, and even in the objections and replies, Aquinas goes systematically through the four causes of virtue, correlating each, more or less adequately, with each part of the Augustinian definition. Indeed, Lombard's formula is hallowed by Augustine's authority, but it also happens to be the one that fits the causal method of definition best (or, rather, least inadequately). Where the Augustinian definition does not quite supply the right answer, Aquinas adapts it to fit the causal schema. Were it not for Aquinas's characteristic reverence for Augustine, the article "Whether the customary definition is fitting?" could have been titled "What are the causes of virtue?"

DOES VIRTUE EXIST?

We have seen how Aquinas defines virtue in general in terms of its four causes. Before we examine these causes in more detail, it is necessary to raise a question that has been held in abeyance for some time namely—the question not of essence but of existence. Does anyone actually possess virtues? The question is far from trivial. Due to the challenge from situational psychology, the question is a live one in contemporary virtue theory, with some authors claiming empirical evidence that people do not exhibit the stable, global dispositions that would constitute the virtues.[19]

Aquinas on Existence

Aquinas's usual method is to establish existence before essence. He does not believe essences exist in some abstract Platonic realm, independent of the individuals that possess them. So one cannot strictly know *what* something is unless one knows *that* it is: "There are no definitions of what does not exist."[20] The correct method of investigation is to begin with the question "*An est?*" (whether something exists), and only when that has been answered may one legitimately move to the question "*Quid est?*" (what something is in its essence).

Aquinas sees the apparent vicious circularity: how to prove *that* something exists before one knows *what* is to be shown to exist? To circumvent this catch-22, Aquinas distinguishes the preliminary knowledge of what something is from the scientific knowledge of its essence provided by a definition. One begins, then, with a nominal definition, proceeds to establish existence, and then finally arrives at a real definition or statement of what a thing is in its essence (I 2.2 ad 2).[21]

Why, then, does Aquinas begin the *Treatise on Virtue* with the definition of virtue, bypassing the prior question of whether there are any virtues?[22] The commentators often found this apparent lacuna difficult to explain.[23] There are various possible reasons for the omission.

One possibility is that Aquinas supposes he has demonstrated the virtues' existence in what has gone before. Aquinas has already argued that habits are "necessary" (I.II 49.4c). Here he is employing the idea of the "necessity of the end" (*necessitas finis*).[24] Something is necessary-simply-speaking when it cannot not be; something is necessary-for-the-end when the end cannot be attained, or attained well, without it (I 82.1c). In this sense, water is necessary for plants and making honey is necessary for bees.[25] For Aquinas, the virtues are necessary to human beings with the necessity of the end: without them a human being cannot attain the rational, human good to which she is oriented by nature. This, indeed, is the reason Aquinas considers the virtues at such length in his moral science. The virtues are the interior principles required to perform those actions by which we may arrive at beatitude (I.II 6 pr; 49 pr). We need the virtues.

Does virtue's necessity-for-the-end answer the question of its existence? Perhaps indirectly, at least within the framework of Aquinas's overall theology. For Aquinas, it is inconceivable that God should create humans and also make it systemically impossible that they find what they need to attain their good (110.2). The existence of virtue as a habit realistically attainable by human beings is an implication of his understanding of the created order as ruled by a provident God.

Aquinas would also acknowledge the direct scriptural testimony to the virtues, as in Paul's hymn to love (1 Corinthians 13). However, for Aquinas there is also a more empirical route to knowing virtues exist. In the *Summa Theologiae* he explicitly refers to virtue as one of those things that are known to us by experience (*nobis per experientiam nota*) (II.II 145.1 ad 2). In the *Commentary on the Sentences* he notes that, while we have no direct knowledge of habits, we can recognize their existence in others or in ourselves when we perceive that someone acts in such a way that she could not have done so without the corresponding habit.[26] So scripture, theology, and daily experience all point to the existence of the virtues. For these reasons, Aquinas may simply have assumed there was no need for a proof.

The Situationist Challenge

Does Aquinas's virtue theory survive the situationist challenge, which claims that there is empirical evidence that there are no virtues? The "situationist critique" of classical virtue theory is a philosophical argument based on interpretations of a body of empirical social psychology. It finds that social situation, not trait of character, has a greater role in explaining human behavior.[27] A strong version of the situationist critique is offered by Gilbert Harman, who claims that our attributions of character "tend to be wildly incorrect and, in fact, there is no evidence that people differ in character traits."[28] Other situationist critiques are more circumscribed. John Doris, for example, argues that the "robust traits" of classical virtue theory do not exist but that fine-grained "local traits" may: someone may be repeatedly helpful in one situation and repeatedly unhelpful in another rather similar situation.[29]

For Harman, as for Aquinas, our ability to affirm the existence of a virtuous habit depends on its success in explaining action. We can say a virtue, rather than situation alone, is the cause of an action only when the stable, operative quality we call a virtue is the best explanation for what is done. A contemporary virtue theory cannot remain hermetically sealed against situationist work that provides empirical evidence that situation plays a stronger role than character in explaining action. Robert Adams is one author who takes the evidence seriously in conceding that human virtue is "fragmentary and frail in various ways."[30] Similarly, we should question, on both theoretical and empirical grounds, one of Aquinas's claims, that a virtue must be extensionally perfect; that is, it must rightly dispose its bearer in regard to its objective matter globally rather than partially (see chap. 10 for a discussion). Doris may be right that our virtues are often "local" rather than "global."

At the same time, a more robust defense of virtue is possible.[31] To begin, it is necessary to ask what traits the situationist psychologists are testing for since they may have misunderstood the nature of the virtues that ethicists like Aquinas believe exist. The situationists often understand character traits in terms of behavioral dispositions, and they tend to assume, for example, that someone possesses the virtue of compassion only if she always helps those in need. Yet, as we have seen, for Aquinas virtues are not to be understood as ready-made behavioral responses to stimulus; they are situationally more sensitive than that. For Aquinas the possession of the virtue of mercy, say, does not require helping every time a person in need appears but rather being disposed to help another when, where, and how it is fitting to help, as judged by the practically wise person; the assessment will not always lead to helping (see II.II 33.2c). Testing for the existence of a virtue is a complex matter since the absence of a helping behavior on a particular occasion is not necessarily evidence of the nonexistence of the corresponding virtue.

A further complicating factor for situationist testing for character is that, as Aquinas points out, a virtuous person may sometimes fail to act on that virtue even when acting is a fitting response (I.II 74.1c). The failure to display a particular behavior is not proof that a person lacks a character; it may simply indicate that a person sometimes acts out of character or that her character trait is as yet imperfectly possessed. It is also worth pointing out that the possession of virtue, for Aquinas, is a relatively rare achievement and gift (35.5 ad 1). Even proving the absence of character in most people would not outright contradict Aquinas's virtue theory. Situationist evidence may point to the notion not that the are no virtuous people, only that virtue, for most of us, is of the germinal and imperfect kind that still needs to grow into complete virtue.

AQUINAS ON THE FOUR CAUSES

Having briefly looked at the question of the existence of the virtues, let us return to the question of essence. If Aquinas defines virtue in terms of its causes, how does he understand "cause"? Here Aquinas is undoubtedly indebted to Aristotle and the Arabic commentators.[32] The Aristotelian causes, however, are put to theological work to understand things in heaven and on earth undreamt of by the philosopher, such as creation, grace, and the sacraments. In the process, there is a resharpening and even retooling that takes place. Jordan is undoubtedly right to state, "The theologian's [Aquinas's] notion of causality both embraces more kinds of causes and deepens the accounts of causes already recognized."[33] What, then, is a cause?

Cause in General

Aquinas's concept of cause is broader than ours. "Explanation" may be a more accurate, if cumbersome, translation since the four causes correspond to four ways of answering the question, Why? As Aquinas puts it, "This question, Why? or, On account of what? asks about a cause."[34] The four causes are really the four *becauses*.[35] Robert Pasnau and Christopher Shields therefore suggest that Aquinas's account of the four causes may best be understood as a "framework of explanation."[36] For, "We do not think that we scientifically know anything, unless we grasp the *Why*, which is to grasp the cause."[37]

However, the doctrine of the four causes is not *merely* a methodological principle. For Aquinas we can explain things only by their causes because the causes themselves are real principles that genuinely influence the nature and existence of their effects. Aquinas's account of cause is not merely methodology; it is metaphysics.

Is it possible to define cause? Since "cause" is so basic a concept, it may be that a genus-difference definition is not possible. Nevertheless, Aquinas seems to identify origin or principle (*principium*) as the quasi-genus of cause. In its general sense a principle is simply "that from which something proceeds" (I 33.1c).[38] It is a "first" in a sequence.[39] Principle is therefore a more general concept than cause: all causes are principles, but not all principles are causes (33.1 ad 1). There are some common-sense reasons for the distinction. As night precedes day, a privation is a "principle" or starting point of change because privation necessarily precedes the acquisition of a new form; clearly, however, night does not cause day. Aquinas is unhappy with what he perceives as Aristotle's loose way of speaking when Aristotle says that every principle is a cause and vice versa.[40] For Aquinas, a cause is only one kind of principle.

Trinitarian theology helps to further refine the idea of causality. Aquinas claims that the Father is the principle but not the cause of the Son, since "this name of cause seems to imply diversity of substance, and dependence of one on the other, which the name of principle does not imply" (I 33.1 ad 1).[41] So a cause is not a mere principle, because it involves a relation of *dependency* between two *distinct* terms. As Aquinas explains in *On the Power of God*, this dependency obtains whether we are talking of material, formal, efficient, or final causation, because dependency is implied in the very concept of cause: "For the effect must depend on its cause. For this belongs to the rationale of effect and of cause."[42] So if C is the cause of E, then C is the *principle* of E, C is *distinct* from E, and E *depends in its being* on C.

Finally, there is another concept that seems to enter into Aquinas's characterization of cause. In the commentary on the *Metaphysics* we find the following statement: "This name of 'cause' implies a certain influence on the being of the caused."[43] A cause, then, is an *influxus*, or "influence." By this term, Poinsot observes, Aquinas distinguishes a cause from a mere necessary condition (*sine qua non*) since a cause is not merely something concomitant or required but rather is a positive influence on the effect.[44] It is therefore necessary to differentiate Aquinas's theory from that of J. L. Mackie, who famously sees a cause as an INUS condition: an insufficient but necessary part of an unnecessary but sufficient condition. Despite the danger of definitional circularity in using the term "influence," Aquinas does seem to be getting at something missed in Mackie's account. A privation, such as the absence of a captain of a ship, may have a real consequence, such as a shipwreck. Yet Aquinas would regard such a privation as an accidental cause only: it causes only in virtue of other *per se* causes—that is, causes that themselves have a causal influence, such as the wind, tide, and rocks.

Aquinas nowhere offers a systematic account of cause. But by piecing his disparate comments together we come to this conclusion: a cause is a principle that influences the being of another, entailing a dependency of the latter on the former. Or, as Poinsot reconstructs Aquinas's view: "A cause is a principle of something by influence or derivation, of such a nature that something follows from it with dependence in being."[45]

The Causal Nexus

How should we understand the four modes or genera of causation? The standard textbook account introduces them via a hackneyed example, albeit one that Aquinas himself employs.[46] The bronze, the being with potential for being shaped, is the *matter*; what makes this bronze into a statue of Socrates rather than, say, a canon, Aquinas calls *form*. For the statute to come into being, an efficient or agent cause is required: the sculptor. Since nothing acts unless it "intends" something, an *end* or *final cause* is needed. The danger in this example is that we take human artifice as the paradigm of causation, whereas for Aquinas natural causation is primary.

For Aquinas the four causes form a nexus. That is, an interrelationship exists among the four causes as expressed in the axiom, "Causes are causes of each other."[47] Matter and form, the "intrinsic" causes, are causes of each other: they both exist only as co-constituents of some whole, and they mutually depend on each other in the exercise of their respective roles in constituting the whole. The relation between efficient and final causes, the "extrinsic" causes, is also mutual. Aquinas argues that all agency is telic: "Every agent acts for an end, otherwise *this* more than *that* would not follow from the action of the agent, unless by chance" (I 44.4c).[48] Not just anything can follow from anything: that would be randomness, not causation. The efficient cause must "intend" the end; that is, it must have an inclination toward that specific end, otherwise it could not act (I.II 1.2c). The end enters into the definition of agency, as the term toward which it tends.

One important aspect of the causal nexus is therefore expressed in the axiom that "every agent acts for the end." In Aquinas's view all efficient causality, whether exercised by conscious beings or not, is telic. This may appear to be a glaring example of the "pathetic fallacy" that ascribes features of human consciousness to nonhuman beings. Yet Aquinas is not guilty of such a blunder. To "intend" is simply "to tend towards some other" (12.5c).[49] His point, then, is that even inorganic things exhibit inclinations toward some activity or end, as, according to now obsolete Aristotelian physics, fire has a natural inclination to rise (I 80.1c). It can be argued that, with current scientific understandings, even inorganic teleology in this very general sense is not implausible.[50] Agency and its correlative final causality is more obviously seen in nonconscious living beings (plants), sensate beings that are capable of acting for an end presented to them by their senses (animals), and rational beings capable of presenting to themselves their own ends (humans). For Aquinas there are degrees of agency that correspond to the degree that the principle of agency is internal to the agent (I 18.3c). Rational agents are self-directing in that they choose the ends for which they act; they exhibit a fuller kind of telic agency than other living beings (I.II 1.2).

In addition to viewing the four causes as a nexus, Aquinas claims that the final cause has a unique priority within this interrelated system. Admittedly, the efficient cause temporally precedes the end: I must exercise before I can become fit and healthy. However, I would not go for my regular jog unless I already had an end in view, such as increased health and fitness. So for Aquinas the final cause, as the object of appetite or desire, is what explains why an efficient cause in potency becomes an efficient cause in actuality. Similarly, the causality of the matter and form are also subsequent to that of the end: "The matter would not receive a form unless through the end, and a form would not perfect the matter unless through the end."[51] Aquinas concludes that the final cause is the cause of the causes (*causa causarum*) because it is "the cause of the causality" in all the other causes.[52]

For Aquinas, then, the ultimate explanation of why anything comes into being is final-causal since it is through the causality of the end that the other causes are causes at all. While the end is the *final* cause temporally speaking, it is the *first* cause causally speaking: "The final cause is the first among all the causes" (1.2c).[53] As will be seen, this thesis of the causal priority of the final cause within the causal nexus is an important element of Aquinas's relentlessly telic virtue theory.

The Causal Reading

How legitimate is it to read Aquinas's account of virtue through the lens of the four causes? Despite appearances to the contrary, his explicit structuring of the *Treatise on Virtue* reflects the nexus of the causes quite closely. The first question defines virtue in terms of the four causes. The second question looks at the subject, which is a material cause. The section on the division of virtue and the specification of the virtues examines the formal differentiation of virtue through the interplay of formal and material causes. Then follows a question on the efficient cause. Finally, while the section on the "properties" of virtue follows on the sections defining its "essence," the properties are explored largely in terms of the formal and material causes of virtue. Admittedly, the final cause is lacking from the schema, but this may be because Aquinas has already largely dealt with this cause in the questions on beatitude, which is the end of virtue (I.II 1–5), or because the proximate end of virtue coincides with its (extrinsic) formal cause (see chap. 7). Furthermore, four-causal explanation permeates the detailed argument of the articles on virtue in general, such as in the description of the way prudence and moral virtue dance together, as it were, in directing a person toward a good end (58.5). Aquinas does not slavishly follow the four-causal schema in structuring his *Treatise on Virtue in General*, but on a deep level causal analysis permeates the whole treatise.

Causal analysis does not impose an arbitrary schema on Aquinas's virtue theory; it has a prominent place in his method of investigation in general and the understanding of virtue in particular. The causal approach to reading Aquinas on virtue therefore yields a promising new way into the riches of his account.

NOTES

1. Carlo Leget, *Living with God: Thomas Aquinas on the Relation between Life on Earth and "Life" after Death* (Leuven: Peeters, 1997), 18.

2. "Virtus est, ut ait Augustinus, bona qualitas mentis, qua recte vivitur, et qua nullus male utitur, quam Deus solus in homine operatur." Peter Lombard, *Sententiae in IV Libris Distinctae*, 3rd ed. (Rome: Editiones Collegii S. Bonaventurae, 1971), Liber II, Dist. XXVII, Cap. 1, 480.

3. *Super Sent.*, lib. 2 d. 27 q. 1 a. 2

4. For Aquinas's references to these characterizations see II.II 56.5, 56.3c, 56.1sc; I.II 110.3; and II.II 57.5 arg 1.

5. Martin Rhonheimer, *The Perspective of Morality: Philosophical Foundations of Thomistic Virtue Ethics* (Washington, DC: Catholic University of America Press, 2011), 197.

6. Ibid., 197n18.

7. 55.4c: "ista definitio perfecte complectitur totam rationem virtutis." Compare *On the Virtues* 1.2.

8. Mark D. Jordan, "Theology and Philosophy," in *The Cambridge Companion to Aquinas*, ed. Norman Kretzmann and Eleonore Stump (New York: Cambridge University Press, 1993), 238.

9. Eleonore Stump, "The Non-Aristotelian Character of Aquinas's Ethics: Aquinas on the Passions," in *Faith, Rationality, and the Passions*, ed. Sarah Coakley (Oxford: Wiley-Blackwell, 2012), 93.

10. Here Aquinas apparently paraphrases Lombard's definition, replacing the final clause, "quam Deus solus in homine operatur," with the more or less equivalent, "quam Deus in nobis sine nobis operatur."

11. Bonnie Kent, "Habits and Virtues (Ia IIae, qq.49–70)," in *The Ethics of Aquinas*, ed. Stephen J. Pope (Washington, DC: Georgetown University Press, 2002), 119.

12. Matthew B. O'Brien, "Review of 'The Second-Person Perspective in Aquinas's Ethics: Virtues and Gifts' by Andrew Pinsent," *Notre Dame Philosophical Reviews* (December 2010).

13. *Super Sent.*, lib. 2 d. 27 q. 1 a. 2 ad 9: "si accipiatur definitio rei quae complectitur totum esse rei, secundum quod ex omnibus causis constituitur, quae est perfecta definitio, tunc unius rei non potest esse nisi una definitio. Dicta autem definitio virtutis complectitur omnes causas ejus."

14. 55.4c: "Perfecta enim ratio uniuscuiusque rei colligitur ex omnibus causis eius."

15. In *Posterior Analytics*: *Expositio Posteriorum Analyticorum*, lib. 1 l. 4 n.5: "Oportet igitur scientem, si est perfecte cognoscens, quod cognoscat causam rei scitae"; ibid., lib. 1 l. 8 n.4.; l. 13 n.8.; l. 13 n.8: "scire est causam rei cognoscere." In *Metaphysics*: *Comm. Metaph.*, lib. 8 l. 4 n.11: "Et oportet causas cognoscere ad hoc quod aliquid sciatur, quia scire est causam cognoscere." In *Physics*: *Comm. Physic.*, lib. 2 l. 5 n.7: "aliquando unius rei assignantur plures definitiones secundum diversas causas; sed perfecta definitio omnes causas complectitur."

16. Robert Pasnau, *Aquinas on Human Nature*, 10.

17. Clifford G. Kossell, SJ, "Natural Law and Human Law (Ia IIae, Qq. 90–97)," in *The Ethics of Aquinas*, ed. Stephen J. Pope (Washington, DC: Georgetown University Press, 2002), 170.

18. Jacobus Ramírez, *De Habitibus*, 1:4–5.

19. For a summary of the debate see Candace L. Upton, "Virtue Ethics and Moral Psychology: The Situationism Debate," *Journal of Ethics* 13, no. 2/3 (2009): 103–15. For strong critiques of classical virtue theory from the situationist perspective see the references to John Doris and Gilbert Harman later in the chapter.

20. *Expositio Posteriorum*, lib. 1 l. 2 n.5: "non entium non sunt definitiones."

21. For a lucid exposition see Christopher F. J. Martin, *Thomas Aquinas: God and Explanations* (Edinburgh: Edinburgh University Press, 1997), 32–49.

22. In a similar way he finds no need to discuss whether habits exist but proceeds directly to the question of their substance or essence (I.II 49); he does the same with vice and sin (I.II 71). When he discusses good and bad human action, he jumps straight to the question of what makes an action morally good or bad without asking whether there are any good human actions in the first place (I.II 18).

23. Salamancans, *Cursus Theologicus*, Tract. 12, *De Virtutibus*, Disp.1 (6:196); Cajetan, in I.II 49.1, n.1.

24. See Aquinas's characterization of *"necessitas finis"* and *"finis rei generatae"* in *De principiis naturae*, cap. 4.

25. See the discussion of "Aristotelian necessity" in Philippa Foot, *Natural Goodness* (Oxford: Oxford University Press, 2001), 15.

26. *Super Sent.*, lib. 3 d. 23 q. 1 a. 2c.

27. For more on situationist psychology see Lee Ross and Richard E. Nisbett, *The Person and the Situation: Perspectives of Social Psychology* (London: Pinter & Martin, 2011).

28. Gilbert Harman, "Moral Philosophy Meets Social Psychology: Virtue Ethics and the Fundamental Attribution Error," *Proceedings of the Aristotelian Society* 99 (January 1, 1999): 330.

29. John M. Doris, *Lack of Character: Personality and Moral Behavior* (Cambridge: Cambridge University Press, 2002), 25.

30. Robert Merrihew Adams, *A Theory of Virtue: Excellence in Being for the Good* (New York: Oxford University Press, 2006), 115.

31. A strong defense of classical virtue theory against situationism is offered by Rachana Kamtekar, "Situationism and Virtue Ethics on the Content of Our Character," *Ethics* 114, no. 3 (April 1, 2004): 458–91.

32. See especially Aquinas's commentaries on Aristotle's *Physics* and *Metaphysics* (*Comm. Physic.*, lib. 2 l. 5 nn.2–8; *Comm. Metaph.*, lib. 1 l. 4 n.2; lib. 5 l. 2 nn.1–13). There is an early systematic account by Aquinas in his own voice in *On the Principles of Nature*. Treatments of other topics in his theological works often also manifest his understanding of causation.

33. Jordan, "Theology and Philosophy," 247–48.

34. "haec quaestio quare, vel propter quid, quaerit de causa" (*Comm. Metaph.*, lib. 5 l. 2 n.9; cf. lib. 1 l. 4 n.2).

35. Compare Gregory Vlastos, "Reasons and Causes in the Phaedo," *Philosophical Review* 78, no. 3 (July 1, 1969): 291–325.

36. Robert Pasnau and Christopher John Shields, *The Philosophy of Aquinas* (Oxford: Westview, 2004), chap. 2.

37. *Comm. Physic.*, lib. 2 l. 5 n.1: "nos non opinamur nos scire unumquodque, nisi cum accipimus *propter quid*, quod est accipere causam."

38. I 33.1c: "id a quo aliquid procedit." Compare De principiis naturae, cap. 3.

39. *De principiis naturae*, cap. 3.

40. *De principiis naturae*, cap. 3.

41. I 33.1 ad 1: "hoc nomen causa videtur importare diversitatem substantiae, et dependentiam alicuius ab altero; quam non importat nomen principii."

42. *De potentia*, q. 5 a. 1c: "Effectum enim a sua causa dependere oportet. Hoc enim est de ratione effectus et causae."

43. *Comm. Metaph.* lib. 5 l. 1 n.3: "Nam hoc nomen principium ordinem quemdam importat; hoc vero nomen causa, importat influxum quemdam ad esse causati."

44. *Cursus Philosophicus* part 1, *De Ente Mobili in Communi* Q.10, and *De Causa in Communi* Art.1 (2:199).

45. Ibid., 2:198: "Causa est principium alicujus per modum influxus seu derivationis, ex qua natum est aliquid consequi secundum dependentiam in esse."

46. *De principiis naturae*, cap.3.

47. See, e.g., *Comm. Physic.* lib. 2 l. 5 n.7 and *De principiis naturae*, cap. 4, in *Metaphysics* 5, lec.2.

48. I 44.4c: "omne agens agit propter finem, alioquin ex actione agentis non magis sequeretur hoc quam illud, nisi a casu."

49. 12.5c: "intendere est in aliud tendere."

50. David Oderberg argues for the existence of inorganic teleology. See Oderberg, "Teleology: Inorganic and Organic," in *Contemporary Perspectives on Natural Law: Natural Law as a Limiting Concept*, ed. Ana Marta González (Aldershot, UK: Ashgate, 2008), 259–79.

51. *De principiis naturae*, cap. 4: "materia non suscipiat formam nisi per finem, et forma non perficiat materiam nisi per finem."

52. De principiis naturae, cap. 4: "Unde finis est causa causalitatis efficientis, quia facit efficiens esse efficiens: similiter facit materiam esse materiam, et formam esse formam, cum materia non suscipiat formam nisi per finem, et forma non perficiat materiam nisi per finem. Unde dicitur quod finis est causa causarum, quia est causa causalitatis in omnibus causis."

53. 1.2c: "Prima autem inter omnes causas est causa finalis."

PART II

Causal Ethics

CHAPTER 5

Exemplar and Object

Suggested reading: *Summa Theologiae* I 77.3, 93.4; I.II
pr, 1.3, 54.2; *On the Virtues* 2.4

A close examination of the four articles in which Aquinas attempts to define virtue (I.II 54.1-4) has revealed that he understands virtue in terms of its causes. Before we look in depth at how Aquinas employs the schema of the formal, material, final, and efficient causes to elaborate a comprehensive virtue theory, a pressing question that is as much systematic as exegetical needs to be considered: Given its dependence on a metaphysical understanding of causation that few today would accept, is it plausible to maintain that Aquinas's causal virtue theory retains its normative significance?

Standing between Aquinas and us is modern philosophy and science and the corresponding wholesale rejection of the scholastic way of understanding causal explanation. As Kenneth Clatterbaugh explains, a number of transformations in thinking about causation occurred in the modern period, from René Descartes onward.[1] First there was a significant simplification, as the moderns reduced talk about the four causes to the explanation of natural phenomena in terms of efficient causation alone. Then came a tendency toward secularization, from the desire to explain and understand the natural world without resorting to divine intention or agency. Eventually there was a move to a greater focus on epistemological questions, such as those concerning how we can know the metaphysical nature of causation and how we can even be sure of the existence of genuine causal interactions. The latter epistemological focus manifests itself in the skepticism of David Hume (1711–1776), who argues that causal inferences are determined by the experience of the constant conjunction of two phenomena only, such as smoke and fire, and not by reason.

Contemporary theories of causation, while influenced by advances especially in physical science, are largely inheritors of the simplification, secularization, and metaphysical skepticism of modern natural philosophy. Some theories, such as the understanding of causes as INUS conditions (insufficient but necessary parts of a condition that is itself unnecessary but sufficient for the effect), take Hume as a starting point.[2] Others explain causation in terms of counterfactual claims, such as the theory put forward by David Lewis.[3] Yet other theories, motivated by problems in such accounts, attempt to define a cause as that which raises the probability of its effect.[4] There is, then, no commonly accepted theory of causation. The diversity of theories "can lead one to suspect that no univocal analysis of the concept of causation is possible."[5]

There are a number of reasons for resisting as too hasty the conclusion that Aquinas's causal approach to virtue is unworthy of serious consideration today. The first is a simple but telling point: modern theories of causation are almost exclusively concerned with efficient causation. What this means is that when moderns refer to the "cause" of something, they are not necessarily talking about the same thing as when Aquinas says the same. For example, Aquinas spends much time on the formal cause of virtue. Yet a formal "cause" for him is simply that which accounts for something being what it is. No one accuses a virtue theorist of employing an obsolete mode of causal explanation if she attempts to say what virtue is, or what justice or some other virtue is.

There is, moreover, a strong motivation for the ethicist to consider seriously the kind of multidimensional account of causation offered by Aquinas, since the "naturalist" alternative seems inimical to an ethical worldview. According to Richard Dawkins, "The universe that we observe has precisely the properties we should expect if there is, at bottom, no design, no purpose, no evil and no good, nothing but pitiless indifference."[6] We shall examine the role, in Aquinas's ethics, of four central causal ideas—exemplar, object, end, and agent—and I shall argue that to discard this wide palette of causal concepts has demoralizing results. Something akin to Aquinas's understanding of causal explanation is needed by normative ethical theory.

THE EXEMPLAR CAUSE

One of the Platonic strands of Aquinas's thought is his recognition that the "exemplar" or "idea" is a cause. In accord with Aristotle, Aquinas rejects Platonic ideas as separate from the beings in which they are realized. But he sees God as the subsistent exemplar cause by which other things, through participation, have their being and goodness. "In this respect, the opinion of Plato can be held."[7]

What is an exemplar cause? Aquinas's fullest characterization of this species of cause in found in his disputed questions *On Truth* (Q3), where he explains that an exemplar cause or idea is a particular kind of form but not in the same way that the soul is the form of a human being or the figure of a statue is the form of bronze. For an idea is not that *by which* something is formed but that *according to* which something is formed.[8] The idea is an exemplary form after whose likeness something is made. Nor is it enough for exemplar causality that one thing resembles another by chance; the likeness must arise from the intention of the agent, as when an artist produces a portrait. Aquinas says, "This therefore seems to be the rationale of *idea*, that it is a form that something imitates from the intention of the agent, who predetermines the end for himself."[9]

Does the exemplar cause fall outside of Aristotle's four-causal schema? Aquinas notes that in some way an exemplar cause is a final cause since the image is intended to be like the exemplar.[10] Similarly, the exemplar also relates to efficient causality since the idea preexists in the mind of the agent who brings the image into being. However, the idea is a particular kind of form in whose likeness something is formed. As Gregory Doolan puts it, the exemplar "is a formal cause, even though it is an extrinsic form."[11]

How can the idea be a form if it is external to what is formed? Aquinas says that the formal cause is related in two ways to what is formed: "In one way as the *intrinsic* form of the thing, and this is called 'species'; in the other way as [the form] *extrinsic* to the thing, after whose likeness, nevertheless, the thing is said to be made; and in this way, the exemplar of a thing is called a form."[12] The exemplar cause, though external to its effect, nevertheless exhibits a kind of formal causality; it is not a fifth species of cause. Poinsot says: "The causality of the idea can be reduced to efficient and final, but specially and properly to formal [causality], insofar as it is an extrinsic form forming, but not *in*-forming."[13] The exemplar cause is an *extrinsic formal cause.*

Exemplars, Images, and Ethics

What role does the exemplar play in Aquinas's theological ethics? Exemplar causation is evident from the outset of his ethical masterpiece, the *Treatise on Morals.* As he begins this central section of the *Summa Theologiae,* Aquinas may well have had in mind Aristotle's famous remark, "A small mistake in the beginning is a big one in the end."[14] The starting point is all-important, as it is present virtually in all that follows. Aquinas begins, then, as follows:

> Because, as Damascene says [De Fide Orth. ii, 12], the human being is said to be made after God's image, insofar as "image" implies "an intelligent being having free judgment and power in himself"; having spoken of the exemplar, namely, of God, and of what proceeds from the divine power according to his will, it remains to consider God's image, that is, the human being insofar as he himself is the principle of his works, having free judgment and power over his own works. (I.II pr)[15]

This dense and intensely holographic text, which sets the stage for Aquinas's most complete statement on moral science, conceives the human person as the image of the exemplar, God.

Why begin ethics with exemplar causality? It is possible to identify at least three advantages. The divine exemplar cause is the efficient, the final, and especially the (extrinsic) formal cause of the human person. So exemplar causality sketches a "theocentric" ethics in which the human person, as the image of God, is made by God, for God, and like God. For, "Everything is treated in sacred doctrine under the rationale of God: either because they are God himself, or because they have an order to God as to the principle and end" (I 1.7c).[16]

A second reason for choosing exemplar causation is that it expresses a remarkably dynamic theological ethics, which Aquinas describes as being "about the *motion* of the rational creature into God" (I 2 pr) (emphasis added).[17] The human person is characterized as made after the image of God (*ad imaginem Dei*) in two senses: an image made *after* the exemplar, on which she is modeled, but also *to be after* the exemplar, as moving toward a more perfect imaging.[18] This is the basis for a developmental ethics: "The human being is not only said to be the image, but also towards the image, by which the motion of someone tending towards completion is designated" (I 35.2 ad 3).[19] Exemplar causation therefore conveys a dynamic process: morality is the created image's movement toward becoming the perfected image in glory (93.4c). Ramírez puts it well: the subject matter of Aquinas's moral theology is not the merely *entitative* but the *dynamic* image of God.[20]

Beginning ethics with the divine exemplar cause also places an accent on human agency. Aquinas sees a connection between being an image of God and being an agent—that is, having mastery over oneself and one's acts (*dominium sui*). Ignatius Theodore Eschmann observes that Aquinas could have begun with the human merely as a creature needing divine direction, indicating an ethics of dependency for a child who by definition never grows up. Instead, Aquinas begins with the idea of a human as made in the image of the creator and governor of the universe, and therefore as an agent in her own right: an ethics of a child who "*by definition* is *growing up.*"[21]

For Aquinas, the exemplar, or that according to which something is formed, is a "cause" in that it is an explanatory principle that helps to account for what something is. There is nothing problematic in the idea itself, and if modern theories of causation fail to acknowledge exemplar causation it is only because they employ a narrower, more reductionistic conception of "cause." Aquinas's employment of the ideas of exemplar and image provide an important motif for a theological ethics that is theocentric, dynamic, and focused on human agency. There is no need to abandon it merely because naturalistic theories of causation fail to consider it.

THE OBJECTIVE CAUSE

We turn now to another species of formal causation—namely, objective causation. This is the causation specific to the object, in Aquinas's technical understanding of "object." The idea of objective causation is closely related to that of *intentionality*, which is derived from the Latin *intendere*, to tend toward. Intentionality is the intrinsic characteristic of being directed toward some object, and since the time the concept was reintroduced by Franz Brentano (1838–1917), from his (evidently incomplete) knowledge of medieval discussions, it is widely seen as an essential mark of the mental.[22] This is not the understanding of Aquinas, who happily ascribes an object even to bodily processes such as growth (I.II 77.3c). Contemporary understandings of intentionality should not be assumed to correspond to Aquinas's understanding of objective causation.[23] Our focus will be on Aquinas as explicated by John Poinsot, whose account has been found to have significant philosophical value today.[24]

Object as Specifier

"Object" (*obiectum*) is evidently a scholastic term of art.[25] To what does it refer? The word was scarcely employed before the year 1240 but was in common use by Aquinas's day.[26] Etymologically, as Joseph Pilsner explains, the Latin word *obiectum* comes from the verb *obiicire*: to throw or place in front of another.[27] An object is therefore something that is distinct from but comes into relation with powers, habits, and acts. For example, one desires various *goods*, thinks about various *things*, or is angry at *a certain person* about *some injustice committed*. Here goods, things, persons, and injustices are all objects since they are what some act of desire, thought, or passion is directed toward.

The crucial role of an object, according to Aquinas, is to specify a power, habit, or act, where "act" includes interior as well as exterior acts.[28] How does one define a power of the soul, such as the power of intellect, will, or sight? In the first place, a power is defined in terms of its *acts*, such as a thinking, willing, or seeing: "In the logic of definition, acts and operations are prior to powers."[29] As Aquinas puts it in his commentary on Aristotle's *De Anima* (the *locus classicus* of the whole discussion), "Acts and operations are prior to powers in their defining rationale. For a power, according to the very thing that it is, implies a certain directedness to act: for it is a certain principle of acting or undergoing. So it is necessary that acts are placed in the definition of powers."[30] For example, to define what the intellect is, one must first define what understanding (*intelligere*) is since a power or potential is defined in terms of what it is a potential *for*. "Each thing takes its species from act, and not from potential" (I.II 1.3c).[31]

If powers are defined by their acts, acts or operations are in turn defined in terms of their objects: "It will be necessary to determine objects before acts, for the same reason that acts are also determined prior to powers."[32] Briefly, Aquinas's argument is that the acts in question are operations of either passive or active powers; in each case it is the object that defines the act (I 77.3c).[33] In the case of a passive power, the object is the principle and "moving" cause of the act; in the case of an active power, the object is its end point or goal. For example, seeing, which is the act of the *passive* power of sight, is defined by its object (namely, color); to see is by definition to perceive some color, which is the proper object of sight. Similarly, growth, which is an act of the *active* power of vegetation, is defined by its object (namely, maturity), since growth is by definition a process toward maturity, or its proper object.

Aquinas applies the principle of specification by object to habits as well as powers: "And so the rationale and species of a power is taken from its object; and the same applies to a habit, which is nothing other than the disposition of a perfected power to its object" (*On the Virtues* 2.4c).[34] As he puts it elsewhere, "Habits imply order to another. However, all things described in terms of their order to another, are distinguished according to the distinction of those things towards which they are described" (I.II 54.2.c).[35] Thus, "species of virtues are distinguished according to objects" in particular (I.II 54.2.c).[36] The way of defining (*via definiendi*), then, is this: first objects, then acts, then powers or habits.

Formal and Material Objects

The principle of specification by object needs to be interpreted with care since there are different aspects under which the object may be considered. Aquinas distinguishes formal and material objects. Take, as an example, the power of sight. The objects of sight include a human being, a stone, and a donkey. However, it is no use defining sight as the apprehensive power that has Peter the human, a stone, and Donald the donkey as its objects, since the same could apply to the power of hearing so long as Peter speaks, the stone falls into the well, and Donald brays. Aquinas therefore makes his first refinement to the principle by distinguishing the *material* from the *formal* objects of a power or habit:

> In the object we find a formal and a material element. The formal element in the object is *that according to which the object is referred to a power or habit*; the

material element, on the other hand, is *that in which this is founded*. For example, if we speak of the power of sight, its formal object is color, or something of this kind, for something is visible insofar as it is colored; but the material element in the object is the body which the color happens to qualify. From this it is clear that a power or habit is referred *per se* to the formal rationale of the object; but to that which is material in the object, *per accidens*. And only what is *per se*, not what is *per accidens* varies the thing; therefore, material diversity of the object does not diversify a power or habit, but only a formal diversity. For there is one power of sight, by which we see both stones and human beings and the sky, because this is a material diversity of objects, and not a diversity according to the formal rationale of the visible. (*On the Virtues* 2.4c)[37]

It is not enough to define sight in terms of its *material* objects (namely, Peter, a stone, and Donald); rather, sight is defined in terms of its *formal object* (that is, whatever in the object makes it an object of sight (namely, color).

Aquinas's preferred term for the formal object is the technical expression "formal rationale of its object" (*formalis ratio obiecti*); it refers to *what makes something an object of some power, habit, or act*. That is, the formal rationale of the object of X is the *ratio* or nature something needs to possess to be an object of X. In the case of sight, this is simply color since color is what makes some bodily thing, such as Peter, a stone, or a donkey, visible. "For the unity of a power and a habit is to be considered according to the object, not indeed materially, but according to the formal rationale of the object; for example, a human being, a donkey, and a stone agree in one formal rationale of colored, which is the object of sight" (I 1.3c).[38] In general, then, a power of the soul or a habit is determined in its species according to the formal rationale of the object toward which it is directed.

The English "rationale" is used here as a placeholder for Aquinas's *ratio*, an important term with a wide semantic field. Alternative translations include "formula," "aspect," "nature," "determinant," and "concept." None is an exact equivalent. As Armand Maurer explains, "The *ratio* of a thing is its definition, or, in other words, the concept that expresses what a thing is. By extension, the term also signifies the intelligible nature of a thing corresponding to its definition."[39] I use "rationale" to translate Aquinas's *ratio*, the formula of a thing's nature, or the intelligible nature itself.

Why is it that the *formal* rationale of the object defines a power, state, or act? A material object, considered as a thing in its own right, may have many different properties and accidents, each with its own rationale: the body that the eye sees may be round, heavy, hard, and blue. The formal rationale of the object makes the object an object since the form is what makes something what it is. For example, the formal rationale of the object of sight is not shape, weight, or hardness. It is color, because that is the rationale under which the object becomes an object of sight. It is not any particular color, such as white or blue, that specifies powers (since then we would need different faculties to perceive white and blue objects); it is only the specific rationale of color (I 59.4c). Thus, the principle of specification by object is this: *Human powers, habits, and acts are specified not by their material objects but by the formal rationale of their objects.*[40]

To complexify still further, Aquinas is prepared to identify different degrees of materiality or formality in the object. The case is once again most easily illustrated by the power of sight. The formal object of sight is that by which something becomes visible. But while a body becomes visible by being colored, it is also true that a colored body becomes visible only when it is manifested to the power of sight through light (I 105.5c).[41] Since it is possible to see light without seeing any colored object, light is the *most* formal object of sight (*De Malo* 2.2 ad 5). Although sight is oriented toward perceiving colored bodies, light seems even more definitive of the object of sight than color.[42]

In the case of sight, then, we have different layers, as it were, of materiality and formality in the object:

(1) The *purely material objects* of the power of sight are bodies since they are visible only insofar as they take on the form of color.

(2) The *somewhat material, somewhat formal* object of sight is color. This is more formal than any body since bodies become objects of sight by being colored. Yet color is a material object of sight when considered in relation to light, in virtue of which a colored body becomes visible.

(3) The *purely formal object* of sight is light. This is the purely formal object of sight since it is ultimately by light that anything becomes visible.

Later Thomists introduce some helpful technical terminology to express the important distinction between (2) and (3). The somewhat material yet somewhat formal object is referred to as the object that is attained (*obiectum quod*), like color in the case of sight. The purely formal object is referred to as the object by which something is attained (*objectum quo*) by a power, habit, or act, like light in the case of sight. [43]

So there is at least a threefold object of any power, habit, or act: the purely material object, the formal rationale of the object that is attained, and the formal rationale of the object by which it is attained. This threefold object provides a powerful method of specifying and distinguishing virtues.

OBJECTIVE CAUSATION

Since the object is clearly a principle of specification, it is natural to ask: Is the object a cause? And if so, of what kind? Poinsot best clarifies the causality of the object by explicitly addressing the key issue: In what genus of cause does the object specify powers, habits, and acts?[44] Poinsot's approach is more penetrating than contemporary accounts, which tend to confuse final and objective causation.

Poinsot characterizes the object as follows: "Object in general [. . .] consists in this, that it is something extrinsic, from which the intrinsic rationale and species of some power or act [or habit] is derived, and upon which it depends; and this is reduced to the genus of formal extrinsic cause, not causing existence, but specification."[45] The object, then, is indeed a cause; more particularly it is a species of *extrinsic formal cause*, like the exemplar cause. Why is this so?

Habits, along with acts and powers, belong to a somewhat unique category of being.[46] The scholastics divide beings into those that are "absolute" or non-relative, in that they have their essence in themselves, and those that are "relative" (*ad aliud*). What falls into the categories of "substance" or "quantity," for example, are absolute beings: while they may depend for their *existence* on another being such as God, their *essence* is, as it were, self-contained. Relations, on the other hand, are purely other-directed: for example, "to be taller than" is by its very nature for one being to be taller than *some other being* without which the relation would not be defined or even exist. Poinsot claims that acts, habits, and powers fall into neither category straightforwardly but rather exist in a kind of in-between or mixed realm, having something absolute in themselves and yet being somewhat relative at the same time. They are indeed ordered to something (*ad aliud*), but they are ordered to this *from their very nature*. As he puts it, "Essentially and intrinsically, that is, from the property of their natures, [powers, habits, and acts] are ordained to another [that is, the object], and therefore are said to be specified by it."[47] It follows that the object must be a formal cause. For the causality proper to a form is precisely that which makes it what it is: the form determines the species (*forma dat speciem*).[48] The object specifies acts, powers, and habits, and so must be a form. As Aquinas puts it, the object "has in some way the rationale of a form, insofar as it determines the species" (I.II 18.2 ad 2).[49] Again, "the object moves [a power] by determining it in the manner of a formal principle" (I.II 9.1c; cf. II.II 4.3c).[50]

Poinsot points out that the object is not the *intrinsic* form of a power, habit, or act but rather something external to which the power, habit, or act is nevertheless intrinsically referred. The intrinsic form is a tendency or directedness to the object; the object, on the other hand, is that to which the power, habit, or act is ordered.[51] The object, then, must be an *extrinsic formal cause* since, while it is extrinsic as that to which a power, habit, or act relates, it nevertheless helps to make a power, habit, or act what it is (cf. I 77.3 ad 1).[52]

Some Objections

A significant objection can be made to this way of conceiving the causality proper to the object. Sometimes the object is an efficient cause, as when a real color causes the act of seeing. At other times the object is a final cause, as in the case of virtues or even acts of the will, which are oriented toward some good act or end as their object. Finally, the object can also be the effect, as when a power, habit, or act gives rise to operation or result. Why identify the object exclusively with the formal cause but not with the final or efficient cause, or even with the effect?

Let us deal with these possibilities in turn. Poinsot discounts the possibility that the object as such can be an efficient cause. Efficient causation concerns the order of existence rather than the order of specification:

> What depends on another in existence, as such, is not specified by it. For specification and definition abstract from existence, because the existence of no created thing is essential or pertains to definition. It is clear, however, that every dependency *from the efficient cause* is only a dependency as regards existence, because the efficient cause as such only regards the thing under existence or to posit it outside its causes. . . . Whence respect to the efficient cause . . . insofar as it is such, does not specify, because it does not regard the definition of the thing according to itself, but only the thing under existence.[53]

The efficient cause, precisely as such, does not determine the nature or species of something but rather bestows existence on it. Yet the role of the object is to specify. The object's characteristic causation is therefore not efficient but formal.

Poinsot concedes that sometimes the object is also sometimes the efficient cause of some act, as when a color is perceived correctly. However, he constructs a thought experiment to show that the causality of the object is not efficient causality. Suppose that God brings about a vision in a person. For example, he makes Paul see Ananias lay his hands on him, even though this event has not yet happened. The perceptions would be efficiently caused by God, not by the object, and yet the object would still specify what is being seen. Paul is seeing Ananias, not God. The causality proper to the object as object, therefore, is not efficient causality.

Admittedly, Aquinas does refer to the object as "moving" a power (I.II 9.1c). However, Poinsot points out that "moving" in this context is applied not merely to efficient causes but to the other genera of causes by a kind of metaphor:

> A great equivocation is committed in that term "motive" when it is applied only to the efficient cause, since it may also be applied to the other causes. For example, the end is said [metaphorically] to "move" [the agent to act], and the object proposed to the will "moves" it, and the exemplar "moves" to its imitation. In this way, therefore, we distinguish "motive" in the manner of *exercise* and in the manner of *specification*, and the first is what characterizes the efficient cause, the second the formal object.[54]

The object "moves" by specifying a power, act, or habit, not by moving it in the manner of an efficient cause (cf. I.II 9.1c). Once again, the characteristic causation of the object is formal, not efficient.

What about the idea that the object causes by final causation? Aquinas claims that human acts receive their species from their end, their final cause (I.II 1.3). Is this not a counterexample to Poinsot's claim that the object specifies by means of formal causation? No, quite the opposite. The reason that human acts that is—acts from deliberate will—are specified by the final cause, is, as Aquinas says, "The object of the will is the good and the end" (ibid.).[55] Poinsot points out, then, that the final cause can specify but only insofar as it "clothes itself," so to speak, in the nature of an object. Thus, in regard to an act of the will, "the end has both offices: both that of *finalizing*, or 'moving' (metaphorically speaking) to the execution and existence of a work, and of *specifying* or *formalizing* the act of a will, insofar as it presents to it the rationale of good and desirable, which is the formal and specifying object of the will."[56] Thus, although the final cause does indeed specify the act of the will, it is by objective not final causation that it does so; to specify is not to "finalize" but to "formalize."

Poinsot's analytic acumen helps to clear up some confusions about object. Joseph Pilsner is the author of the most thorough treatment of object in contemporary literature. On the basis of various texts where Aquinas seems to identify the object with the immediate goal of an action, Pilsner claims that "object" sometimes means "the proximate end of an act."[57] This leaves Pilsner puzzled as to why Aquinas appears to use "object" in two senses: sometimes connoting that to which a power, habit, or act relates, and sometimes connoting the end of a power, habit, or act.

If Poinsot is right, there is no equivocation in Aquinas's terminology. "Object" and "end" can sometimes coincide in reference, but never in sense.

Even when the object happens to be an end because of the appetitive nature of the power, habit, or act to which it belongs, "object" only ever *means* a particular kind of formal cause namely—that to which a power, habit, or act is intrinsically and essentially related as something to be done, desired, known, effected, or in some other way attained. Even when the object happens to be an end, the object *as object* only ever lies in the order of formal and never final causation.

There is one final possibility to consider, that the object *as effect* specifies a power, act, or habit. This moves us toward consequentialist accounts of moral action: an action is right or wrong insofar as it produces good or bad effects. Poinsot points out that this does not work: "The effect, as effect, does not specify an act or power, but presupposes them as specified. For an effect, insofar as it is an effect, receives being and nature or species from its cause, it does not give them to it."[58] Since to count as the efficient cause of some effect something must already exist and therefore already have a specific nature, the efficient cause cannot receive its nature from its effect: this would be to put the cart before the horse. In regard to specification, as well as existence, the effect is the beneficiary rather than the benefactor. Effects may be the sign and manifestation of a power, habit, or act, but they can never be what essentially defines them.[59] Because consequentialism fails to distinguish objective from efficient causation, it mistakenly locates morality in the efficient effect of an action rather than the action's object. The unfortunate result is a morality that eclipses the way every action is already specified by its object—that is, before it brings about any effect. Consequentialism, then, tends to fail to consider the all-important intentionality in which morality is formally located.

For Poinsot the object may sometimes be an efficient cause, a final cause, or an effect, but it is only the object *as object*, not the object under any of these other causal descriptions, that specifies. This is the crucial importance of understanding the specificity of the causation proper to the object. The object as object does not bring about existence, or attract desire, or come into existence; it only specifies. Thus specification by object must be a distinct kind of causality, one that is not reducible to final or efficient causality or being an effect. Poinsot calls it *objective* causality.

Let us review the central point. Why must objective causality be a kind of formal causality? The answer is simple: formal causality is the causality that makes something what it is. The object is that which the power, habit, or act intrinsically regards by its very nature as making it what it is. Hence the causality exercised by the object as such is a formal causality. Because the object is that to which a power, habit, or act is essentially referred, rather than an intrinsic form constituting its essence, it is a kind of *extrinsic* formal causality.

OBJECTIVE CAUSATION AND ETHICS

How important is objective causation in ethics? Its relevance lies in addressing what we can call "the problem of specification." When Elizabeth Anscombe wrote the essay widely credited as the origin of the renewal of virtue, she made the following observation: "It would be a great improvement if, instead of 'morally wrong,' one always named a genus such as 'untruthful,' 'unchaste,' 'unjust.'"[60] Specificity matters in ethics, and modern moral philosophy had for her remained too abstract, making do with an impoverished moral vocabulary of actions that are only "right" or "wrong." A recovery of the richer language of the virtues and vices was needed.

Aquinas is a primary reference point for the retrieval of a differentiated yet integrated vocabulary of virtue. He recognizes that abstract ethics is not, by itself, enough. The extensive first part of his ethical treatise (I.II 6–114), which describes a "universal consideration" of human acts and their principles, is merely a preparation for the even vaster second part (II.II 1–189), which examines them specifically. This is a necessary movement: "For general moral discourse is less useful, since actions exist in the particular" (II.II pr).[61] Aquinas calls this procedure of moving from the general to the specific the way of "determination" (I.II 95.2): "Every operative science is perfected in particular consideration" (II.II pr).[62]

Just as Albert Einstein proposed both a general and a special theory of relativity, so virtue theory has its general and special varieties.[63] Aquinas's general theory of virtue (I.II 55–70) says what virtue in general is; the special theory (II.II 1–170) offers accounts of the specific virtues.

How, though, do we get from a general account of what virtue is to an account of the specific virtues and their interrelationships? It is part of the task of general virtue theory to address this question. Aquinas devotes six questions (I.II 57–62), a large part of the *Treatise on Virtue in General*, to the task: "We have now to consider the *distinction* of virtues: first, as regards the intellectual virtues; second, as regards the moral virtues; third, as regard the theological virtues" (57 pr).[64] His aim is not merely to begin the process of determination but to uncover the methodological principles that govern the specification and distinction of the virtues. In addition, he is careful to order the virtues into an overall structure and so discusses the "connectivity" (*connexio*) or mutual interdependence of the virtues (65) and how they are to be placed on scales of relative importance (66). He attempts, then, to outline the principles of a structured differentiation of virtue, respecting both their oneness and their multiplicity.

It is in this context that the importance of objective causation becomes clear. As discussed earlier, the causality proper to form is to specify (*forma dat speciem*).

Since by definition virtues are the kind of things that are tendencies toward some morally good object (that is, an object that conforms to reason), it is by their objects that virtues are specified and distinguished from one another. Each virtue has a material object (the "matter-about-which" the virtue is), a formal object that is attained by the virtue (the "target"), and a formal object by which the target is attained (the "mode"). These objective causes are both interrelated and relate to the efficient, final, and material causes. The idea of objective causation, therefore, provides a means to the generation of the rich moral vocabulary that Anscombe and others have recognized as so necessary for ethics today.

NOTES

1. Kenneth Clatterbaugh, *The Causation Debate in Modern Philosophy, 1637–1739* (New York: Routledge, 1999), 1–15.

2. John L. Mackie, "Causes and Conditions," *American Philosophical Quarterly* 2, no. 4 (October 1965): 245–64.

3. David Lewis, "Causation," *Journal of Philosophy* 70, no. 17 (1973): 556–67. Lewis has revised his theory a number of times since his original statement.

4. Jon Williamson, "Probabilistic Theories," in *The Oxford Handbook of Causation*, ed. Helen Beebee, Christopher Hitchcock, and Peter Menzies (Oxford: Oxford University Press, 2009), 185–212.

5. Helen Beebee, Christopher Hitchcock, and Peter Menzies, eds., *The Oxford Handbook of Causation* (Oxford University Press, 2009), 1.

6. Richard Dawkins, *River Out of Eden: A Darwinian View of Life* (New York: Basic, 1995), 132–33.

7. *De Veritate*, q. 21 a.4c: "Et quantum ad hoc opinio Platonis sustineri potest."

8. *De Veritate*, q. 3 a. 1c.

9. *De Veritate*, q. 3 a. 1c: "Haec ergo videtur esse ratio ideae, quod idea sit forma quam aliquid imitatur ex intentione agentis, qui praedeterminat sibi finem."

10. *De Veritate*, q. 1. a. 1c.

11. Gregory T. Doolan, *Aquinas on the Divine Ideas as Exemplar Causes* (Washington, DC: Catholic University of America Press, 2008), 42. As Doolan explains, the exemplar is not only a formal cause, since it exercises final and efficient causality; "an exemplar idea, in its capacity as an exemplar, is reduced to the order of formal causality since the characteristic that is proper to it as an exemplar is its imitability" (43).

12. *Comm. Metaph.*, lib. 5 l. 2 n.2: "Alio modo sicut extrinseca a re, ad cuius tamen similitudinem res fieri dicitur; et secundum hoc, exemplar rei dicitur forma." Compare *De Veritate*, q. 3 a. 3c.

13. *Cursus Philosophicus*, part 1, *De Ente Mobili in Communi*, Q.11, Art.3 (Reiser 2:245b): "Nihominus dicendum est causalitatem ideae reduci posse ad efficientem et finalem, sed specialiter et proprie ad formalem, quatenus est forma extrinseca formans, sed non informans."

14. Aquinas begins his *De Ente et Essentia*: "Quia parvus error in principio magnus est in fine, secundum philosophum in I caeli et mundi."

15. I.II pr: "Quia, sicut Damascenus dicit, homo factus ad imaginem Dei dicitur, secundum quod per imaginem significatur *intellectuale et arbitrio liberum et per se potestativum*; postquam praedictum est de exemplari, scilicet de Deo, et de his quae processerunt ex divina potestate secundum eius voluntatem; restat ut consideremus de eius imagine, idest de homine, secundum quod et ipse est suorum operum principium, quasi liberum arbitrium habens et suorum operum potestatem."

16. I 1.7c: "Omnia autem pertractantur in sacra doctrina sub ratione Dei, vel quia sunt ipse Deus; vel quia habent ordinem ad Deum, ut ad principium et finem."

17. I 2 pr: "de motu rationalis creaturae in Deum."

18. What I say here draws on my essay "Spirituality and Virtue in Christian Formation: A Conversation between Thomistic and Ignatian Traditions," *New Blackfriars* 97, no. 1068 (March 2016): 202–17.

19. I 35.2 ad 3: "homo non solum dicitur imago, sed ad imaginem, per quod motus quidam tendentis in perfectionem designatur."

20. Jacobus M. Ramírez, *De Hominis Beatitudine: In I–II Summae Theologiae Divi Thomae Commentaria (QQ. I–V)* (Madrid: Vives, 1972), 1:88–89.

21. Ignatius Theodore Eschmann, *Ethics of St. Thomas Aquinas*, ed. Edward A. Synan (Toronto: Pontifical Institute of Mediaeval Studies, 1997), 163–64.

22. Franz Brentano, *Psychology from an Empirical Standpoint* (New York: Routledge, 2014), 92–95, 181, 205.

23. Robbie Moser, "Thomas Aquinas, Esse Intentionale, and the Cognitive as Such," *Review of Metaphysics* 64, no. 4 (June 2011): 763–88; and Stephen L. Brock, "Intentional Being, Natural Being, and the First-Person Perspective in Thomas Aquinas," *The Thomist* 77 (2013): 103–33.

24. John Deely, *Purely Objective Reality* (Berlin: Walter de Gruyter, 2009).

25. Although his focus is on action rather than on virtue, the best contemporary treatment of object as specifying is that by Joseph Pilsner, *The Specification of Human Actions in St. Thomas Aquinas* (Oxford: Oxford University Press, 2006), chap. 5. My approach is influenced by Poinsot: *Cursus Philosophicus, Ars Logica (Prima Pars), Summul. Lib. I. Cap. II* (Reiser 1:9); *Ars Logica (Secunda Pars)*, Q.21; *De Signo Secundum Se*, Art. IV (Reiser 1:670–79); Q.27, *De Unitate et Distinctione Scientiarum*, Art.1 (Resider 1:818–20); *De Ente Mobili Animato*, Q.2, Art.3, *Utrum potentiae specificentur et distinguantur per actus et obiecta* (Reiser 3:74–83); and *Cursus Theologicus*, in I–II, Disp.1, *De fine ultimo et morali*, Art.3, nn.5–7 (Solesmes 5:39). See also Salamancans, *Cursus Theologius*, Tract. 8, *De Ultimo Fine*, Disp.1, Dub.3, §1, nn.27–32 (Solesmes 5:18–21); Tract. 14, *De Fide*, Disp.1, nn.1–4 (11:5–6); Ramírez, *De Beatitudine*, 1972, pt. I, 60ff.; and *De Fide Divina: In II–II Summae Theologiae Divi Thomae Expositio (QQ. I–VII)* (Madrid: Vives, 1972), 24–27.

26. Lawrence Dewan, "'Obiectum': Notes on the Invention of a Word," in *Wisdom, Law, and Virtue: Essays in Thomistic Ethics* (New York: Fordham University Press, 2007), 403–43.

27. Pilsner, *Specification*, 73.

28. *Comm. De Anima*, lib. 2 l. 6 nn.6–9; I.II 77.3; Quaestiones de anima, Articulus 13.

29. *Comm. De Anima*, lib. 2 l. 6 n.6: quia secundum rationem definitivam, actus et operationes sunt priores potentiis.

30. *Comm. De Anima*, lib. 2 l. 6 n.6: "secundum rationem definitivam, actus et operationes sunt priores potentiis. Potentia enim, secundum hoc ipsum quod est, importat habitudinem quamdam ad actum: est enim principium quoddam agendi vel patiendi: unde oportet, quod actus ponantur in definitionibus potentiarum."

31. I.II 1.3c: "unumquodque sortitur speciem secundum actum, et non secundum potentiam."

32. *Comm. De Anima*, lib. 2 l. 6 n.8: "prius oportebit determinare de obiectis quam de actibus, propter eamdem causam, propter quam et de actibus prius determinatur quam de potentiis."

33. On the distinction between active and passive powers, and indeed on the concept of powers itself, see Pasnau, *Thomas Aquinas on Human Nature*, 143–51.

34. *On the Virtues* 2.4c: "Et sic ratio et species potentiae ex obiecto accipitur; et similiter est de habitu, qui nihil est aliud quam dispositio potentiae perfectae ad suum obiectum."

35. I.II 54.2.c: "Habitus autem importat ordinem ad aliquid. Omnia autem quae dicuntur secundum ordinem ad aliquid, distinguuntur secundum distinctionem eorum ad quae dicuntur."

36. I.II 54.2.c: "species virtutum distinguuntur secundum obiecta."

37. *On the Virtues* 2.4c: "Sed in obiecto consideratur aliquid ut formale et aliquid ut materiale. Formale autem in obiecto est id secundum quod obiectum refertur ad potentiam vel habitum; materiale autem id in quo hoc fundatur: ut si loquamur de obiecto potentiae visivae, obiectum eius formale est color, vel aliquid huiusmodi, in quantum enim aliquid coloratum est, in tantum visibile est; sed materiale in obiecto est corpus cui accidit color. Ex quo patet quod potentia vel habitus refertur ad formalem rationem obiecti per se; ad id autem quod est materiale in obiecto, per accidens. Et ea quae sunt per accidens non variant rem, sed solum ea quae sunt per se: ideo materialis diversitas obiecti non diversificat potentiam vel habitum, sed solum formalis. Una est enim potentia visiva, qua videmus et lapides et homines et caelum, quia ista diversitas obiectorum est materialis, et non secundum formalem rationem visibilis."

38. I 1.3c: "Est enim unitas potentiae et habitus consideranda secundum obiectum, non quidem materialter, sed secundum rationem formalem obiecti, puta homo, asinus et lapis conveniunt in una formali ratione colorati, quod est obiectum visus."

39. Armand A. Maurer, *The Division and Methods of the Sciences* (Toronto: Pontifical Institute of Mediaeval Studies, 1986), 36.

40. For a detailed list of texts throughout Aquinas's works where the formal rationale of the object is said to specify and distinguish powers, habits, and acts, see Pilsner, *Specification*, 91.

41. Ibid., 97–102.

42. On Aquinas's understanding of the role of light in percpetion, see ibid., 98n.252.

43. Ramírez, *De Hominis Beatitudine*, 1:60–61.

44. *Cursus Philosophicus, De Ente Mobili Animato*, Q.2, Art.3 (Reiser 3:74).

45. *Cursus Philosophicus, Ars Logica (Secunda Pars)*, Q.21, Art.4 (Solesmes 1:670).

46. Ibid. Also, *Cursus Theologicus*, in I.II, *De fine morali et ultimo*, Disp.1, Art.3, nn.5–7 (Solesmes 5:39).

47. *Cursus Philosophicus, De Ente Mobili Animato*, Q.2, Art.3 (Reiser 3:74).

48. E.g. I.II 18.2c, ad 2, 3c.

49. I.II 18.2 ad 2: "habet quodammodo rationem formae, inquantum dat speciem."

50. I.II 9.1c: "obiectum movet, determinando actum, ad modum principii formalis."

51. *Cursus Theologicus*, in I.II, *De fine morali et ultimo*, Disp.1, Art.3, n.5 (Solesmes 5:39).

52. *Cursus Philosophicus, De Ente Mobili Animato*, Q.2, Art.3 (Reiser 3:74).

53. *Cursus Philosophicus, De Ente Mobili Animato*, Q.2, Art.3 (Reiser 3:75).

54. *Cursus Philosophicus, Ars Logica (Secunda Pars)*, Q.21, Art.4 (Reiser 1:670).

55. I.II 1.3: "Obiectum autem voluntatis est bonum et finis."

56. *Cursus Theologicus*, in I.II, *De fine morali et ultimo*, Disp.1, Art.3, n.32 (Solesmes 5:45).

57. Pilsner, *Specification*, 133–40.

58. *Cursus Theologicus*, in I.II, *De fine morali et ultimo*, Disp.1, Art.3, n.19 (Solesmes 5:42).

59. *Cursus Philosophicus, De Ente Mobili Animato*, Q.2, Art.3 (Reiser 3:74).

60. G. E. M. Anscombe, "Modern Moral Philosophy," *Philosophy* 33, no. 124 (1958): 8–9.

61. II.II pr: "Post communem considerationem *On the Virtues* et vitiis et aliis ad materiam moralem pertinentibus, necesse est considerare singula in speciali, sermones enim morales universales sunt minus utiles, eo quod actiones in particularibus sunt."

62. II.II pr: "Sed quia operationes et actus circa singularia sunt, ideo omnis operativa scientia in particulari consideratione perficitur."

63. Daniel C. Russell, *Practical Intelligence and the Virtues* (Oxford: Oxford University Press, 2009).

64. 57 pr: "Deinde considerandum est de distinctione virtutum. Et primo, quantum ad virtutes intellectuales; secundo, quantum ad morales; tertio, quantum ad theologicas."

CHAPTER 6

End and Agent

Suggested reading: *Summa Theologiae* I 2.3, 18.3;
I.II 1pr, 1.1–8, 14.2, 21.2 ad 2.

The final cause is an especially controversial yet crucial issue in causal virtue theory. Aquinas explains the overall agenda in theological ethics in final-causal terms: "In the first place we must consider the ultimate end of human life, and then those things by which a human can advance towards this end, or deviate from it. For the rationale of what is ordained to the end must be taken from the end" (I.II 1pr).[1] Aquinas's ethics, therefore, presuppose a naturally and indeed supernaturally given end to human life and that the actions and virtues by which we advance toward that end are conceived teleologically. The modern scientific worldview, in contrast, is often understood to be incompatible with a cosmology of natural and supernatural finality. In the modern era, final causes were expunged from physical science as having no explanatory value, and in the one kind of scientific endeavor where teleology remained plausible—biological science—Charles Darwin's theory of evolution offered an alternative account of the genesis of complex life forms, thereby apparently eliminating the need for appeal to final causes. Today philosophers often assume that teleological talk must either be eliminated or interpreted in terms of efficient causes. Can the kind of causal approach to ethics and virtue theory found in Aquinas, one that takes final causality seriously, be sustained today?

EXTRINSIC FINALITY

Margaret Osler has argued that while many of the early modern figures such as Francis Bacon and René Descartes did make a point of explicitly rejecting final-causal explanation in scientific investigation, their rejection of teleology

92

was not done as wholesalely as is generally thought.[2] Even those who rejected teleological explanation in scientific and philosophical argument struggled to do without it altogether. More important, many key figures, such as Pierre Gassendi, Robert Boyle, Gottfried Leibniz, and Isaac Newton, retained some kind of appeal to final causation in their theories of natural philosophy. Final causality was not eliminated as such, only the final causality immanent to the natural world.

A confirmation of this historical interpretation is found in the tendency of seventeenth-century philosophers to compare the cosmos to a machine, usually a clock or watch. A watch, though made of pieces of inert matter with no inherent purposes of their own, nevertheless possesses a function deriving from the mind that made it. Notwithstanding their skepticism about immanent finality, the mechanistic philosophers saw the natural world as possessing a kind of extrinsic teleology derived from the creator. As Osler explains, "With the mechanical reinterpretation of final causes, the idea of individual natures that possess immanent finality was replaced with the idea of nature as a whole which is the product of the divine artificer. Nature becomes a work of art."[3] The design argument for God's existence, as advanced most famously by William Paley, is therefore a modern one. Just as the complex ordering of an artifact to a single function is evidence of the artisan, so the complexity of living beings is evidence of the divine artificer. This argument is the ancestor of intelligent design theory, which argues that the "irreducible" or "specified" complexity of the world indicates an ordering by a divine intelligence.[4]

Once this move has been made, it is difficult to find a way back. The elimination of immanent final causation, while not initially meant to deny divine teleology, opens the door to wholesale skepticism about final causes. Any inference to a divine intelligence as the best explanation of complexity in the universe is always vulnerable to the possibility of a still more-successful scientific explanation. For many this is precisely what Darwin provides. Adaptation and evolution do not occur in order to produce organisms better-suited to their environment. Rather, of the different traits that arise in individuals through variation, those more suited to survival and reproductive success tend to be inherited. Evolution by natural selection is an efficient-causal, not a final-causal process. As Richard Dawkins puts it, "If [natural selection] can be said to play the role of watchmaker in nature, it is the *blind* watchmaker."[5]

Intelligent design theorists infer the existence of a divine watchmaker; Dawkins asserts that evolution is a blind watchmaker; for Aquinas there is no watchmaker, blind or otherwise. As Christopher Martin comments, "In the eight million words Thomas Aquinas definitely wrote, and the three million words he may have written besides, the universe is never compared to a clock."[6]

INTRINSIC FINALITY

Modern thinkers tend to acknowledge (at most) two kinds of finality: rational finality and design. Rational finality is the intrinsic finality exhibited by rational agents that are capable of freely aiming at goals; design is a purely extrinsic finality, such as that exhibited by artifacts. The advantage of this dualism is that one can be explained in terms of the other: the extrinsic finality of a clock or a computer is something imposed on inert matter by a purposive mind.

In the following passage from *On Truth*, Aquinas seems to propose a similar dualism: "Something may be ordered or directed to something, as to an end, in two ways: in one way, *by itself*, as a human being who directs himself to the place to which he tends; in another way, *by another*, as an arrow that is directed by the archer to a determinate place" (emphasis added).[7] However, Aquinas subdivides the finality that comes from a directing intelligence into two species, one of which is purely extrinsic or "violent," and one which is not:

> Sometimes that which is directed into an end is only impelled and moved by the director, without acquiring any form from the director by which such a direction or inclination belongs to it; and such an inclination, as when an arrow is inclined by the archer to a determinate mark, is "violent." Sometimes, however, what is directed or inclined into an end acquires from the director or mover some form by which such an inclination belongs to it; and such an inclination will be "natural," as having a natural principle, just as he who gave gravity to the stone inclined it to be borne down naturally. . . . It is in this way that all natural beings are inclined to what is fitting for them, having in themselves some principle of inclination, by reason of which their inclination is natural, so that in a way they go about their own way to their due ends, and are not merely led.[8]

Here, then, is where Aquinas differs from the early moderns: he sees the basis for the final causality of natural beings in the formal causality of nature. It is because of what they are—that is, because of their substantial forms—that natural beings have a directedness toward an end. Natural finality is intrinsic, not extrinsic. As the Aristotelian maxim has it, "Nature acts for an end."[9]

If Aquinas sees finality as intrinsic to nature, how can he argue from natural finality to the existence of God, as he does in the famous Fifth Way (I 2.3)? Edward Feser has pointed out that this teleological argument is not a design argument as some would have it. Aquinas's argument starts by establishing the existence of finality on the basis that natural bodies always act, or nearly always act (unless prevented from doing so by some defect or intervening circumstance), in a certain way so as to obtain the best result. Feser makes the observation, which is obvious once made but otherwise easily missed, that "Aquinas is not referring here to an intelligent designer; he does not get to God until the second half of the argument."[10] Finality is established on the basis of how things tend to behave, and an argument still has to be made for the existence of a divine intelligence responsible for this already established intrinsic finality. Aquinas's argument for God proceeds *from* finality, not *to* finality.

While the universe for Aquinas is not like a clock with its purely extrinsic finality, Aquinas does draw an important analogy between created beings and artifacts. In one of his most important characterizations of nature he states: "And so it is clear that nature is nothing other than the rationale of a certain art, namely, the divine art, instilled in things, by which the things themselves are moved to a determined end, just as if a shipbuilder were to be able to bestow on the timbers that by which they could move themselves to take on the form of a ship."[11] Natural telic activity for Aquinas arises from an internal source (*principio intrinseco*), which itself is derived from an external source (*principio extrinseco*) (cf. I 104.5). Where Aristotle sees a purely intrinsic principle, Aquinas goes further and traces the origin of this intrinsic principle back to God's intelligence and power.

The recovery of this kind of cosmology of immanent finality is attractive to theological ethics in part because of its ability to address certain modern problematics. On the "divine watchmaker" viewpoint, the divine will is purely extrinsic and heteronomous, and we risk reducing God to a manipulator who uses humans for His own purposes. Nature, lacking any intrinsic finality, becomes devoid of its own intrinsic moral status and is therefore open to human domination. Immanent finality, in contrast, opens up the possibility of reconciling human autonomy with divine heteronomy, as the moral life fulfills God's wise plan precisely by fulfilling human desires instilled into human nature. A nature invested with finality is also one with meaning and its own good and therefore not lacking any moral status of its own, as "Green Thomism" contends.[12] If we are in search of a moral basis on which to resist attributing to God the instrumentalization of humanity and a simultaneous instrumentalization of nature by humanity, the recovery of immanent final causation may well be a good place to begin.

Immanent teleology is attractive to more than theologians alone. Philippa Foot, for example, begins with the "natural goodness" of living beings, which is distinguished from any goodness they possess merely in reference to human concerns. In her view this natural goodness has to do with what serves the natural teleology of the species to which an individual belongs, although she is careful to distinguish this teleology from conscious purpose, whether of living beings or some creator deity. If living beings have a natural goodness, then moral goodness can be understood in terms of the natural goodness specific to the human species.[13] How tenable is it, though, to see nature, including human nature, as permeated by natural finality?

ASSESSING INTRINSIC FINALITY

Immanent finality is controversial. It is seen by its opponents as unscientific and as a projection of mental qualities onto mere things, and as a philosophical concept its problems involve an ontologically mysterious backward causation. Let us briefly examine these three problems in turn.

The main scientific challenge to immanent teleology comes from evolutionary theory. Darwin's theory of natural selection is widely interpreted as doing away with the need for design or final-causal explanation. According to Darwin, evolution by natural selection occurs when there is variation in a species that fits individuals better or worse for surviving and reproducing, together with the possibility of inheriting such variable traits. The origin of the different species, then, is accounted for not by the direct intervention of a deity but by a purely natural process.[14] Since natural selection is an entirely nonteleological process that accounts for the *apparent* teleology of the evolution of a species' traits, it is often inferred that natural selection does away with the need to posit immanent teleology or a divine creator.

From a Thomistic perspective, there is little problem in seeing evolution as having natural causes. For Aquinas, God gives creatures causal powers and endows them with the dignity of being agents in their own right: the divine primary causality operates, therefore, through creatures' secondary causality without bypassing it (I 105.5 ad 1). As Armand Maurer points out, Darwin himself, at points in his career, appealed to the idea of secondary causation as an alternative to the view that God creates individual species by a singular intervention.[15] Furthermore, while the rejection of final-causal explanation in the generation of the species seems incompatible with a William Paley design argument, it is less clear that Darwinian natural selection is incompatible with immanent teleology.[16]

Many philosophers of biology do see teleological concepts as an ineliminable part of biological explanation. As Ernst Mayr points out, biologists frequently employ teleological language to talk about organs' functions, physiological processes, and the behavior of individuals and species; they often insist that "they would lose a great deal, methodologically and heuristically, if they were prevented from using such language."[17] On this basis, Thomists such as Jean Porter have argued that Aquinas's "teleological conception of the human person" remains defensible as a grounding for ethics. Porter argues that even to conceive of a particular kind of creature it is necessary to form a conception of the way of life proper to a mature instance of that kind. She shows that this viewpoint receives support from scientists and philosophers who, independent of particular moral or theological concerns, take a stance on teleology that differs from that of Dawkins.[18] While the philosophical interpretation of teleological language within the biological sciences remains contested, it is at least plausible to reject as too hasty the widespread assumption that the Darwinian theory of evolution, and its contemporary inheritors, has ruled out immanent teleology as inherently unscientific.

There are other objections to final causality, however. Is Aquinas's idea of intrinsic finality not an anthropomorphic projection of mental qualities onto nonrational and even nonconscious beings?

One should not be misled by Aquinas's language. Terms such as appetite (*appetitus*) and intention (*intentio*) in their common English translations, "appetite," "desire," and "intention," convey consciousness. Aquinas, however, adopts a very general definition of both. An appetite is simply an inclination toward something on the part of its bearer (I.II 81.1c); to intend is nothing other than to tend toward something (I.II 12.5 arg 3). Aquinas claims that all natural things manifest appetite or intention in the sense of directedness or inclination toward some goal; he is not thereby attributing some conscious end to them.[19] Paul Hoffman distinguishes in Aquinas a "full-bodied notion of final causation" from a "stripped-down understanding."[20] The former is applicable to rational agents, whereas the latter extends to all natural beings. While the deliberate, self-directive agency of humans requires acting for something viewed as a good, finality in nonrational and even inanimate beings requires merely tending to a certain effect. Aquinas does not project the kind of finality characteristic of human agency onto natural beings.

More can be said against the accusation of anthropomorphism, however. Aquinas understands himself not to be attempting to understand nature in terms of human consciousness but rather the opposite: rational agency is seen as a special case of a more general phenomenon of telic agency. As Robert Pasnau explains: "Rather than attribute to human beings an obscure volitional power, and leave it at that, Aquinas wants to account for the will in terms of concepts that play a familiar role elsewhere. In the case of the will, as in so much else, it is important to Aquinas that he situate his theory within a broader account of the workings of nature."[21] When Aquinas writes of a natural inclination of the will (*naturalis inclinatio voluntatis*) toward the good (I 1.8 ad 2), natural philosophy is being used to throw light on human psychology, not vice versa.

This approach is more scientifically respectable than one that views teleology as a projection of the human mind. As Robert Spaemann notes, the rejection of natural teleology "allows the dimension of finality in man to suddenly, so to speak, appear, and it excludes man from the natural context."[22] Simon Oliver makes a similar point: "Ascribing teleological orientation to human intentionality—in other words, to mind—presents a particular problem [for the naturalist] for it renders 'mind' or 'consciousness' anomalous in the face of an otherwise inert and non-teleological material universe."[23] It would be odd were the naturalist to claim that teleology springs ex nihilo with the evolutionary emergence of humankind. The Thomistic claim of immanent finality, according to which human intentionality is a specific and developed instance of a more generally observable phenomenon in nature, is therefore more conducive to modern scientific assumptions than the supposedly naturalistic viewpoints that see natural finality as the projection of human attributes onto a purposeless natural world.

A more radical philosophical objection to final causation sees the very concept of finality as incoherent. How can the end of an action, which by definition does not exist before the agent acts, move it to act? It seems odd to ascribe causation to possible future existents, which may or may not come to be.

Aquinas recognizes this problem of backward causation: "A cause is naturally prior [to the effect]. But the end has the rationale of last, as its very name implies" (I.II 1.1 arg 1).[24] He resolves the problem by making a distinction: "The end, even though last in execution, is nevertheless first in the intention of the agent. And in this latter way it has the rationale of cause" (ad 1).[25] A child wants to build a model helicopter and sets about doing so. After much labor she completes her task. But the end as it exists at the temporal end point of the process is not a *cause* of the child's action; it is its *effect*. The helicopter that rests in all its glory on the bedroom floor is the result of intentional action, not its principle. The final cause of the child's hard work is not the end as a future real existent but the end as the object of desire and thought, which as such temporally preexists the helicopter. There is no backward causation.

TELEOLOGICAL ETHICS

How does the final-causal viewpoint affect ethics? As we have seen, for Aquinas it is from the final cause that the causality of all the other causes derives: "The final cause is the first among all the causes" (I.II 1.2).[26] Correspondingly, the idea of the *finis* or end of human life is the primary, if not the solitary, organizing principle of Aquinas's moral thought: right action, the virtues, and the law all derive their nature from order to the end. As he says, "The principle of the entire moral order is the last end" (I.II 72.5).[27] Without its orientation to the overall end of human life, Aquinas's ethics would collapse like a decorative mobile that has come loose from its hook and fallen in a tangled heap on the floor.

To say that Aquinas's ethics is teleological can leave it open to misinterpretation because of an unfortunate tendency to conflate "teleological" and "consequentialist" ethics. Aquinas's ethics is teleological in that morality concerns the ordering of actions to the overall end of human life. "Good and evil [in moral acts and habits] are said in relation to the end."[28] However, this ethics is not consequentialist, since it does not locate morality in the value of the overall effects of an action. A foreseen consequence affects the morality of an action primarily because it is a sign of the goodness or badness of the will: the "input" of an action is therefore more important, morally speaking, than its "output" (I.II 20.5, 73.8).[29]

If the effect does not specify an action, what is left of Aquinas's thesis that an action is specified by the end or terminus of an action (1.3)? As we saw above (see chap. 5), an action's effect is the beneficiary, rather than the benefactor, of existence and nature, so it cannot be the cause of the act's species. Poinsot explains, however, that the end or terminus of an action can indeed specify an action, not as its effect but only insofar as it "clothes itself in the rationale of cause, or principle, or object." "For the terminus to specify an action, it must be considered, not as executively proceeding from the action, but as contained in the causative power and principle of the action: for there the terminus is itself contained virtually and radically, and as in the principle; and thence, primarily and immediately, the action takes its species."[30] As Aquinas himself puts it, "The end, insofar as it is prior in intention, in this respect pertains to the will; and in this way it gives species to a human act" (I.II 1.3 ad 2).[31]

Aquinas's ethics is teleological in the legitimate, nonconsequentialist sense that sees the final cause of human life as the governing principle of the moral order. The moral goodness and badness of acts are therefore defined in terms of their due or undue relation to this end: "In morals, where what matters is the order of reason to the overall end of human life, sin and evil are understood in terms of deviation from the order of reason to the overall end of human life" (21.2 ad 2).[32] The same can be said for habits: "True unqualified virtue is that which orders to the principal good of the human being" (II.II 23.7).[33]

TELIC AGENCY

A final-causal approach also affects the understanding of agency and therefore, once again, has ramifications for ethics. The dominant theory of agency is what is termed the "causal" theory, which analyzes intentional action in terms of the efficient causality of internal psychological states, such as desires and beliefs. The best-known proponent of this account is Donald Davidson, according to whom "an action is performed with a certain intention if it is caused in the right way by attitudes and beliefs that rationalize it."[34] One problem of this reduction of intentional agency to the efficient causality of psychological states is that of the vanishing of the agent: actions, on the efficient-causal viewpoint, seem to be events that happen to us rather than things we actively do ourselves.[35] As Stefaan E. Cuypers has proposed, Aquinas can be seen as offering an account that is simultaneously "agent-causal" and teleological and is therefore an attractive alternative to the causal theory; it is more successful in accounting for what it means to act *actively*.[36]

Aquinas holds a teleological theory of agency: to act is to act for some end (I.II 1.2c). However, he contrasts the way humans and nonrational animals tend to the end: "It is characteristic of a rational nature that it tend into the end *as acting*, or *as leading oneself to the end*; whereas it is characteristic of irrational nature to tend into the end *as acted or led by another*" (1.2c, emphasis added).[37] The telic nature of active agency comes out in a contrast between animal and human agency. The agency of nonrational animals is a mixture of agency and passivity. A robin does act when it builds a nest to shelter its young, but it does not actively choose this end over another. The agency of humans, in contrast, is more purely active: humans act for an end and actively choose the end(s) for which they act. Whereas animals tend to the end "as acted," humans tend to the end "as acting."

For Aquinas the scale of agency goes from the minimal agency of plants through growth to the perfect agency of God, whose activity involves no passivity at all (I 18.3c). Once again, teleology is the key. On this scale, animals are more perfectly agents than plants because they can move toward objects perceived by the senses—that is, by pursuing food, or a mate, or escape from enemies. However, the ends of their actions are not determined by the animals themselves, but by nature: a sheep cannot choose to befriend a wolf instead of fleeing it. For humans, it is different: "Above such [non-rational] animals are those that move themselves *even in regard to the end, which they determine in advance for themselves*. This only happens by reason and intellect, which knows the proportion of the end and of what is for the end, and to order the one in regard to the other" (18.3c, emphasis added).[38] One might put it this way: animals are *self-moving*, but only humans are *self-directing* and able to choose the end for which they act.

What is the root of the difference between merely animal and self-directive human agency? Aquinas says, "Those beings that lack reason tend to the end by a natural inclination, as if moved by another, and not by themselves, since they do not think about the rationale of the end, and therefore cannot order anything to the end, but only are ordered by another to the end" (I.II 1.2c).[39] The difference between nonrational and human agents, then, lies in the fact that, "whatever a human being desires, he desires under the rationale of the good"

(1.6c).[40] Humans, because of their capacity for reason, can evaluate different potential goals and choose to direct themselves to one or other accordingly.

This conception of human agency as truly active because self-directive is equally evident in Aquinas's analysis of deliberation. Aquinas accepts the Aristotelian thesis that deliberation is always about the means, or "those things that are for the sake of the end," rather than about the end itself (14.2). Deliberation has to begin from an end that is already "given" and proceed to determine how best to realize that end: if an agent did not already have some end in mind, there would be no start to the process of reasoning. Yet Aquinas does nevertheless claim that there can be deliberation about the end: "Having apprehended the end, someone can, deliberating about the end and about the means, be moved or not be moved to the end" (6.2c).[41] What does Aquinas mean, then, by "deliberating about the end"?

There are at least two ways in which means-end reasoning takes place: one is about what would *constitute* a given end, and one is about what *steps* need to be taken to realize that end. Take the example of someone wanting to have an enjoyable day of leisure. The primary question here is what would constitute such a day: would it be hiking a mountain, or meeting friends, or reading a book, or some combination of these? Once this prior question has been answered, it is possible to determine the steps that need to be taken (pack a rucksack or take a certain train). Both processes are examples of means-end reasoning, but the first step concerns what constitutes the end to be achieved, while the second concerns the actions that can realize that end.

It is reasonable to think that, when Aquinas says that we can deliberate about ends as well as means, he means that we can deliberate about what constitutes some end.[42] Poinsot puts it in the following way. Admittedly, one may not deliberate about the end *formally speaking*, since there is no doubt, and therefore no deliberation, that the good in general is to be desired and willed. Yet it is possible to deliberate about the end *materially* speaking—that is, about what happens to constitute the end: "Thus all desire to live happily, but many doubt about where that happiness may be found: whether in riches, or in pleasure, or in God. And many desire to establish life rightly, but whether that life is to be chosen in celibacy or marriage, or in studies, or in the military, is the subject of deliberation."[43] The chosen constitutive means to happiness then, whether it be wealth, honor, pleasure, or knowing and loving God, may in turn become the organizing goal of one's life.

Aquinas's teleological account of human agency as self-directive and deliberate helpfully sets morality within an overall teleological context. Moral theologians today rightly critique the old moral manuals for focusing exclusively on acts in an atomistic way—that is, divorced from a broader context of a person's orientation toward the overall goal of human life.[44] One of the contributions of the return to virtue has been to set human actions within this narrative context rather than focusing exclusively on the "freeze frame" of a specific action. Aquinas avoids the trap of the atomistic approach precisely because of his teleological vision of agency. The moral manuals invariably begin with a treatment of human action and omit the *Treatise on Beatitude*, whereas Aquinas situates his definition of human action within a consideration of the overall end of human life (I.II 1–5). His account of human agency is teleological from the beginning, in seeing that human action is the motor of the journey of the dynamic *imago Dei* toward God. For him, truly human moral agency flows from deliberation about ends, as well as how best to realize those ends. Ethics must therefore begin not with the question of what to do but with the deeper final-causal question of what ends are worth pursuing in the first place.

ASSESSING CAUSAL ETHICS

A full-scale evaluation of Aquinas theory of causation, one that engages contemporary science, philosophy of science, and metaphysics, is beyond the professional competency of the ethicist. Yet at the same time it is not possible for the ethicist to ignore these questions altogether. It has been rightly observed that, for Aquinas, "there is no fundamental separation between metaphysics and ethics."[45] Causal concepts such as those of exemplar, object, end, and agent all have significant contributions to Aquinas's ethics. My aim has been to make these ideas intelligible today and to indicate their potential contribution to contemporary theological and philosophical ethics.

Alfred J. Freddoso and Edward Feser have boldly argued that Thomistic and scholastic theories of causation stand up well in relation to alternative accounts.[46] A less defensive and more dialogical approach is also possible. As observed above, the diversity of theories of causation "can lead one to suspect that no univocal analysis of the concept of causation is possible."[47] One strength of Aquinas's theory is that it is not a univocal, reductionistic account, and so it is able dialectically to acknowledge the insights of different perspectives. Aquinas's account has something in common with pluralistic accounts, as it recognizes more than one form of causation; it also resembles "primitivist" accounts in some way because it recognizes causation as a basic concept that, while to some extent is analyzable, nevertheless resists strict definition. Michael Rota has argued that Aquinas's account of efficient causation has much in common with contemporary "dispositional" accounts. Gabriele De Anna argues that the four causes can be seen as at least INUS conditions; he thereby draws connections with J. L. Mackie's analysis of causation.[48] Michael Dodds identifies "burgeoning expansion of the idea of causality in contemporary science" as conducive to Thomistic understandings.[49] We should not expect the dialogue between Aquinas and contemporary theories of causation to leave Thomistic understandings unchanged, but it is a strength that Aquinas's analogically nuanced account is open to dialogue on these and many other fronts.

Finally, it is worth returning to the initial consideration: the four causes are simply four ways of answering the question, "Why?" A cause, for Aquinas, is some principle in virtue of which something can be understood or explained. The explanatory framework of the four causes opens up a number of interrelated, promising lines of investigation into the nature of virtue. To Aquinas's causal inquiry into virtue, therefore, we now turn.

NOTES

1. I.II 1pr: "Ubi primo considerandum occurrit de ultimo fine humanae vitae; et deinde de his per quae homo ad hunc finem pervenire potest, vel ab eo deviare, ex fine enim oportet accipere rationes eorum quae ordinantur ad finem."

2. Margaret J. Osler, "Renaissance Humanism, Lingering Aristotelianism and the New Natural Philosophy: Gassendi on Final Causes," in *Humanism and Early Modern Philosophy*, ed. Jill Kraye and Martin William Francis Stone (London: Routledge, 2000), 193–208.

3. Ibid., 194.

4. William A. Dembski, *The Design Revolution: Answering the Toughest Questions about Intelligent Design* (Downers Grove, IL: InterVarsity Press, 2004); and Michael J. Behe, *The Edge of Evolution: The Search for the Limits of Darwinism* (New York: Simon and Schuster, 2008).

5. Richard Dawkins, *The Blind Watchmaker: Why the Evidence of Evolution Reveals a Universe Without Design* (New York: Norton, 1996), 5.

6. Christopher Martin, *Thomas Aquinas: God and Explanations* (Edinburgh: Edinburgh University Press, 1997), 180.

7. *De Veritate*, q. 22 a. 1 c: "Dupliciter autem contingit aliquid ordinari vel dirigi in aliquid sicut in finem: uno modo per seipsum, sicut homo qui seipsum dirigit ad locum quo tendit; alio modo ab altero, sicut sagitta quae a sagittante ad determinatum locum dirigitur."

8. *De Veritate*, q. 22 a. 1 c: "Sed ab alio possunt dirigi in finem determinatum etiam quae finem non cognoscunt sicut patet de sagitta. Sed hoc dupliciter contingit. Quandoque enim id quod dirigitur in finem, solummodo impellitur et movetur a dirigente, sine hoc quod aliquam formam a dirigente consequatur per quam ei competat talis directio vel inclinatio; et talis inclinatio est violenta, sicut sagitta inclinatur a sagittante ad signum determinatum. Aliquando autem id quod dirigitur vel inclinatur in finem, consequitur a dirigente vel movente aliquam formam per quam sibi talis inclinatio competat: unde et talis inclinatio erit naturalis, quasi habens principium naturale; sicut ille qui dedit lapidi gravitatem, inclinavit ipsum ad hoc quod deorsum naturaliter ferretur;

per quem modum generans est motor in gravibus et levibus, secundum philosophum in Lib. VIII Physic. Et per hunc modum omnes res naturales, in ea quae eis conveniunt, sunt inclinata, habentia in seipsis aliquod inclinationis principium, ratione cuius eorum inclinatio naturalis est, ita ut quodammodo ipsa vadant, et non solum ducantur in fines debitos."

9. *Comm. Physic.*, lib. 2 l. 15 n.1.

10. Edward Feser, "Teleology: A Shopper's Guide," *Philosophia Christi* 12, no. 1 (2010): 156.

11. *Comm. Physic.*, lib. 2 l. 14 n.8: "Unde patet quod natura nihil est aliud quam ratio cuiusdam artis, scilicet divinae, indita rebus, qua ipsae res moventur ad finem determinatum: sicut si artifex factor navis posset lignis tribuere, quod ex se ipsis moverentur ad navis formam inducendam."

12. Christopher Thompson, "Perennial Wisdom: Notes Toward a Green Thomism," *Nova et Vetera* 10, no. 1 (Winter 2012): 74. English edition.

13. Philippa Foot, *Natural Goodness* (Oxford: Oxford University Press, 2001).

14. For an explanation of Darwinian and modern theories of natural selection, see Ernst Mayr, *Toward a New Philosophy of Biology: Observations of an Evolutionist* (Cambridge, MA: Harvard University Press, 1988), chaps. 6, 12, 13.

15. Armand A. Maurer, "Darwin, Thomists, and Secondary Causality," *Review of Metaphysics* 57, no. 3 (2004): 491–514.

16. André Ariew, "Teleology," in *The Cambridge Companion to the Philosophy of Biology* (Cambridge: Cambridge University Press, 2007), 160–81.

17. Mayr, *Toward a New Philosophy of Biology*, 38–41.

18. Jean Porter, *Nature as Reason: A Thomistic Theory of the Natural Law* (Grand Rapids, MI: Eerdmans, 2005), 82–103.

19. Michael Rota, "Causation," in *The Oxford Handbook of Aquinas*, ed. Brian Davies and Eleonore Stump, 105–14 (Oxford: Oxford University Press, 2012), 107.

20. Paul Hoffman, "Does Efficient Causation Presuppose Final Causation? Aquinas vs. Early Modern Mechanism," in *Metaphysics and the Good: Themes from the Philosophy of Robert Merrihew Adams*, ed. Samuel Newlands and Larry M. Jorgensen (Oxford: Oxford University Press, 2009), 295–312.

21. Robert Pasnau, *Thomas Aquinas on Human Nature: A Philosophical Study of Summa Theologiae 1a* (Cambridge: Cambridge University Press, 2002), 201.

22. Robert Spaemann, "The Unrelinquishability of Teleology," in *Contemporary Perspectives on Natural Law: Natural Law as a Limiting Concept*, ed. Ana Marta González (Aldershot, UK: Ashgate, 2008), 288.

23. Simon Oliver, "Teleology Revived? Cooperation and the Ends of Nature," *Studies in Christian Ethics* 26, no. 2 (May 1, 2013): 161.

24. I.II 1.1 arg 1: "Causa enim naturaliter prior est. Sed finis habet rationem ultimi, ut ipsum nomen sonat."

25. Ad 1: "finis, etsi sit postremus in executione, est tamen primus in intentione agentis. Et hoc modo habet rationem causae."

26. I.II 1.2: "Prima autem inter omnes causas est causa finalis." Compare I.38.8 arg 4 et c.; 44.4 arg 4.; In De divinis nominibus, cap. 1 l. 3.

27. I.II 72.5: "Principium [autem] totius ordinis in moralibus est finis ultimus."

28. *De Potentia* 3.6 ad 12: "Bonum vero et malum dicuntur per comparationem ad finem."

29. For the characterization of consequentialism as a moral theory claiming that the rightness of an action depends on its "output" rather than its "input," see the anti-consequentialist argument of Jorge L. A. Garcia, "The Right and the Good," *Philosophia* 21, no. 3 (1992): 235–56.

30. Ibid.

31. I.II 1.3 ad 2: "finis secundum quod est prior in intentione, ut dictum est, secundum hoc pertinet ad voluntatem. Et hoc modo dat speciem actui humano sive morali."

32. 21.2 ad 2: "Sed in moralibus, ubi attenditur ordo rationis ad finem communem humanae vitae, semper peccatum et malum attenditur per deviationem ab ordine rationis ad finem communem humanae vitae."

33. II.II 23.7: "virtus vera simpliciter est illa quae ordinat ad principale bonum hominis."

34. Donald Davidson, *Essays on Actions and Events* (Oxford: Oxford University Press, 2001), 87.

35. J. David Velleman, "What Happens When Someone Acts?," *Mind* 101, no. 403 (1992): 461–81.

36. Stefaan E. Cuypers, "Thomistic Agent-Causalism," in *Mind, Metaphysics, and Value in the Thomistic and Analytic Traditions,* ed. John Haldane (Notre Dame, IN: University of Notre Dame Press, 2002), 90–108.

37. 1.2c: "proprium est naturae rationalis ut tendat in finem quasi se agens vel ducens ad finem, naturae vero irrationalis, quasi ab alio acta vel ducta, sive in finem apprehensum, sicut bruta animalia, sive in finem non apprehensum, sicut ea quae omnino cognitione carent."

38. 18.3c: "supra talia animalia sunt illa quae movent seipsa, etiam habito respectu ad finem, quem sibi praestituunt. Quod quidem non fit nisi per rationem et intellectum, cuius est cognoscere proportionem finis et eius quod est ad finem, et unum ordinare in alterum."

39. I.II 1.2c: "Illa vero quae ratione carent, tendunt in finem per naturalem inclinationem, quasi ab alio mota, non autem a seipsis, cum non cognoscant rationem finis, et ideo nihil in finem ordinare possunt, sed solum in finem ab alio ordinantur."

40. 1.6c: "quidquid homo appetit, appetit sub ratione boni."

41. 6.2c: "apprehenso fine, aliquis potest, deliberans de fine et de his quae sunt ad finem, moveri in finem vel non moveri."

42. Terence Irwin, *The Development of Ethics: A Historical and Critical Study,* vol. 1: *From Socrates to the Reformation* (Oxford: Oxford University Press, 2007), 572.

43. *Cursus Theologicus,* in I.II, Disp. 3, Art.2, n.10 (Solesmes 5:279).

44. John Mahoney, *The Making of Moral Theology: A Study of the Roman Catholic Tradition,* Martin D'Arcy Memorial Lectures, 1981–82 (Oxford: Clarendon, 1987).

45. Rebecca Konyndyk DeYoung, Colleen McCluskey, and Christina Van Dyke, *Aquinas's Ethics: Metaphysical Foundations, Moral Theory, and Theological Context* (Notre Dame, IN: University of Notre Dame Press, 2009), 188.

46. See Freddoso's extensive discussion in Francisco Suárez, *On Efficient Causality: Metaphysical Disputations 17, 18, and 19*, trans. Alfred J. Freddoso (New Haven, CT: Yale University Press, 1994); and Edward Feser, *Scholastic Metaphysics: A Contemporary Introduction* (Heusenstamm: Editiones Scholasticae, 2014).

47. Helen Beebee, Christopher Hitchcock, and Peter Menzies, eds., *The Oxford Handbook of Causation* (Oxford: Oxford University Press, 2009), 1.

48. Gabriele De Anna, "Causal Relations: A Thomistic Account," in *Analytical Thomism: Traditions in Dialogue*, ed. Craig Paterson and Matthew S. Pugh, 79–100 (Aldershot, UK: Ashgate, 2006).

49. Michael J. Dodds, *Unlocking Divine Action* (Washington, DC: Catholic University of America Press, 2012), 1.

The Causal Analysis of Virtue

PART III

The Causal Analysis of Virtue

CHAPTER 7

Rational Virtue

Suggested reading: *Summa Theologiae* I.II 55.4,
60, 61, 64, 85.3; II.II 27.6, 48, 128, 143, 161.1;
On the Virtues 1.13c

Aquinas analyzes the Augustinian definition of virtue in terms of the four causes (I.II 55.4c): A virtue is:

a good quality	formal cause
of the mind	material cause
by which we live rightly and no one can use badly	final cause
which God works in us without us	efficient cause

So many anomalies emerge from this line of reasoning that it may seem that Aquinas is attempting to hammer an Augustinian round peg into an Aristotelian square hole. Yet his overriding goal is not exegesis; rather, it is to give an account of virtue in general. The result replicates neither Aristotle nor Augustine. Instead, it offers a third position that neither would have recognized and is all the worthier of attention for this reason.

In Aquinas's ordering, each of virtue's causes can be understood only in relation to the others. For the sake of exposition it is necessary to treat them individually in the hope that it will be meaningful to deal with parts that, finally, make sense only in terms of the whole.

The formal cause is what makes something what it is. *Forma dat speciem*: the form specifies (I.II 18.2). Aquinas states, then, "The formal cause of virtue, as also of anything, is taken from its genus and difference, when it is said [in the Augustinian definition, that virtue is] 'a good quality.' For virtue's genus is *quality*, and its difference is *good*. It would however be a more fitting definition if quality were replaced by *habit*, which is the proximate genus" (55.4c, emphasis added).[1] Thus the characterization of virtue as a good habit (see chaps. 2 and 3) is incorporated into the causal account as providing virtue's formal cause. It is important to remember, then, that "good" in the definition of virtue refers to the moral or rational good (*bonum rationis*) (55.4 ad 2). Virtue's most formal element is the moral goodness that lies in its conformity with human agency's rule and measure—that is, divine and human reason.

Aquinas conceives of this formal cause of virtue in at least two distinct ways: as object and as exemplar. Since a virtue is a disposition or habit, it is good insofar as it is directed toward a good human action and object. So a virtue's goodness or its consonance with reason is derived from its object's goodness or consonance with reason. For example, the virtue of mercy, which inclines to acts that offer aid to the suffering, is good because its object (to give aid to the suffering when and in the manner it is fitting to do so) is consonant to divine and human reason. Also, a habit is good insofar as it participates in, or imitates, the divine goodness in some respect, albeit in a manner suited to human rather than divine nature. Both approaches to virtue's formal cause contribute to the causal theory of virtue.

VIRTUE'S OBJECT

Virtue theory must provide a way of specifying and distinguishing virtues.[2] Since Aquinas defines virtue causally, he specifies particular virtues causally as well. Moral virtues can be divided into those about other-regarding operations, such as justice, and those about the passions, like temperance; here virtues are divided on the basis of *objective matter* (60.2). The *subjective matter* is one way to distinguish the cardinal virtues: prudence is in the practical intellect, justice in the will, fortitude in the irascible power, and temperance in the concupiscible power (61.2). The *efficient cause* differentiates virtues acquired by habituation and those infused by God (63.4). Virtues disposing to perfect beatitude must differ from those disposing only to the imperfect beatitude of this life; this is distinction by means of *final cause* (51.4). There is also the distinction of virtues into different kinds based on degrees of similitude to the *exemplar cause* (61.5). Aquinas also distinguishes divine and human virtues as fitting for *diverse natures*: human nature and the superior nature of grace (54.3, 61.5, 63.4).

There is a serious question of interpretation to be addressed here. Are there multiple, conflicting principles? If so, the coherence of the virtue theory would be at risk. William Mattison focuses on three principles of division: efficient cause, ultimate end, and object. He claims that these three methods of "categorization" do "graft onto each other," but it is left unclear how they are related.[3]

The causal approach offers a solution. The formal cause is what directly specifies (*forma dat speciem*). Where different causes suggest different categorizations,

Aquinas prioritizes the formal (II.II 157.3 ad 2). The other causes specify virtue only indirectly and mediately and as indicating a different formal cause—namely, the object. As Aquinas puts it, "Just as the form gives species in natural things, so also in morals the object gives species to an act, and consequently to a habit."[4] He often repeats this principle (e.g., 54.2; 60.5; 72.1 ad 2), which unifies the diverse ways of specifying and distinguishing virtues under one grand principle: the object (*obiectum*), which is the extrinsic formal cause. How then does the object specify a virtue?

A VIRTUE'S MATERIAL OBJECT

As discussed earlier, different levels of formality and materiality inhere in the object. It helps to begin with a virtue's material object, or "matter-about-which" (*materia circa quam*): "The *matter-about-which* is the object of a virtue. This could not be placed in the above definition, since it is through the object that a virtue is fixed to a species, whereas here we are supplying the definition of virtue in general" (55.4c).[5] To what does this phrase, "matter-about-which," refer?

Martha Nussbaum notes that Aristotle defines virtues by identifying "spheres of life" in which we may do well or badly. A virtue is a state that disposes us to choose and respond well in some sphere of experience.[6] Similarly, Christine Swanton talks of a virtue's "field": "The *field* of a virtue consists of those items which are the sphere(s) of concern of the virtue, and to which the agent should respond in line with the virtue's demands. These items may be within the agent, for example, the bodily pleasures which are the focus of temperance, or outside the agent, for example, human beings, property, money, or honors."[7] The corresponding term in Aquinas is not "sphere of life" or "field" but rather the "matter-about-which" a virtue disposes a person (55.4c). It is what the virtue is about. For example, justice is about exchanges with others; temperance is about the desires and pleasures of food, drink, and sex; and fortitude is about fear and daring in the face of the danger of death (61.3c).

From its constituent terms the concept of matter-about-which can be understood as the combination of two distinct concepts: *matter* (potentiality to receive some form) and *object* (that which an act, power, or habit is about). The material aspect implies the potential to receive some form from virtue. Since a moral habit is formally a virtue insofar as its act conforms to reason (58.2), the matter of the moral virtues is human acts, which of their nature ask to be conformed to the rule of reason.

Take, for example, a passion such as anger. Anger can be considered as morally good, morally bad, or neutral. Anger can be a disordered passion contrary to reason and virtue, as when someone is willfully enraged over a small slight.

Anger can be a well-ordered and entirely reasonable passion, as when someone is duly angered by an injustice. Finally, abstracting from both, anger can be considered as capable of being manifested either way.[8] Anger considered thusly, as potentially either morally good or bad, is the matter of the virtue of gentleness: it is matter suited to and capable of receiving from virtue the form of rationality, just as a malleable but hard material like steel is matter fit to receive from the metalsmith the form of a sword. As Aquinas says, "The matter of each moral virtue is that about which [the virtue] imposes the mode of reason."[9]

The second integral part of the concept of matter-about-which is that of object, or that which it is about. For example, the proximate matter of temperance is the greatest appetites and pleasures, whereas its remote matter is the objects of those passions—namely food, drink, and sexual intercourse.[10] Or, the immediate matter of magnanimity is the hope for great honors, whereas the mediate matter is the object of the passion—namely, the great honors themselves (II.II 129.1).

Is the matter-about-which material or formal? In relation to virtue, the matter-about-which is a hybrid, since as matter it is material but as object it is formal. It is material as that which virtue "works on" since the operations are given a form by virtue through reason. Yet it is also formal as specifying a virtue since, as object, it is an exterior formal cause that defines the habit that is directed toward it. Aquinas explains, "The object is not the matter-out-of-which but the matter-about-which, and has in a way the rationale of a form, insofar as it gives species" (18.2 ad 2).[11] We can therefore term the matter-about-which either the "objective matter" or the "material object" of a virtue.

Peter Lombard's definition contains no element corresponding to the material object, so Aquinas provides a rationale for its absence: a virtue's matter-about-which, he says, fixes its species and so belongs to the definition of this or that virtue, not to virtue in general (55.4c). This is a weak post hoc rationalization because unqualified virtue, while it lacks *specific* matter, does possess *generic* proximate matter: the human passions and operations that participate to a greater or lesser degree in freedom and the potentiality to conform to reason. Aquinas even has a name for the generic matter of virtue: *agibilia et appetibilia*, or the doings and desirings that fall within the sphere of human agency (e.g., II.II 27.6c). Aquinas could have specified the material object of virtue in general; had he been constructing his own definition rather than relying on Lombard's, he no doubt would have.

Is the Material Object Enough?

Aquinas claims that the material object determines the species of a virtue. Does this, then, solve the problem of specification? It is roughly the method

Nussbaum ascribes to Aristotle: first identifying a distinctive sphere of life in which it is possible to do well or badly; then defining a virtue as the state disposing us to do well in that sphere. Aquinas adopts a similar method. Virtue, like art, concerns "the difficult and the good": "Art and virtue are about the more difficult matters in which we need to act well, which is what art and virtue dispose us to do. For in easy matters anyone can act well. But to act well in difficult matter belongs only to the one who possesses virtue and art."[12] A moral matter, in contrast to a technical one, is a difficult matter in which we need to act well with a view to the overall end of human life. Wherever there is such a matter, there must be a virtue: "There can be a moral virtue about every [matter] that can be ordered and moderated by reason" (I.II 59.4c).[13]

However, the material object alone is not enough to specify the virtues. To understand a virtue we must know not merely how to identify its sphere of life but also what doing well in that sphere consists in. A virtue's matter at best provides a "thin" account of that virtue, and the task of the ethicist is to find a "thick" specification of what constitutes choosing and responding well in each sphere.

Relying on the matter alone to specify virtues also fails to account for the possibility of overlap in two virtues' material object. Take the moral matter of "appetite for a difficult good." We need to be both humble (not desiring what is beyond us) and magnanimous (being willing to strive for great things in a reasonable way) in regard to this matter (II.II 161.1c). Because Aquinas recognizes the priority of form over matter as a principle of specification, the material identity of humility and magnanimity does not disconcert him. While humility and magnanimity share the same matter, they differ in rationale since "humility restrains the appetite, lest it tend to great things beside right reason, whereas magnanimity impels the soul according to right reason" (161.1 ad 3).[14] For a full definition of a virtue one needs to identify not merely its material object but also its formal rationale.

Aquinas therefore rejects the view that J. O. Urmson once proposed in interpretation of Aristotle—namely, that virtues are individuated by emotion: one type of emotion, one type of virtue.[15] Urmson's thesis is doubly wrong: just as two virtues can concern the same passion, as with humility and magnanimity, so also one virtue can concern two or more passions, as fortitude holds back fear and moderates daring (123.3c). Aquinas states the reason in the following, characteristically terse statement: "The objects of the passions cause diverse species of passions insofar as they are related in different ways to the sensitive appetite; they cause diverse species of virtues insofar as they are related to reason" (I.II 60.5c).[16] A moral matter specifies a moral virtue only *indirectly* by indicating its required form.

THE MOST FORMAL OBJECT: THE MODE

What, then, is the formal object of virtue? The object of virtue, formally speaking, is the good (I.II 56.3 arg 2, ad 2). (We will begin by examining the *most* formal object of virtue; the somewhat formal and somewhat material object will be considered when we examine virtue's final cause.) What makes a habit virtuous is precisely its orientation to good (*On the Virtues* 1.7c). Therefore the formal object of a moral virtue will be the good at stake in some specific moral matter or sphere: "The object of any virtue is the good considered in its proper matter. For example, the object of temperance is the good of pleasurable things in the desires of touch. The formal rationale of this object is from reason, which institutes the mode in these desires, whereas the material element is that which is on the part of the desires" (63.4).[17] The material object of temperance is the desires of touch; its formal object, called the "mode" or "the mode of reason," is from practical reason. As Aquinas puts it elsewhere, "Habits are not distinguished by material objects, but by the formal rationales of objects. However, the formal rationale of the good to which moral virtue is ordered is one, namely, the mode of reason" (60.1 arg 2).[18] The most formal object of virtue, then, is the mode.

The concept of the mode (*modus*) is a neglected but important concept in Aquinas's virtue theory. From Cicero onward, "mode" was especially associated with temperance, as a kind of "moderation." As Helen North explains, "The noun *modus* ("limit") and its numerous derivatives—especially *modestia*, a very ancient abstract noun, *moderatio*, *moderare* and *moderari*—expressed one of the central themes of sophrosyne [temperance] from the very beginning of Latin literature."[19] There are remnants of this connection in Aquinas. For example, he distinguishes temperance from the other cardinal virtues because "temperance is a certain disposition of the mind that imposes the mode [= limit] on diverse passions or operations" (61.4).[20] However, Aquinas also extends this mode to all the moral virtues, just as Aristotle had done with the mean (e.g., 60.1 arg 2, ad 2). Since having a mode is characteristic of the good as such (I 5.5c), every virtue (moral, intellectual, or theological) must have a mode.

What, then, is a virtue's mode? For Aquinas, mode is almost synonymous with "measure" (*mensura*): "The good in the case of human passions and operations is that they attain the mode of reason, which is the measure and rule of all human passions and operations" (*On the Virtues* 1.13c).[21] However, this concept of mode adds a new thought to the idea of rule or measure: application to a more specific sphere. Following Augustine, Aquinas's definition is that "mode signifies a certain determination of a measure" (I.II 27.3c).[22] "Determination" here means a specification: if prudence is the measure of human acts, the mode is the determination, the specification, of this generic rule in a more particular sphere. A moral virtue's mode is the prudential wisdom specific to some specific matter.

It is this note of specification or determination that makes mode important for virtue theory. As its *measure*, the mode is the most formal element of a virtue since it is by conformity to the mode that a habit becomes good and therefore a virtue. However, since the mode is more precisely the *determination* of a measure—that is, the measure as applied to a specific matter—the mode therefore specifies different virtues differently. How, then, do we identify the mode of each virtue?

Differentiating the Modes of the Virtues

The basic principle for identifying mode is this: as the form of a virtue, its mode is correlative to its matter. The principle is evident from an analogy Aquinas develops among and between the sciences, the arts, and the moral virtues. What is a mode, for example, fitting for ethics? Aquinas notes that, for Aristotle, matter and form are mutually proportional: "The mode of manifesting the truth in any science ought to fit what is treated as the matter in that science."[23] This principle of mode-matter fit within science is explained by a comparison with the arts. A craftsman will employ a different method with wax, with clay, or with iron; similarly, the mode of ethics, which treats of contingent human actions, differs from the mode of mathematics, which deals with necessary things and so offers demonstration.[24]

For Aquinas, the arts and sciences in turn provide an analogy for the virtues: "Just as in the sciences it is necessary to investigate the mode according to the matter, so also in regard to the virtues, as [Aristotle] says in *The Nicomachean Ethics* (Bk I)."[25] A moral or theological virtue's mode is therefore not a static form; it is more akin to a scientific or artistic *modus operandi* or method. But it is a method for establishing the good in some specific matter, not a way to produce an artifact or to determine the truth.

The Cardinal Virtues

How does this mode or method work out more concretely? Aquinas identifies four general modes of moral virtue, which constitute the "generic" cardinal virtues (I.II 61.2–4). Remembering that the material object is some sphere of "the difficult and the good," the four generic cardinal virtues are responses to the generic moral matters and universal challenges we all must face in achieving the rational good. To act well in life we must rise to the challenge of deliberating, judging, and deciding well what is to be done and desired—this is the office of prudence. In addition, one must learn to embody practical wisdom in one's volitional and emotional life. Justice answers the challenge of rightly ordering one's actions; fortitude responds to the emotional test of standing firm in the rational good despite dangers, toils, and sorrows; temperance responds to the challenge posed by the passions of attraction, which can tend to overrun their bounds, by modulating them. Discretion, rectitude, strength, and moderation: these generic cardinal virtues are the qualities we need in order to face the four universal challenges of living a good life.

For Aquinas these four challenges are not merely integral to human nature; they correspond to the four "wounds" that followed from original sin. Prudence, justice, fortitude, and temperance correct the ignorance, malice, weakness, and concupiscence to which the post-lapsarian human is prone (85.3c). The generic cardinal virtues are healings as well as perfections of human nature.

This dividing of the mode of reason into four general modes results in four generic formal virtues. However, while they are "virtues" in a sense (61.2), Aquinas clarifies that, they are not such strictly speaking (61.4). Each virtue, as an operative habit, needs a determinate and proper act; a generic virtue is too general to count (*On the Virtues* 1.12 ad 27). The general modes operate together in specific virtuous habits and so are better regarded as constituents of virtues (I.II 61.4). Aquinas ingeniously identifies the four generic cardinal "virtues" with the necessary conditions of acting virtuously that Aristotle lays down.[26] To act virtuously one needs to know what is to be done (prudence), act from choice and not mere passion (temperance), do so for a due end (justice), and act firmly and immovably (fortitude) (61.4 arg 3, ad 3; *On the Virtues* 1.5c). Every morally virtuous act whatsoever requires the four general modes of virtue.[27]

Accordingly, Aquinas identifies a more proper way of speaking of the cardinal virtues: "The cardinal virtues are understood in two ways. In one way, insofar as they are special virtues having determinate matters. In another way, insofar as they signify certain general modes of virtue" (II.II 58.8 ad 2).[28] The generic cardinal virtues apply reason to some generic matter of the moral life; the specific cardinal virtues, which are virtues in the strictest sense, apply reason in some more specific sphere (I.II 61.4c). For example, specific fortitude is not about standing firm despite any obstacle whatsoever, but it is about standing firm against the greatest obstacle—namely, the fear of death (61.3). Specific temperance is moderation and restraint as applied to the greatest pleasures—namely those of touch (that is, to do with food, drink, and sex) (II.II 141). It is to the most intense specifications of the four generic moral matters that the specific cardinal virtues are addressed.

The differentiation of virtue does not stop with the identification of four specific cardinal virtues. Prudence and fortitude are unitary and indivisible virtues. However, specific justice and specific temperance, while determinate in comparison with their respective general virtues, are nevertheless generic in relation to their own subdivisions. Justice as a (semi-) specific virtue can be divided into distributive, commutative, and legal justice, together with its companion *epikeia* (equity) (II.II 61.1, 58.6, 120.2); temperance can be divided into abstinence, sobriety, chastity, and *puditia* (what today we might term "modesty") (143). Aquinas calls these more specific virtues the "subjective parts" of justice and temperance: the species of a genus.

Aquinas also acknowledges many moral virtues, such as humility, perseverance, and religion, that are not subspecies or subjective parts of the four cardinal virtues. How does he specify and differentiate these? By referring to them as the principal virtues' "potential parts" (*partes potentiales*) (II.II 48c): they are participants in the "power" or "capacity" (*potentia*) of a principal virtue.[29] As he puts it in *On the Virtues*, "Other adjunct or secondary virtues are posited as 'parts' of the cardinal virtues, not as integral [parts] or subjective [parts]; for they have a determinate matter and a proper act; but as potential parts, insofar as they *participate* in a particular and partial way what principally and more perfectly belongs to a cardinal virtue" (1.12 ad 27).[30] These power-participants share the mode or generic rationale with a principal virtue but differ in respect to matter: "Potential parts of any principal virtue are called secondary virtues, which observe the same mode the principal virtue observes concerning some principal matter, but in certain other less challenging matters" (II.II 143).[31] For example, gentleness is counted as a power-participant of temperance: it participates in the mode of restraint and applies it not to the concupiscences of touch but rather to anger. The secondary virtues, then, consist of a general mode or rationale of the good as applied to some "secondary" or less challenging matter.

Since each of the modes of the moral virtues is a participation in the virtue of prudence suited to a specific moral matter, it follows that this intellectual virtue is somehow involved in all the moral virtues: "Prudence places the mode and form in all other moral virtues."[32] Prudence is the practical wisdom of the moral virtues.

The arts, sciences, and moral virtues have a mode. Do the theological virtues of faith, hope, and love also have a mode? In his later works, at least, Aquinas insists on finding a sense in which the love of God does have a mode, albeit not a limit: "In the love of God there is no mode as it exists in what is measured . . . but only as it exists in the measure" (27.6c).[33] Thus, "charity, which has the mode as the measure, excels the other virtues, which have the mode as measured" (ad 1).[34] Love of God has a mode in the same way that water, not a sidewalk after a downpour, is wet: essentially, not derivatively.

Every virtue has its own characteristic mode, whether we are talking of the intellectual, the moral, or the theological virtues. The mode of the sciences and arts is the method suited to each of their specific matters; the mode of the moral virtues is the mode of reason; the mode of the theological virtues is a limitless mode that knows no bounds since it is not possible to believe in, hope in, and love God too much (compare I.II 64.4).

From the Mode to the Mean

What do we make of the doctrine of the mean that Aquinas inherits from Aristotle? According to Aristotle, "Virtue is an elective state existing in the mean relative to us, determined by reason and as the prudent one would determine it."[35] This Aquinas takes to be an accurate definition of moral virtue. As with the mode, Aquinas frequently identifies the rational mean as the form of the moral virtues (I.II 66.2; II.II 47.7 ad 2; 61.2 arg 2; On the Virtues 1.10 arg 8, ad 8).

In Aquinas's virtue theory, the mean is secondary to the mode of reason. This becomes evident in his most extensive argument for the mean:

> The good in the case of human passions and operations is that they attain the mode of reason, which is the measure and rule of all human passions and operations. . . . The bad, on the other hand, is that someone exceeds the mode of reason or falls short of it in their human passions and operations. Therefore, since the human good is human virtue, it follows that moral virtue lies in a mean between excess and deficiency, where "excess," "deficiency" and "mean" are understood in relation to the rule of reason. (On the Virtues 1.13c)[36]

Here "mean," "excess," and "deficiency" are simply the application of a quantitative metaphor to the mode. The mean at which virtue aims is just conformity of virtue's matter to the mode; excess and deficiency are two ways of its matter failing to equal the mode. Aquinas can therefore mention mode and mean in the same breath: "the mode of a virtue, that is, a certain mean" (On the Virtues 1.13 ad 4).[37]

Contemporary virtue theorists argue about how to interpret the doctrine of the mean, and are often skeptical of its value. Aquinas's understanding of the mean of moral virtue may help clear up some of the difficulty; moreover, it is worth examining here for the light it sheds on the formal cause of moral virtue. Aquinas distinguishes two aspects of the doctrine of the mean:

> Virtue is called a mean in two ways. First, by reason of its objective matter, insofar as virtue makes it equal to right reason. And this mean belongs per se to every moral virtue. . . . Second, virtue is called a mean by reason of habit, that is, insofar

as it is a mean between the habits of two evils. . . . And this is accidental to a virtue, nor is it necessary that it exist in all virtues.[38]

The core doctrine of the mean, then, is that a moral virtue makes its objective matter equal to right reason, as when temperance moderates the desires of food, drink, and sex. That temperance lies between two vices—intemperance and insensibility—is secondary.

Rosalind Hursthouse says it would be "a deeply mysterious fact" if each virtue were opposed by two and only two vices.[39] This criticism does not seem to touch on Aquinas's accounting. For him, justice has only one vice by excess (*On the Virtues* 1.13 ad 12). In contrast, there are at least four vices of excess opposed to magnanimity: presumption, ambition, vainglory, and pride. This poses no problem, because "it is no contradiction for there to be, for one mean, multiple excesses in diverse respects" (II.II 119.1 ad 1). Even more interestingly, Aquinas thinks that a vice opposed to a virtue can be a mixture of excess and deficiency. Someone can possess a mixture of prodigality and miserliness (opposite vices that are both contrary to liberality) since "Nothing prevents opposites from being in the same thing in diverse respects" (119.1 arg 1, ad 1).[40] Aquinas would agree with Hursthouse, then, that moral virtue is not by some mysterious symmetry necessarily opposed by two and only two contrary vices. What is essential for Aquinas is that a virtue causes its objective matter to be "equal" but not "exceed" or "fall short" of the rule of reason.

How can we understand this equality with reason? Aquinas states that the mean is to be understood "according to circumstances" (*secundum circumstantias*) (64.1 ad 2). Indeed, it is "in relation to [circumstances that] the mean of virtue is found or lost in human actions and passions" (7.2 ad 3).[41] The circumstances of a human act are "whatever conditions are outside the substance of the act, yet touch in some way the human act" (7.1c).[42] They are, in a sense, the "accidents" of an act, not its substance.

Aquinas, drawing on Cicero and Aristotle, lists seven or eight circumstances of a human act (depending on how one counts) that are relevant to its moral evaluation (7.1).[43] They are *when* the action takes place (time), *where* it is done (place), *how* it is performed (manner), *what* it brings about (effect), *why* it is done (reason), *about what* it concerns (material object), *who* performs it (person), and *by what means* (instrument). For Aquinas it is impossible to determine what is virtuous without a consideration of all of these contingencies: "Acts of virtue ought not be done anyhow, but by observing the due circumstances that are required for an act to be virtuous" (II.II 33.2).[44] For example, temperance will regulate appetite for food according to the circumstances of *material object* (not craving excessively luxurious or gourmet foods), the *quantity* (not desiring too much food), the *manner* (not being too eager to eat), and *time* (not desiring to eat too early) (48.4).

Hursthouse worries that a "quantitative" doctrine of the mean is implausible.[45] Similarly, Aquinas repeatedly states, "The mean of virtue is not understood according to quantity, but according to right reason" (147.1 ad 2).[46] The occasion for this assertion is the objection that certain virtues seem to lie in a maximum rather than a mean. Fortitude concerns the greatest dangers; magnanimity the greatest honors; magnificence the greatest in expenses; piety the great reverence that is due to parents, to whom we can never make a return of equal value. The same applies to religion since no matter how greatly we honor God, we can never give God the honor that is His due (*On the Virtues* 1.13 arg 5). The virtues of poverty and celibacy also seem to lie in an extreme, as they reject all possessions and sexual pleasures (arg 6). None of these moral virtues seem to lie in a mean, but rather in an extreme. Aquinas's reply is that virtue lies not in the quantitative mean but rather in the rational mean (*medium rationis*). What, then, is the rational mean?

The rational mean is determined but by *what is fitting in the circumstances*, not by absolute quantity. Even when a virtue tends to something great, as with magnanimity, it is still a mean because "virtues of this kind tend to this [object] according to the rule of reason, that is, where it is fitting, when it is fitting, and for the reason it is fitting" (I.II 64.1 ad 2).[47] A great-souled person fittingly aims at the greatest honors, as reason recognizes. As Aquinas puts it later, "The magnanimous man is indeed an extreme in *magnitude*, insofar as he tends to what is greatest, but in point of *fittingness*, he is a mean, because he tends to the greatest according to reason" (II.II 129.3 ad 1).[48] The rational mean in regard to a set of circumstances, then, is defined nonquantitatively and simply as what is fitting according to reason.

This insight, that the "mean" is to be defined primarily in terms of fittingness as determined by reason, relativizes the value of the quantitative metaphors of "mean," "excess," and "deficiency," and points to what Hursthouse calls the valuable "central doctrine of the mean."[49] Cajetan, in a display of analytic clarity that impressed his successors, also explains this nonquantitative definition of the rational mean as follows:

> The rational mean . . . requires two things: namely, the matter, and the conditions of reason. So the rational mean lies in the affirmation of both, namely of the proper matter, and of all the conditions regarding right reason. For example, the rational mean in temperance is to take pleasure when it is fitting, in the manner that is fitting, for a fitting reason, and so on. But the extremes are understood as the negation of one, and the affirmation of the other: so that "excess" affirms

the matter, with the conditions negated; "deficiency" however negates the matter, with the conditions affirmed. For example, to use pleasures when it is unfitting, for an unfitting reason, where it is unfitting, and so on, is "excess": for it is to use pleasures, which are the matter of temperance, "more" than is fitting. But not to use pleasures when it is fitting, for a fitting reason, and so on, is "deficiency": for it is to take pleasure "less" than is fitting. (in I.II 64.2)

Even if we question the value of the quantitative metaphors as Hursthouse does, the core idea of the rational mean remains helpful: moral virtue aims at the affirmation of both matter and the conditions of reason. For example, magnanimity aims at great things when, with whom, and in the manner it is fitting. Any failure in adjusting this ambition to what reason judges to be fitting is a failure in moral virtue.

The important contribution of the concept of the rational mean is that it shows the situation relativity in the mode of reason, and therefore also in all the moral virtues. The good at which a virtue aims, Aquinas says, "can be enacted in many different ways, and not in the same way in all situations; whence the judgement of prudence is required for this: that the right mode be established" (*On the Virtues* 1.6c).[50] The mode or mean of reason is, as it were, the GPS of the virtuous life that helps work out the next step toward the destination in the particular location or circumstances of life.

The Principle of Unification

Together the material and formal objects of virtue address the problem of specification: each virtue is defined by the combination of its proper material object and the corresponding mode of reason that delineates what constitutes doing well in that sphere. However, the mode and the matter also help us address another related issue: unification.

Christine Swanton proposes a "pluralistic theory" of virtue. Two ways in which this account is "pluralistic" are first, that it acknowledges that a virtue may have multiple fields, and second, that it may respond to those multiple fields in a number of ways or "modes" (for example, by loving, or promoting, or respecting).[51] This pluralistic approach has an advantage in that it recognizes a virtue may be exhibited in different ways. Yet this pluralism threatens to undermine any virtue's unity. If a virtue exercises *diverse* modes of response to items in *diverse* fields, what ties these responses or items to the same virtue? Swanton refers to "constellations" of characteristic modes of responsiveness, which make up the "profile" of a virtue. Yet in the absence of any unifying feature that can tie these modes of responsiveness together, her view runs the risk of undermining the integral identity of any single virtue. Virtues become accidental assortments rather than unified dispositions.

Aquinas's account, in contrast, insists that each virtue has its own unified object: "For one habit does not extend itself to many things, except in order to one thing, from which it has unity" (I.II 54.4c).[52] A virtue is a disposition *ad unum*, toward a single thing (that is, one object, or one act) of the same moral species (*On the Virtues* 1.9). Temperance inclines to temperate acts, fortitude to brave ones.

How, then, is it possible to define the specific moral unity of a virtue's acts in light of its diversity of manifestations? The solution lies in the causal account. The formal object of a virtue provides not only its principle of specification and distinction but also its *principle of unification* since while a virtue may extend to many different material objects, these all agree in a single formal rationale. As Aquinas puts it, "For the unity of a power and a habit is to be considered according to the object, not indeed materially, but according the formal rationale of the object" (I 1.3c).[53] Feasting and fasting can be acts of the same virtue of temperance since these materially diverse acts intend the same formal object—namely, fitting moderation of consumption in the circumstances. Aquinas's analysis of specific virtues in terms of their form and matter allows for a healthy pluralism without giving up the unifying principle that maintains the integrity of each distinct virtue.

VIRTUE'S EXEMPLAR

The exemplar is an "extrinsic formal cause" after which the image is modeled and in which it participates (see chap. 5). Exemplar causation is important in Aquinas's theological ethics, as it focuses on the dynamic image of God on the way to becoming more like the exemplar. To what extent does exemplar causation influence virtue theory?

Aquinas follows Augustine in arguing that the exemplar of human virtue must preexist in God: "As Augustine says (*On the Morals of the Catholic Church*, Ch.vi), 'it is necessary that there be something that the soul follows, in order that virtue may be born in her, and this is God: if we follow him, we live well.' There must therefore be an exemplar of human virtue pre-existing in God, just as the rationales of all things pre-exist in him" (I.II 61.5c).[54] The human virtues are therefore modeled on their exemplar in God but allow for the distance between God and creature, which makes this exemplarity analogical rather than univocal. Humans are not virtuous in the way that God is virtuous; rather, insofar as humans are virtuous, they participate in God's goodness in a manner fitting to human beings. It is by becoming like God through grace and the virtues and acts that flow from grace that we progress toward our true end. The exemplarity of the divine goodness is therefore a primary principle of the dynamic of human formation in virtue: "It belongs to the human being to drag himself as much as he can even to divine things, as even the Philosopher recognizes (*Nichomachean Ethics* X.7); and it is frequently commended to us in sacred Scripture, as in Matthew 5:48, 'Be perfect, just as your heavenly Father is perfect'" (61.5c).[55] Since the exemplar cause is the agent, end, and form, virtue finds its origin, end, and nature in its divine exemplar.

Exemplar causality enables Aquinas to conceive of a radical dependence of all virtue on God: a dependence that is not merely efficient-causal and final-causal but even formal-causal. Aquinas says:

> Just as we are said to be good by the goodness that is God, and wise by the wisdom that is God, because the goodness by which we are formally good is a certain participation in the divine goodness, and the wisdom by which we are formally wise is a certain participation in the divine wisdom, so also the charity by which we formally love the neighbor is a certain participation in divine charity. (II.II 23.2 ad 1)[56]

Virtue is formally a participation in God, the perfect exemplar of all goodness. It is difficult to conceive of a more radically theocentric account of virtue.

It makes sense to see justice, wisdom, mercy, and charity as participations in divine virtue since God is just, wise, and loving. However, it is not clear that God can be temperate (having no bodily appetites), brave (needing nothing to fear), or religiously devout (having no superior to worship). The Salamancans suggest that the moral virtues, which by definition belong to a subject possessing some imperfection, are nevertheless present in God—not formally, but "eminently" and "virtually."[57] By saying God possesses these virtues "eminently" it appears they mean that He possesses these virtues in some analogous and higher sense. For example, God's "fortitude" is His immutability (I.II 65.5c). The "virtual" presence of the moral virtues in God can be interpreted, they say, through the conditional: "If God *could* be devout, brave, and temperate, he *would* be." The doctrine of the Incarnation helps us to make sense of this idea: by becoming human, God further expresses His divine goodness through His human virtues.

Aquinas recognizes there is a problem of "distance" between the divine and human, if God is to be the exemplar of human virtue in any practical way, and he appeals to the Incarnation as the necessary bridge: "This exemplar, God, was previously truly remote from us. As it is said, 'What is a human being, that he could follow the King his maker?' (Ecclesiastes 2:12).

And therefore he willed to become a human being, to present to humans a human exemplar."[58] The divine virtues become more accessible to us through their divine-human exemplar.

Aquinas points to the value of Jesus as an exemplar who is not only accessible but also trustworthy:

> Someone's words and examples are more efficacious in leading to virtue the firmer is our opinion of his goodness. But we could have no infallible opinion of any mere human being's goodness, because even the holiest men are found lacking in certain things. And so it was necessary for humans, so that they be strengthened in virtue, that they receive teaching and examples of virtue from God humanized. For this reason, the Lord himself said, "I have given you an example, that just as I have done, so also you might do" (John 13:15).[59]

Theological virtue theory has this advantage over its philosophical cousin: it can point with confidence to at least one human exemplar of virtue to be imitated, Jesus Christ.[60]

There are parallels to this idea in contemporary philosophy and theology. Linda Zagzebski proposes an "exemplarist virtue theory." For Zagzebski a moral exemplar is a person who is admirable and therefore imitable. Drawing on the Kripke-Putnam theory of direct reference, she proposes that basic moral concepts such as virtue are anchored in direct reference to exemplars of moral goodness: "Good persons are persons *like that*, just as gold is stuff *like that*."[61] If God is seen as the supreme exemplar, then God incarnate provides a moral exemplar within reach, so to speak, of humankind.[62]

Exemplarist virtue theory is attractive to moral theologians as well, especially those with a Thomistic leaning. Patrick M. Clark sees the exemplarist approach as responsive to the Second Vatican Council's desire to recenter moral theology on Christ. Clark traces exemplarist themes in recent work, especially that of Liva Melina, even arguing for a "Thomistic moral exemplarism."[63] Brian Shanley has also referred to "Aquinas's exemplar ethics," arguing that understanding the human person as the image of the Trinity is "the key for an understanding of Aquinas's moral thinking."[64]

Can Aquinas's virtue theory accurately be described as an exemplarist virtue theory? Zagzebski observes that her theory is "foundational in structure," like others in modern Western philosophy.[65] Its foundation is direct reference to moral exemplars through the experience of admiration. Zagzebski is perceptive in recognizing that while the ancient ethical approaches of Aristotle or Confucius (or, one might add, Aquinas) place a great deal of importance on moral exemplars, it is only in the modern era that foundational moral theory has arisen, due to the need to justify the practice of morality by reference to an uncontroversial basis. For this reason Aquinas's virtue theory, though having an exemplarist strand, is not exemplarist strictly speaking. Aquinas's ethics is holistic, and virtue within it is not defined *foundationally* by its relation to the exemplar. While the exemplar cause is important, a comprehensive definition of virtue can be attained only by one that embraces all the causes.

NOTES

1. 55.4c: "Causa namque formalis virtutis, sicut et cuiuslibet rei, accipitur ex eius genere et differentia, cum dicitur qualitas bona, genus enim virtutis qualitas est, differentia autem bonum. Esset tamen convenientior definitio, si loco qualitatis habitus poneretur, qui est genus propinquum."

2. In contemporary philosophy this is referred to as the problem of "individuation" or "enumeration." See Daniel C. Russell, *Practical Intelligence and the Virtues* (Oxford: Oxford University Press, 2009), pt. 2.

3. William C. Mattison III, "Thomas's Categorizations of Virtue: Historical Background and Contemporary Significance," *The Thomist* 74, no. 2 (2010): 189–235.

4. *On the Virtues* 4.4c: "Sicut autem forma in rebus naturalibus datspeciem, ita et in moralibus obiectum dat speciem actui, et per consequens habitui."

5. 55.4c: "Materia autem circa quam est obiectum virtutis; quod non potuit in praedicta definitione poni, eo quod per obiectum determinatur virtus ad speciem; hic autem assignatur definitio virtutis in communi."

6. Martha C. Nussbaum, "Non-Relative Virtues: An Aristotelian Approach," in *Moral Relativism: A Reader,* ed. Paul K. Moser and Thomas L. Carson (New York: Oxford University Press, 2001), 202–3.

7. Christine Swanton, *Virtue Ethics: A Pluralistic View* (New York: Oxford University Press, 2003), 20.

8. See Poinsot, *Cursus Theologicus, Isagoge ad D. Thomae Theologiam,* in I.II 59 (Solesmes 5:171).

9. *Comm. Ethic.*, lib. 2 l. 3 n.3: "Materia enim uniuscuiusque virtutis moralis est id circa quod modum rationis imponit."

10. Ibid.; compare *Super Sent.* lib. 3 d. 33 q. 2 a. 2 qc. 2 arg 2, ad 2; qc.3c and ad 3.

11. 18.2 ad 2: "obiectum non est materia ex qua, sed materia circa quam, et habet quodammodo rationem formae, inquantum dat speciem."

12. *Comm. Ethic.*, lib. 2 l. 3 n.14: "Ars autem et virtus est circa difficilius, in quo magis requiritur quod aliquis bene operetur, ad quod ordinatur ars et virtus; nam in facilibus quilibet potest bene operari. Sed bene operari in difficilibus est solum habentis virtutem et artem."

13. I.II 59.4c: "circa omne id quod contingit ratione ordinari et moderari, contingit esse virtutem moralem."

14. 161.1 ad 3: "humilitas reprimit appetitum, ne tendat in magna praeter rationem rectam. Magnanimitas autem animum ad magna impellit secundum rationem rectam."

15. J. O. Urmson, "Aristotle's Doctrine of the Mean," *American Philosophical Quarterly* 10, no. 3 (July 1, 1973): 226. For a critique of this view see Russell, *Practical Intelligence and the Virtues*, 181.

16. I.II 60.5c: "Obiecta igitur passionum, secundm quod diversimode comparantur ad appetitum sensitivum, causant diversas passionum species, secundum vero quod comparantur ad rationem, causant diversas species virtutum."

17. 63.4: "Obiectum autem virtutis cuiuslibet est bonum consideratum in materia propria, sicut temperantiae obiectum est bonum delectabilium in concupiscentiis tactus. Cuius quidem obiecti formalis ratio est a ratione, quae instituit modum in his concupiscentiis, materiale autem est id quod est ex parte concupiscentiarum."

18. 60.1 arg 2: "habitus non distinguuntur secundum materialia obiecta, sed secundum formales rationes obiectorum. Formalis autem ratio boni ad quod ordinatur virtus moralis, est unum, scilicet modus rationis."

19. North, *Sophrosyne*, 263.

20. 61.4: "temperantia vero sit quaedam dispositio animi quae modum quibuscumque passionibus vel operationibus imponit, ne ultra debitum efferantur."

21. *On the Virtues* 1.13c: "bonum in passionibus et operationibus humanis est quod attingatur modus rationis, qui est mensura et regula omnium passionum et operationum humanarum."

22. I.II 27.3c: "modus importat quandam mensurae determinationem." Compare I. 5. 5 c; scg. III 97, 100.

23. *Comm. Ethic.*, lib. 1 l.3 n.1: "Modus manifestandi veritatem in qualibet scientia, debet esse conveniens ei quod subiicitur sicut materia in illa scientia."

24. *Comm. Ethic.*, lib. 1 l. 3 n.5.

25. *Super Sent.*, lib. 3 d. 33 q. 3 a. 2 qc. 1c: "Sicut enim in scientiis modum oportet secundum materiam inquirere, ut dicitur in 1 Ethic., ita et in virtutibus."

26. *Nicomachean Ethics* II.4.

27. Terence Irwin comments, "These claims do not fit the passage in Aristotle that Aquinas cites, but they fit Aristotle's intentions in his account of virtue as a whole." Irwin, *The Development of Ethics: A Historical and Critical Study,* vol. 1: *From Socrates to the Reformation* (Oxford: Oxford University Press, 2007), 592.

28. II.II 58.8 ad 2: "virtutes cardinales dupliciter accipiuntur. Uno modo, secundum quod sunt speciales virtutes habentes determinatas materias. Alio modo, secundum quod significant quosdam generales modos virtutis."

29. Compare the helpful discussion of *partes potentiales* in Robert Pasnau, *Thomas Aquinas on Human Nature: A Philosophical Study of Summa Theologiae 1a, 75–89* (Cambridge: Cambridge University Press, 2002), 144–45.

30. 1.12 ad 27: "alie virtutes adiunctae vel secundariae ponuntur partes cardinalium, non integrales vel subiectivae, cum habeant materiam determinatam et actum proprium; sed quasi partes potentiales, in quantum particulariter participant, et deficienter medium quod principaliter et perfectius convenit virtuti cardinali."

31. II.II 143: "Partes autem potentiales alicuius virtutis principalis dicuntur virtutes secundariae, quae modum quem principalis virtus observat circa aliquam

principalem materiam, eundem observant in quibusdam aliis materiis, in quibus non est ita difficile."

32. *Super Sent.*, lib. 3 d. 27 q. 2 a. 4 qc. 3c: "prudentia ponit modum et formam in omnibus aliis virtutibus moralibus."

33. 27.6c: "in dilectione Dei non potest accipi modus sicut in re mensurata, ut sit in ea accipere plus et minus, sed sicut invenitur modus in mensura."

34. Ad 1: "caritas, quae habet modum sicut mensura, praeeminet aliis virtutibus, quae habent modum sicut mensuratae."

35. *Nichomachean Ethics* VII.6: "Est igitur virtus habitus electivus in medietate existens quoad nos, determinata ratione et ut utique sapiens determinabit." Here I use the Latin text of the *Ethics* available to Aquinas. I translate "sapiens," wise one, as "prudent one" because that is how Aquinas interprets it: wise, not simply speaking, but in human affairs. *Comm. Ethic.*, lib. 2 l. 7 n.5. When he discusses the definition, sometimes he switches from "wise" to "prudent." E.g., I.II 58.2 ad 4.

36. *On the Virtues* 1.13c: "bonum in passionibus et operationibus humanis est quod attingatur modus rationis, qui est mensura et regula omnium passionum et operationum humanarum. . . . Quod autem in passionibus et operationibus humanis aliquis excedat modum rationis vel deficiat ab eo, hoc est malum. Cum igitur bonum hominis sit virtus humana, consequens est quod virtus moralis consistat in medio inter superabundantiam et defectum; ut superabundantia et defectus et medium accipiantur secundum respectum ad regulam rationis."

37. *On the Virtues* 1.13 ad 4: "modus virtutis quasi medium quoddam."

38. *Super Sent.*, lib. 3 d. 33 q. 1 a. 3 qc. 1 ad 5: "virtus dicitur medium dupliciter. Uno modo ratione materiae circa quam est, inquantum adaequat eam rationi rectae; et hoc per se convenit omni virtuti morali. . . . Alio modo dicitur medium ratione habitus, inquantum scilicet habitus virtutis est medium inter habitus duarum malitiarum . . . et hoc accidit virtuti, nec oportet quod sit in omnibus virtutibus."

39. Rosalind Hursthouse, "A False Doctrine of the Mean," *Proceedings of the Aristotelian Society* 81 (1980): 59–60.

40. 119.1 arg 1, ad 1: "nihil prohibet eidem inesse opposita secundum diversa."

41. The fuller text: "Consideratio circumstantiarum pertinet ad moralem, et politicum, et ad rhetorem. Ad moralem quidem, prout secundum eas invenitur vel praetermittitur medium virtutis in humanis actibus et passionibus." Compare I.II 64.1 ad 2; II.II 33.2, 58.10; *De Malo*, q. 14 a.3c.

42. 7.1c: "quaecumque conditiones sunt extra substantiam actus, et tamen attingunt aliquo modo actum humanum, circumstantiae dicuntur."

43. There is a helpful list of texts in Joseph Pilsner, *The Specification of Human Actions in St. Thomas Aquinas* (Oxford: Oxford University Press, 2006), 178.

44. II.II 33.2: "actus virtutum non quolibet modo fieri debent, sed observatis debitis circumstantiis quae requiruntur ad hoc quod sit actus virtuosus."

45. Rosalind Hursthouse, "The Central Doctrine of the Mean," in *The Blackwell Guide to Aristotle's Nicomachean Ethics*, ed. Richard Kraut (Oxford: Blackwell, 2006) 96–115.

46. 147.1 ad 2: "medium virtutis non accipitur secundum quantitatem, sed secundum rationem rectam."

47. I.II 64.1 ad 2: "in hoc tendunt huiusmodi virtutes secundum regulam rationis, idest ubi oportet, et quando oportet, et propter quod oportet."

48. II.II 129.3 ad 1: "magnanimus est quidem magnitudine extremus, inquantum scilicet ad maxima tendit, eo autem quod ut oportet, medius, quia videlicet ad ea quae sunt maxima, secundum rationem tendit."

49. Hursthouse, "Central Doctrine of the Mean," 109.

50. *On the Virtues* 1.6c: "Unumquodque autem horum contingit multipliciter fieri, et non eodem modo in omnibus; unde ad hoc quod rectus modus statuatur, requiritur iudicii prudentia."

51. Swanton, *Virtue Ethics*, 93.

52. I.II 54.4c: "Non enim unus habitus se extendit ad multa, nisi in ordine ad unum, ex quo habet unitatem."

53. I 1.3c: "Est enim unitas potentiae et habitus consideranda secundum obiectum, non quidem materialiter, sed secundum rationem formalem obiecti." See also I.II 54.2 ad 1; *On the Virtues* 2.4c; and Pilsner, *Specification*, 101–2.

54. I.II 61.5c: "sicut Augustinus dicit in libro de moribus Eccles., oportet quod anima aliquid sequatur, ad hoc quod ei possit virtus innasci, et hoc Deus est, quem si sequimur, bene vivimus. Oportet igitur quod exemplar humanae virtutis in Deo praeexistat, sicut et in eo praeexistunt omnium rerum rationes."

55. 61.5c: "ad hominem pertinet ut etiam ad divina se trahat quantum potest, ut etiam philosophus dicit, in X Ethic.; et hoc nobis in sacra Scriptura multipliciter commendatur, ut est illud Matth. V, estote perfecti, sicut et pater vester caelestis perfectus es."

56. II.II 23.2 ad 1: "sicut dicimur boni bonitate quae Deus est, et sapientes sapientia quae Deus est, quia bonitas qua formaliter boni sumus est participatio quaedam divinae bonitatis, et sapientia qua formaliter sapientes sumus est participatio quaedam divinae sapientiae; ita etiam caritas qua formaliter diligimus proximum est quaedam participatio divinae caritatis."

57. *Cursus Theologicus*, Tract. 12, *De Virtutibus*, Disp.3, Dub.3, n.48 (Solesmes 6:357).

58. Super I Cor., cap. 11 l. 1: "Hoc autem exemplar Dei prius erat a nobis valde remotum, secundum illud Eccle. II, v. 12: quid est homo, ut sequi possit regem factorem suum? Et ideo homo fieri voluit, ut hominibus humanum exemplar praeberet."

59. *Contra Gentiles* IV.54: "Exempla autem alicuius et verba tanto efficacius ad virtutem inducunt, quanto de eo firmior bonitatis habetur opinio. De nullo autem homine puro infallibilis opinio bonitatis haberi poterat: quia etiam sanctissimi viri in aliquibus inveniuntur defecisse. Unde necessarium fuit homini, ad hoc quod in virtute firmaretur, quod a Deo humanato doctrinam et exempla virtutis acciperet. Propter quod ipse dominus dicit, Ioan. 13–15: *exemplum dedi vobis, ut quemadmodum ego feci, ita et vos faciatis.*"

60. Brian J. Shanley, "Aquinas's Exemplar Ethics," *The Thomist* 72, no. 3 (2008): 345–69.

61. Linda T. Zagzebski, "Exemplarist Virtue Theory," *Metaphilosophy* 41, no. 1–2 (January 1, 2010): 51.

62. Linda T. Zagzebski, *Divine Motivation Theory* (Cambridge: Cambridge University Press, 2004), 228–70.

63. Patrick M. Clark, "The Case for an Exemplarist Approach to Virtue in Catholic Moral Theology," *Journal of Moral Theology* 3, no. 1 (2014): 54–82.

64. Shanley, "Aquinas's Exemplar Ethics," 369.

65. Zagzebski, "Exemplarist Virtue Theory," 47.

CHAPTER 8

Passionate Virtue

Suggested reading: *Summa Theologiae* I 81.2–3;
I.II 23.1, 24.1, 24.3, 56, 58.2, 58.5; II.II 25.7;
On the Virtues 1.3–5

A virtue is the perfection of a potential or power (*perfectio potentiae*) (I.II 66.3). Virtue's material cause is not the perfection itself but the potential for it. The material cause corresponds to the "plasticity" of human nature, to use William James's term: the capacity of the human psyche to be formed well or badly, like the matter the craftsman shapes and forms.

As with the formal cause, Aquinas introduces an initially bewildering number of distinctions:

> Virtue, like any other accident, does not have a *matter-out-of-which*, but it does have a *matter-about-which*, and a *matter-in-which*, namely, the subject. The *matter-about-which* is the object of a virtue, which could not be placed in the above definition, since it is through the object that a virtue is fixed to a species, whereas here we are supplying the definition of virtue in general. This is why the subject is put in the place of the material cause, when it is said [in the Augustinian definition that virtue] is a "good quality *of the mind*." (55.4c)[1]

Aquinas distinguishes three matters. First is the *matter-out-of-which* something comes to exist, such as a cake's flour, egg, and sugar out of which the cake is made; this is its "substantial matter." Since a virtue is a person's quality rather than a substance, virtue has no substantial matter out of which it comes to be. Second is the *matter-in-which* a quality exists, such as a statue's initial lump of bronze, which receives the form of the statue or what we may call its "subjective matter": the subject or bearer of the form or quality. Third is the *matter-about-which* an act, power, or habit stands: this is its "objective matter" or "material object." For example, color is the objective matter of the power of sight. We turn now to a virtue's subjective matter: its bearer or subject.

THE SUBJECTIVE MATTER

Virtues, like their acts, belong strictly only to persons. While it is the hand that strikes or the eye that sees, strictly speaking it is only the integral human person who strikes or sees (II.II 58.2). Actions belong, in the last analysis, to "supposits," or whole subjects only (*Actiones sunt suppositorum*). Similarly, strictly speaking virtue has only one bearer or subject (*subiectum*): the human person. It is Clarence or Gwen who is just, prudent, or temperate. We should avoid hypostasizing or reifying the soul's powers, as though the intellect could be prudent, or the will just, as Clarence is prudent and Gwen is just. As Eleonore Stump puts it, the faculties of the soul are not "homuncular."[2]

However, Gwen can possess virtuous qualities only because she is a human with apprehensive and appetitive capacities that can be formed well or badly. By a kind of analogy, then, these powers can be seen as the subjects of virtue. While Aquinas prefers not to say a power *is* the subject of a virtue, he is prepared to say this: "Human virtue is in a power of the soul *just as* in a subject" (I.II 56.1, emphasis added).[3] Gwen, in terms of an old scholastic distinction, is the whole subject *that* has the virtue and exercises it (*subiectum quod*); but some faculty or power is the subject *by which* the virtue is possessed and exercised (*subiectum quo*).

What, then, are the virtues' "subjects"? The Augustinian definition says that virtue is a quality "of mind." Aquinas explains, "Virtue cannot exist in the irrational part of the soul, except insofar as it participates in reason (*Nichomachean Ethics* I.13). And therefore reason, or mind, is the proper subject of virtue" (55.4 ad 3).[4] The mind is virtue's subject. From the next question onward he switches to a more Aristotelian vocabulary: a virtue is a quality that has a power or capacity of the soul (*potentia*) as its subject (56).[5]

It is the powers of intellect, will, and the sensitive appetite (the locus of the passions, which is in turn divided into the irascible and concupiscible) that Aquinas claims can serve as the subjects of virtue (56.3–4, 56.6). The concupiscible power is the subject of the passions of desire and aversion; in contrast, the irascible power has to do with the more spirited passions of impulse and resistance. The distinction between "concupiscible" and "irascible" is often misunderstood as a division of the passions into positive and negative, or between those that tend to good versus those that tend away from evil. In fact, there are concupiscible passions, such as hate, that are "negative" and tend away from evil; there are irascible passions, such as hope, that are "positive" and tend toward some good. Aquinas's distinction is subtler: the difference lies in whether the good or evil object is *arduous* to attain or avoid: if so, the passions are irascible, if not, they are concupiscible (I 81.2; I.II 23.1). The passions of simple attraction (or repulsion) to good (or evil) are concupiscible. The spirited passions of pursuit (or avoidance) of some arduous good (or evil) are irascible. Peter King gives the example of Jones teasing his dog, Rover, with a bone: Rover begins with a concupiscible desire for the bone but then develops the irascible passion of anger, directed toward the teasing Jones, as a threat to his desired pleasure.[6] The irascible serves the concupiscible as its "champion and defender" (I 81.2).[7]

Which subjects connect with which virtues? The general principle is this: "A certain power is the subject of a virtue when this virtue aims at rectifying the act of that power" (I.II 58.4).[8] For example, justice's subject is the will: Gwen is a just person and is inclined to just acts because of the way her will is disposed to give others their due.

A corollary is that a virtue's subjective and objective matter correspond. For example, since temperance modifies certain concupiscible passions, its subject is the concupiscible power (II.II 141.3; I.II 61.2c). There is an apparent (although not genuine) exception to this rule: continence is about the concupiscible appetite for the pleasures of touch (155.2); its subject, however, is the will (155.3). There is a simple solution: the desires for the pleasures of touch are the *mediate* matter of continence; its *immediate* matter are the acts of the will by which one controls one's desires. Even with continence, then, subject and immediate matter correspond.

Aquinas identifies three necessary conditions for a power of the soul counting as the subject of a virtue. First, since a virtue is an operative habit, its subject must be a power or capacity for operation (I.II 56.1c). Second, since a virtue is necessary only where a power can be disposed either well or badly to its operation, its subject must be a power that exists with some indifference or indeterminacy (49.4c). Finally, if the form of human virtue is the rational good, then only those powers that are potentially rational will qualify as subjects (61.2c). In sum, to be virtue's subject, a power must be operative, indeterminate, and potentially rational.

One argument, a distant ancestor of which was offered by Plato in *The Republic*, seems to make the correlation of powers of the soul and virtues a relatively simple matter. Aquinas argues that there are four cardinal virtues corresponding to the four potentially rational powers of the soul: prudence is subjected in the practical reason, justice in the will, fortitude in the irascible, and temperance in the concupiscible appetite (61.2). This argument establishes that there are *at least* four principal virtues, as there is no reason why there could not be more than one principal virtue in each subject (54.1).

Could a virtue not have more than one subject? It may seem so. For example, to be a just person one needs not only a good will but also an ability to judge what is due to another; to be prudent one needs not only to be able to reason well but also to have a good heart; and so on. While Aquinas would acknowledge these points, he claims that a virtue cannot exist in two powers equally. Since virtues actualize the powers of the soul, their objects must be specifications of those powers. As Aquinas puts it, "Diversity of powers follows the generic conditions of objects, whereas diversity of habits follows their specific conditions; and so wherever there is diversity of powers, there is diversity of habits, but not conversely" (56.2).[9] If temperance exists equally in the will and in the sensitive appetite, for example, there would be two virtues that are distinct in species, not one.

Yet Aquinas does recognize that a virtue can exist in two powers, not equally in each but "by a certain order." For example, prudence has practical reason as its immediate subject but also presupposes a rightly ordered will (56.2 ad 1). One does not reason well about what should be done unless one is first moved by a rightly channeled desire for the ends that are the principles of practical reason (56.3c; 57.4). Thus the subject of prudence, Aquinas says, is the practical intellect "as moved by the will" or "in order to right will" (56.3c). He is prepared to examine the complex interaction of the capacities of the human soul for thought and desire that enter into most of the virtues. Except with very few virtues, the subject will involve more than one power, albeit "in a certain order" (56.2c).

THE VIRTUOUS WILL

Which virtues lie in the will as their primary subject? Aquinas claims no virtue is required to perfect the will in order to achieve the agent's own good: "The object of the will is the good of reason proportionate to the agent, [and] to this extent the will does not require any perfecting virtue" (I.II 56.5).[10] Every being naturally loves itself, and so each being has a natural inclination toward its connatural and fitting good (*bonum proprium*). A virtue in the will is required only for other-regarding virtues to will the good of another (as with justice) or to love a higher supernatural good (as with charity), but not to love the agent's connatural good, which it does naturally and spontaneously.

We know by experience, however, that the will does not always choose the agent's good; indeed, many of life's miseries are due to self-destructive choices, such as entering the wrong relationship or becoming addicted. Is there no need for a virtue that directs and strengthens the will in loving the agent's own good?

Cajetan defends Aquinas's idea that there is no moral virtue of self-love; he argues that while the *agent* is not always inclined to choose her own good, the *will* nevertheless always retains this natural inclination (in I.II 56.6). Though the will can be turned to what is against the agent's good, the deviation is due not to any deficiency in the natural inclination of the will itself but rather in the disordered sensitive appetite that, like undesirable company, turns the will away from its natural bent to the agent's long-term good. One might say that the will's love for the agent's own good is *elastic* rather than *plastic*: absent the corrupting force of disordered passion, the will returns to its desire for the agent's good. Lacking plasticity, self-love is not a suitable matter of moral virtue. Thus, Cajetan argues, there is no connatural virtue of self-love needed in the will.

While Cajetan's solution is elegant, I am not entirely convinced. Aquinas admits that only the virtuous truly love themselves, being friends, as it were, to themselves, whereas the wicked "do not rightly love themselves, but love what they [wrongly] think themselves to be" (II.II 25.7).[11] This disordered self-love, which is really a kind of self-hate, could be the fault of a will distorted by passion. Yet why point the finger of blame at the passions rather than at the will itself, given that, as Aquinas admits, the will itself also suffers disorder due to original sin (I.II 83.3)? True self-love is a love formed by a correct knowledge of one's self and one's good, and it is therefore an attainment of virtue. It seems at least as plausible to claim that the will requires a virtue to love well the agent's own true and proper good.[12]

VIRTUOUS PASSION

Aquinas claims that the irascible and concupiscible appetites—the seats of the passions—can serve as the subject of virtues (I.II 56.4). For example, fortitude and its parts are located in the irascible appetite as its subject, whereas temperance and its parts are located in the concupiscible appetite, at least as a general rule (61.2).[13]

By identifying the subject of these virtues as lying in the sensitive rather than in the intellectual appetite, Aquinas is affirming both the possibility of intrinsically virtuous passion and the positive moral role of passion even within the cardinal virtues such as fortitude and temperance. His virtue theory suggests an ethics of reason and will, but also of passion. When viewed from the angle of its formal cause, moral virtue is rational in that it consists in conformity to the rational good; when viewed from the perspective of the material cause, many moral virtues are not merely rational, but passionate. But how tenable is this pro-passion viewpoint?

As Hursthouse observes, there is no better source than Aquinas for exploring the relation between virtue and passion.[14] When it was written, the *Treatise on the Passions* (22–48) probably constituted the most sustained treatment of the passions to date, and it continued to be influential for centuries. Its relative neglect in modern times has now been corrected more than amply, through at least three monographs on the topic.[15] However, judging from its location in the *Summa Theologiae*, the *Treatise* is not intended as a self-standing tract. Rather, it serves as a preparation for the study of the role of the passions in the life of virtue. Our own focus must be on how Aquinas relates moral virtue and the passions in his *Treatise on Virtue in General*.

The "core thesis" is that the irascible and concupiscible appetites are subjects of moral virtues. Aquinas notes a significant objection. It is a necessary condition of a habit being a moral virtue that it be an "elective habit" that is capable of resulting in right choice or election (I.II 56.4 arg 4). But election or choice is substantially an act of the will, as informed by reason (13.1). Its subject lies, therefore, in the "higher" part of the soul of reason and will (as contrasted with the "lower" part of the soul, where the sensitive appetite lies). Because of its subject, a habit located in the concupiscible or irascible appetite seems to fail to fulfil one of the necessary conditions for being a moral virtue. As Aquinas puts it: "The principal act of moral virtue is election (*Nichomachean Ethics* VIII.13). But election is not the act of the irascible or concupiscible, but of reason, as we have said. Thus moral virtue is not in the irascible or concupiscible, but in reason" (56.4 arg 4).[16] John Duns Scotus was later to locate the moral virtues in the will precisely on this basis.[17]

Here Aquinas gets to the heart of the twofold challenge presented by a positive account of the relationship between passion and virtue. First is the problem of the relation between passion and reason. Passions seem to be somewhat chaotic impulses that often conflict with reason; virtue, on the other hand, is characterized by its harmony with practical reason. How, then, can virtue incorporate psychic phenomena that are so nonrational, even irrational? Second is the problem of the relation between passion and the will. We tend to think of passions as phenomena that happen *to* us: they are precisely passions rather than actions. Virtue, on the other hand, is a principle of voluntary human action. How, then, can virtue be concerned with something we undergo rather than something we voluntarily execute ourselves?

Aquinas's solution is to add precision to the core thesis that the concupiscible and irascible appetites can be the subject of virtue. His modified core thesis depends on a distinction between two ways in which the irascible powers and concupiscible powers, as they exist in human beings, can be considered:

> The irascible and the concupiscible can be considered in two ways. First, in themselves, insofar as they are parts of the sensitive appetite. And in this way, they are not able to be a subject of virtue. Second, they can be considered insofar as they participate in reason, through this: that they have a natural aptitude to

obey reason. And thus the irascible or concupiscible can be the subject of human virtue: for thus each is a principle of a human act, insofar as it participates in reason. (56.4)[18]

Aquinas's modified core thesis, then, is that the irascible and concupiscible can be subjects of virtue *insofar as they participate in reason through their natural capacity to obey reason*. As such, they can be principles of a human act and of right election (56.4c and ad 4). How successful is the modified core thesis in explaining the possibility of passionate virtue?

INCOMMENSURABLE READINGS?

Fergus Kerr alleges that Aquinas's text contains "Janus-like ambiguities" that result in "incommensurable yet equally plausible" readings.[19] One such locus of competing interpretations is Aquinas's claim that the passions can be integrated into virtue because they "participate in reason, through their having a natural aptitude to obey reason" (I.II 56.4).[20]

In Aquinas's theology, the cosmos, human society, and the human soul are all ordered in a hierarchy in which the "higher" move the "lower" as ordained by God (II.II 104.1; I 77.4). Cosmology, politics, and moral psychology all portray an analogous hierarchy. The metaphors of "higher" and "lower" *describe* how things are by nature and as they have been created by God and ordered by His providence; they also *prescribe* how things should be, to conform to His wisdom. As he says, "The virtue of any subordinate thing is that it be well subordinated to that by which it is governed, just as we see that the virtue of the irascible and concupiscible faculties lies in this, that they are well obedient to reason" (I.II 92.1).[21] By this accounting, the moral virtues are habits of obedience: "The moral virtues are certain habits, by which the appetitive powers are disposed to obeying reason promptly" (I.II 68.3c).[22]

The question is how to interpret this obedience. Two possible readings stand out in the literature. The first is the rationalist reading, which sees total and immediate rational control of passion as the ideal. Giuseppe Butera's interpretation of Aquinas tends in this direction, as he rejects the idea of spontaneous virtuous passion independent of reason's immediate command. The second reading is "the pure spontaneity view," which looks for a more positive role for the passions in moral virtue. It claims virtues such as temperance and fortitude incline a person to spontaneous well-ordered passion and consequently to the virtuous action that flows from this passion. Jean Porter, in her early writing on Aquinas, tends to this viewpoint: the virtuous person's "immediate responses will reliably direct him to act appropriately, at least in normal circumstances."[23]

The spontaneity viewpoint posits that formed emotional responses bypass reason and will and the need for continual deliberation.

How to decide between these two readings? The pure spontaneity view does not seem to correspond to Aquinas's, which sees deliberation as necessary for all virtuous acts, even spontaneous ones. He states: "Nor is this [sudden virtuous action] to be understood as meaning that operation according to the habit of virtue can be completely without deliberation, since virtue is an elective habit; but [it means] that the possessor of the habit already has the end determined in his choice; so whenever something suited to that end occurs, it is chosen immediately, unless blocked by some more attentive and weighty deliberation."[24] While virtuous human action may happen without *forethought*, it cannot lack *thought* altogether (see chap. 2). Though the pure spontaneity viewpoint runs aground in light of Aquinas's understanding that will and reason are always involved in virtuous action, the rationalist viewpoint is also problematic, as it gives too little a role to passion in virtue and is difficult to reconcile with some of Aquinas's more positive statements.

I propose a third viewpoint: the "moderate spontaneity view," which acknowledges the place of reason and will in all morally virtuous action but also finds a more positive place for the participation of habits subjected in the sensitive appetite. Moral virtues such as temperance do incline to rectified passion of themselves, and therefore contribute to virtuous deliberation, election, and execution—but only in conjunction with reason and will. This third viewpoint is both a proper reading of Aquinas and the more attractive position. Butera's critique, in my view, only undermines the pure, not the moderate spontaneity viewpoint.

My argument will focus not on the interpretation of texts alone but also on four substantive points in Aquinas's account of virtuous passion: the idea of participative rationality, the distinction between despotic and political authority, the distinction between antecedent and consequent passion, and the contribution of passion to deliberation.

Participative Rationality

To understand the "moderate spontaneity view" it helps to refer to Robert C. Roberts's critique of Aquinas on moral passion. Roberts distinguishes *intrinsic* from *derivative* rationality: beliefs, actions, and people are intrinsically rational because they are the sorts of things that can be both rational and irrational; bodily movements and buildings are derivatively rational because they derive their rationality from prior events or actions.[25] Roberts interprets Aquinas as making the emotions only derivatively rational since their rationality comes from obedience to reason.[26] Roberts effectively accuses Aquinas of too rationalistic a position that does not acknowledge the genuine or "intrinsic" rationality of the passions that could make them genuine contributors to virtuous action. Bodily movements are derivatively rational, but the body is not a subject of virtue; if the irascible and concupiscible are only derivatively rational, neither can they be the subject of virtue.

Roberts's dichotomy between intrinsic and merely derivative rationality leads to a dilemma. Either the passions are seen as possessing merely derivative rationality, in which case virtue is attributed purely to the reason and will controlling passion, or the passions possess intrinsic rationality, in which case the degree to which virtuous action can issue from well-formed, rationalized passion without rational deliberation is exaggerated.

Aquinas offers a way out of this dilemma. He would agree that the body's movements have a merely derivative rationality in that "the whole motion of the body is referred back to the soul" (I.II 56.4 ad 3).[27] Reason, in contrast, is intrinsically or "essentially" rational (61.2c). Aquinas in effect proposes a third category: *participative* rationality (58.3). By ascribing participatory rationality to the passions, Aquinas evades Roberts's charge of rationalism without sliding into the opposite extreme that attributes to passion too great a role in virtuous action.

Aquinas characterizes participation as follows: "To participate is, as it were, to take part; and therefore when something particularly receives that which belongs to another universally, it is said to participate in that."[28] To participate in a quality is to acquire that quality to some extent. As he says, "Everything participating in something is related to that in which it participates as potency to act: for through that in which it participates, the participant becomes actually such."[29] For Aquinas it is a general principle that "a lower nature, at its highest point, attains to that which is proper to a higher nature, imperfectly participating in it" (*De Veritate* 16.1).[30] Thus through its participation in reason, the human capacity for passion becomes, to some extent, a capacity for *rational* passion: "The irascible and concupiscible take the name of reason or the rational insofar as they participate in some way in reason" (*On the Virtues* 1.10 ad 3).[31] There is a distinction between what is rational *essentially*, such as reason itself, what is rational *derivatively*, like bodily movements, and what is rational *through participation*, or the sensitive and intellectual appetites.[32]

For Aquinas it is a fact of experience that this participative rationality of the sensitive appetite exists: "Anyone can experience this in himself, for by applying certain universal considerations, anger or fear or other things of this kind may be tempered or excited" (*On the Virtues* 1.10 ad 3).[33] One may voluntarily change one's passions, at least to some extent, by reasoning about the object(s) of one's passions and seeing them as more or less unjust or threatening or attractive than one initially feels them to be. Aquinas's account can explain this phenomenon since, for him, the object is presented to the sensitive appetite with the aid of the "particular reason" or "cogitative power" whose function is to apply universal concepts to the particulars perceived by the external and interior senses.[34] As Robert Pasnau suggests, the cogitative power is the capacity of "seeing as."[35] When someone is angry because she sees a thief run off with a poor man's possession, she is responding to an action *seen as* unjust. The sensitive appetite participates in reason insofar as reason influences the object of our passions.

It is because human passions can be originatively rational in this way that they can be measured against the normatively rational and therefore judged as morally good or bad, virtuous or vicious (I.II 24.1). Indeed, "The irascible or concupiscible can be the subject of human virtue, for thus it is the principle of a human act, insofar as it participates in reason" (56.4c).[36]

The participatory rationality of the sensitive appetite suggests a position between rationalism and the pure spontaneity interpretation. Aquinas's viewpoint is not rationalism, because virtuous agency is not attributed to reason and will alone: the sensitive appetite is a principle of a human action, not merely its consequence. However, neither does Aquinas advocate the "pure spontaneity view," according to which the sensitive appetite, when formed by virtue, can issue in virtuous action without reason and will. If the irascible and concupiscible, as perfected by virtuous habits, can participate in reason, they can also *take part* in virtuous election and action. But they cannot *take over* from reason and will. As Aquinas puts it, the sensitive appetite, to the extent that it participates in reason and will, is capable of being a "participant in an election" (*particeps electionis*).[37]

Habits subjected in the sensitive appetite can contribute to election and also to the execution of virtuous action: "An act of virtue cannot belong to the irascible or concupiscible alone, without reason. . . . A virtue is not said to be in the irascible or concupiscible as if, through them, the whole act of virtue or its more principal part were completed, but only insofar as, by the habit of virtue, the ultimate completion of goodness is conferred to the act of virtue" (*On the Virtues* 1.4 ad 2).[38] Once again, a virtuous habit in the irascible or concupiscible does not take over from reason and will in the performance of virtuous action, but it does take part in the consummation of a virtuous act. Temperate and brave action is more than simply reason's control alone, but it does not happen without it. Just as the concupiscible and irascible cannot be the subjects of mortal sin by themselves, even if they can "concur" in it (*On the Virtues* 1.4 ad 1), so these powers can be subjects of virtue but only as "concurring" with reason and will.

In the moderate spontaneity view, because the sensitive appetite can be participatively rational, it can take part in virtuous decision and action, together with reason and will.

Despotic versus Political Authority

Aquinas distinguishes two kinds of rule or authority within the human soul: tyrannical and political. He introduces the ideas in response to an objection (I.II 56.4 arg 3). If a coachman, obeying my instructions, directs the horses in the right way, it is I who am responsible. In the same way, if the irascible and concupiscible powers are rightly ordered, this is entirely due to the directing power of reason and will. Does not the virtue lie with these commanding powers rather than with those that obey?

Aquinas replies that reason rules the sensitive appetite and the soul rules the body, but in different ways. The soul rules the body with a "despotic authority," just as a master rules a slave, since the response of the body to the soul is immediate and without contradiction, at least in matters such as moving a limb. Aquinas continues:

> The irascible and concupiscible do not obey at the nod of reason, but have their own proper motions, by which they sometimes go against reason. Whence ... the Philosopher says that "the reason rules the irascible and concupiscible by a politic authority," by which they are ruled as freemen, who have in some respects their own will. And for this reason it is necessary that there be in the irascible and concupiscible certain virtues, by which they are well disposed to act. (56.4 ad 3)[39]

It is only a particular kind of obedience that enables the sensitive appetite to be perfected by virtue. The question is how to interpret this political authority (*principatus politicus*) as opposed to despotic authority (*despoticus principatus*).

There is evidence for a rationalist interpretation. Aquinas says reason's rule over the sensitive appetite is politic, not despotic, because the lower power *resists* reason, "inasmuch as we sense or imagine something pleasant that reason forbids, or unpleasant that reason commands" (I 81.3 ad 2; cf. I.II 17.7).[40] This suggests that passion's resistance is what Robert Miner calls a "negative resistance," or the irrational against the rational.[41] While Aquinas concedes that reason's authority over the passions is merely political, the norm is tyrannical domination. This mirrors Butera's interpretation: "The ideal limit of temperance is despotic rather than political control, where the former is the sort of control a master exercises over his slave, who has no power to resist his master's will."[42] Steven J. Jensen concurs with Butera's interpretation, claiming that "in every instance in which I have found Aquinas using this metaphor, he uses the metaphor precisely as Butera would have him do."[43] In this viewpoint, the reason there is a need for virtue in the sensitive appetite is solely to remove passion's unfortunate tendency to fight against and obscure reason. The norm is a despotic rather than political obedience.

However, there is also evidence in favor of a different interpretation. It is better to be like a freeman than a slave. Indeed, Aquinas contrasts the body, which is like the slave who does not have the right of speaking against his master, with the appetitive powers, which are like freemen who have some right (*ius*) to resist (I.II 58.2). This suggests that the passions may even engage in what Miner terms a "positive resistance" to (erroneous) reason: the capability to correct reason when it is faulty, just as a subordinate may correct someone in a place of higher authority at times without usurping his role as a subordinate. Reason should be "authoritative" rather than "authoritarian." In saying that, unlike the body, the irascible and concupiscible passions have their own "proper motions," Aquinas is implying that they are in some way active and have something of their own to contribute; they are not like puppets, as pure instruments of reason, but more like willing partners. In this interpretation the ideal is not despotic but rather political obedience.

One attractive feature of this second interpretation is that it strikes the mean. A rationalism that dominates passion risks suppressing it. A romanticism that rejects reason's authority altogether paves the way for a different kind of tyrannical domination of bodily and emotional cravings over the mind and will. The ideal is of proper authority over one's passions, neither making them otiose nor letting them run loose.

Interestingly, Poinsot advocates the political rather than the tyrannical authority of reason over passion and offers a compelling argument.[44] He assumes, in accord with Aquinas, that Adam, in the state of innocence, and Christ, in his earthly life, both possessed the moral virtues of temperance and fortitude. However, in these the obedience of the sensitive appetite to reason could not have been despotic. Were it so, the sensitive appetite of Adam or Christ would have been no more capable of virtue than each's body, which despotically serves the reason; the passions themselves would not have been any more praiseworthy than movements of the body. He concludes:

> Wherefore, the appetite's being made submissive and rendered non-resistant [to the rule of reason] in this way is not a despotic obedience, that is, a natural slavery, but very much a political obedience. For, the appetite is completely subjected to reason while remaining in its indifference and perfection, and so there

is a moral obedience and submission, and therefore also a virtuous one, derived however [in Adam and in Christ] from the gift of grace, specifically the gift of original justice.[45]

Butera sees temperance and fortitude as purely corrective virtues: they remove from the concupiscible and irascible powers the disorder that is due to original sin and restore their natural tendency to obey reason without resistance. However, in this case Adam and Christ, as free from original sin, would have no need of such virtues. Since they did possess these virtues, these virtues are more than habits of despotic obedience—in Adam, in Christ, and in us.

Butera's temperate person seems excessively controlled in his emotional life. The person in whom there is a political and moral obedience of passion to reason is more emotionally balanced and morally virtuous than one in whom the passions, like slaves, only appear when and how they are summoned to do so by despotic reason.

Antecedent and Consequent Passion

Dispute also exists over another distinction. Aquinas says the passions of the soul are related to reason in two ways: either antecedently or consequently. Passions that are antecedent to the judgment of reason "obscure the judgment of reason, on which the goodness of the moral act depends" (I.II 24.3 ad 1).[46] Antecedent passions, he adds, diminish the goodness of a virtuous act. Only passions consequent to the judgment of reason have positive moral value, either as a sign of an intense good will that has overflowed into corresponding passion or as a kind of additional impetus to action (ibid.).

The distinction between antecedent and consequent passions seems to ascribe to passion a rather minor role in virtue. Antecedent passions cannot contribute positively, and even consequent passions are reduced to assisting in the execution of actions already decided on by reason.

Can passions ever positively influence the will and the intellect? Aquinas recognizes that will and intellect can be affected by passion since "insofar as someone is in some passion, something seems fitting to him that does not seem so without this passion" (9.2).[47] Initially there seems to be no room in the doctrine of antecedent and consequent passion to account for this as anything but a usurpation of proper order. Will and reason should rule over the sensitive appetite rather than vice versa. As Pasnau sees it, Aquinas cannot seem to acknowledge that the passions "help illuminate features of a situation that intellect alone would never grasp."[48]

However, Pasnau makes the following suggestion for allowing a greater role for the passions within the framework of Aquinas's theory: "[Aquinas] can allow the emotions some weight when they are governed by a disposition that itself has been cultivated over the years through discipline and intelligence. . . . This is not a point that I have found him making, but it is a point that we can easily make on his behalf, using the resources of his theory."[49] While Pasnau concedes that antecedent passions have no moral weight, he interprets "consequent passion" in a broad sense to include not only passions that follow immediately from the command of reason but also those that result from a habit that has been formed by reason. This is similar to training in tennis: while actions initially have to be constantly monitored and corrected, through training those actions eventually become second nature. Instinct and the "feel" of the shot become reliable guides in their own right.

Butera objects to what he calls this "spontaneity view." However, the moderate spontaneity viewpoint does not say that "the antecedent passions of the temperate are controlled by reason via habituation."[50] The argument is not that antecedent passions can be controlled by reason; it is clear that antecedent passion is defined as not so controlled. Rather, passions arising from virtuous habits in the sensitive appetite are consequent passions because they arise from a habit in the sensitive appetite formed by reason.

The textual evidence Pasnau needs does exist, in Aquinas's *Commentary on the Sentences*.[51] There Aquinas notes that the lower powers can receive their rectitude from the higher powers in two different ways. The first is in the manner of a *transient passion*, as when the sensitive appetite contributes nothing to the act. In such a case, the rectitude of the consequent passion is purely extrinsic and lasts no longer than the duration of the act that produces it; it is not accompanied by the ease and delight that is characteristic of virtuous acts. In the second, as when the sensitive appetite receives its rectitude after the manner of an *inherent quality*, there arises a habitual form existing in the power itself; it is an imprint, as it were, of reason. In such a case, delight and ease characterize the production of virtuous passion: the quality has been "turned, as it were, into nature" (*quasi in naturam versa*).[52]

The virtues of the sensitive appetite are therefore more than dispositions to respond promptly to the immediate command of reason (as Butera would claim) since the perfected sensitive appetite, as participating in reason, is itself a principle of rectified and rationalized passion. As Aquinas puts it in *On the Virtues*: "A virtue of the appetitive part is nothing other than a certain disposition or form sealed and impressed on the appetitive power by reason" (1.9).[53] In temperance and fortitude the sensitive appetite itself receives the form of reason, at least participatively, and does not need to wait for the actual command of the power of practical reason to operate and contribute positively to a moral act.

Passion and Deliberation

Can the passions contribute positively to deliberation? We have seen that Aquinas thinks that antecedent passion clouds the judgment of reason and diminishes the moral goodness of an action. At first sight this seems to be evidence that Aquinas does not want even to consider the possibility that passion might have a positive role in deliberation. Butera references a passage from *On Truth*: "And so it is that passion anteceding an election impedes the act of virtue insofar as it impedes the judgement of reason, which is necessary in choosing; after the election has already been completed by a pure judgment of reason, a passion that follows helps more than harms, because if in some way it may disturb the judgment of reason, it nevertheless produces promptness in execution" (*De Veritate* 26.6 ad 3).[54] Butera takes this as decisive evidence that any passions disturb rather than help deliberation. The ideal is the "pure judgment of reason" lacking any influence from passion.

The interpretation of the cited text is not as straightforward as it may seem. Aquinas is replying to the Stoic position, here represented by the Roman historian Sallust, which sees passion as inevitably corruptive of reason (arg 3). Aquinas can defeat the Stoic position even when conceding that passion disturbs deliberation since he can argue that passion following the judgment of reason may contribute positively to virtuous action and aid in execution. A temporary concession to an opposing viewpoint for the sake of argument is not strong evidence of Aquinas's own position. Once placed in context, Butera's proof-text is not compelling.

Is there any evidence that passion and the habits of the sensitive appetite may contribute positively to rational judgment? It is necessary to attend carefully to the definition of "antecedent" and "consequent" passion. Steven Jensen, who largely shares Butera's rationalist interpretation, suggests passion causally influenced by the judgment of reason is consequent, whereas passion that influences judgment is antecedent.[55] Note that on this definition a passion could be simultaneously consequent (in relation to one judgment) and antecedent (in relation to another).

There are problems with Jensen's interpretation of antecedence. Given that Aquinas claims that antecedent passion obscures judgment, the critical question of whether consequent passion could contribute positively to deliberation is resolved negatively and purely by stipulation: it would be an antecedent passion and therefore cloud judgment. But why even a rational passion must necessarily cloud judgment is left obscure. Furthermore, Jensen's definition leaves open the possibility of a third kind of passion, which is neither antecedent nor consequent and that neither influences nor is influenced by reason. This is something of a slight on Aquinas's acuity since he explicitly claims that passions stand in a twofold, not a threefold, relation to reason.

Is there a better way to interpret antecedent and consequent passions? A causal definition is necessary, as Jensen suggests, but what is the relevant genre of cause? It is not effective but rather formal or participative causality. The following definition is proposed: A consequent passion is one that participates in reason and therefore is, in a way, rational; an antecedent passion is one that does not participate in reason and therefore is irrational, or at least nonrational. Unlike Jensen's definition of antecedence, this definition helps in explaining why Aquinas insists that antecedent passion inevitably clouds rational judgment. It is also an adequate division of all passions and does not lead to the confusing case of passions that are simultaneously antecedent and consequent. And, most important, it also leaves open the substantive question, Can consequent passion (consequent either because it derives from the immediate command of reason or because it flows from a virtuous habit subjected in the sensitive appetite) contribute positively to judgment and deliberation?

There is evidence that Aquinas acknowledges that passion can indeed contribute positively to judgment. Aquinas contrasts purely rational knowledge from a more affective kind: "Rectitude of judgment can come about in two ways: first, following the perfect use of reason; second, on account of a kind of connaturality toward those things about which one must judge in the now. Thus he who has acquired knowledge of moral science rightly judges about matters of chastity by the inquiry of reason, whereas he who has the habit of chastity rightly judges about such matters by a kind of connaturality" (II.II 45.2).[56] For Aquinas, prudence depends radically on this knowledge through connaturality, or affective knowledge, since it is through one's ordered appetitive dispositions that one rightly perceives the end that is the principle of prudential deliberation (I.II 58.5). Prudential judgment is the judgment of someone possessing a connaturality with what is good and honorable. Aquinas, then, allows a significant and indispensable cognitive role for the passions in prudential deliberation. Pasnau's suggestion is confirmed again: Aquinas can and does allow that the passions have cognitive value when arising from a disposition cultivated by reason and will.

What are we to conclude, then, about Aquinas's attempt to incorporate passion into virtue by claiming that habits subjected in the irascible and concupiscible, insofar as they participate in reason by obedience to it, can be virtues? This central thesis can stand only if such habits incline to choice and fully human action. Aquinas's texts generate competing interpretations. As an interpretation of Aquinas, and as an attractive position in its own right, the middle position acknowledges the spontaneity of virtuous passion flowing from habit while also recognizing that reason and will are not short-circuited in virtuous action. Rather, passion flowing from habits in the sensitive appetite becomes a *participant*, together with reason and will, in virtuous election and action. Habits of passion do not contribute to virtuous action merely by adding motor power and promptness to execution; they do so by inclining the will toward the right ends and, crucially, by supplying connatural knowledge of the ends from which prudential deliberation begins. Moral virtue, for Aquinas, is passionate virtue.

NOTES

1. 55.4c: "Virtus autem non habet materiam ex qua, sicut nec alia accidentia, sed habet materiam circa quam; et materiam in qua, scilicet subiectum. Materia autem circa quam est obiectum virtutis; quod non potuit in praedicta definitione poni, eo quod per obiectum determinatur virtus ad speciem; hic autem assignatur definitio virtutis in communi. Unde ponitur subiectum loco causae materialis, cum dicitur quod est bona qualitas mentis."

2. Stump, *Aquinas*, 535.

3. I.II 56.1: "virtus humana est in potentia animae sicut in subiecto."

4. 55.4 ad 3: "virtus non potest esse in irrationali parte animae, nisi inquantum participat rationem, ut dicitur in I Ethic. Et ideo ratio, sive mens, est proprium subiectum virtutis humanae."

5. On the soul's powers see Robert Pasnau, *Thomas Aquinas on Human Nature: A Philosophical Study of Summa Theologiae 1a, 75–89* (Cambridge: Cambridge University Press, 2002), 143–70.

6. Peter King, "Aquinas on the Passions," in *Thomas Aquinas: Contemporary Philosophical Perspectives*, ed. Brian Davies (Oxford: Oxford University Press, 1998), 362.

7. I 81.2: "quasi propugnatrix et defensatrix concupiscibilis."

8. I.II 58.4: "illa potentia est subiectum virtutis ad cuius potentiae actum rectificandum virtus ordinatur."

9. 56.2: "diversitas potentiarum attenditur secundum generales conditiones obiectorum, diversitas autem habituum secundum speciales; unde ubicumque est diversitas potentiarum, est diversitas habituum, sed non convertitur."

10. I.II 56.5: "obiectum voluntati sit bonum rationis voluntati proportionatum, quantum ad hoc non indiget voluntas virtute perficiente." See also *On the Virtues* 1.5.

11. II.II 25.7: "non recte cognoscentes seipsos, non vere diligunt seipsos, sed diligunt id quod seipsos esse reputant."

12. Another question concerns whether the will *alone* is the subject of justice (II.II 58.4). For helpful discussion, see Thomas J. Bushlack, *Politics for a Pilgrim Church: A Thomistic Theory of Civic Virtue* (Grand Rapids, MI: Eerdmans, 2015), chap. 3.

13. There are some exceptions to this general rule. For example, the virtue that concerns anger is considered a potential part of temperance, not of fortitude, even though

it is located in the irascible. The reason is that form, as what determines species, is more essential to a virtue than matter (II.II 157.3 ad 2). While this virtue shares its subjective matter with the cardinal virtue of fortitude, it shares its form or mode with temperance, being a kind of restraint or moderation.

14. See Rosalind Hursthouse, *On Virtue Ethics* (Oxford: Oxford University Press, 1999), chaps. 4 and 5.

15. Diana Fritz Cates, *Aquinas on the Emotions* (Washington, DC: Georgetown University Press, 2009); Robert Miner, *Thomas Aquinas on the Passions: A Study of Summa Theologiae, 1a2ae 22–48* (Cambridge: Cambridge University Press, 2009); Nicholas E. Lombardo, *The Logic of Desire: Aquinas on Emotion* (Washington, DC: Catholic University of America Press, 2010). In addition, see Paul Gondreau, *The Passions of Christ's Soul in the Theology of St. Thomas Aquinas* (Scranton: University of Scranton Press, 2002). Pasnau's study of the powers of the soul is important background. See Pasnau, *Thomas Aquinas on Human Nature.*

16. 56.4 arg 4: "principalis actus virtutis moralis est electio, ut dicitur in VIII Ethic. Sed electio non est actus irascibilis et concupiscibilis, sed rationis, ut supra dictum est. Ergo virtus moralis non est in irascibili et concupiscibili, sed in ratione."

17. Bonnie Kent, "Rethinking Moral Dispositions: Scotus on the Virtues," in *The Cambridge Companion to Duns Scotus*, ed. Thomas Williams (Cambridge: Cambridge University Press, 2006), 368–69.

18. 56.4: "irascibilis et concupiscibilis dupliciter considerari possunt. Uno modo secundum se, inquantum sunt partes appetitus sensitivi. Et hoc modo, non competit eis quod sint subiectum virtutis. Alio modo possunt considerari inquantum participant rationem, per hoc quod natae sunt rationi obedire. Et sic irascibilis vel concupiscibilis potest esse subiectum virtutis humanae, sic enim est principium humani actus, inquantum participat rationem."

19. Fergus Kerr, *After Aquinas: Versions of Thomism* (Malden, MA: Blackwell, 2002), 210.

20. I.II 56.4: "participant rationem, per hoc quod natae sunt rationi obedire." Compare I.59.4 ad 3; I.79.2 ad 2; and II.II 50.3 ad 1.

21. I.II 92.1: "Cuiuslibet autem subditi virtus est ut bene subdatur ei a quo gubernatur, sicut videmus quod virtus irascibilis et concupiscibilis in hoc consistit quod sint bene obedientes rationi."

22. I.II 68.3c: "Virtutes autem morales habitus quidam sunt, quibus vires appetitivae disponuntur ad prompte obediendum rationi."

23. Jean Porter, *The Recovery of Virtue: The Relevance of Aquinas for Christian Ethics* (Louisville, KY: John Knox, 1990), 115. See also Porter, *Moral Action and Christian Ethics* (Cambridge: Cambridge University Press, 1999), 172–73.

24. *De Veritate*, q. 24 a. 12c: "Nec hoc est intelligendum quod operatio secundum habitum virtutis possit esse omnino absque deliberatione, cum virtus sit habitus electivus; sed quia habenti habitum iam est in eius electione finis determinatus; unde quandocumque aliquid occurrit ut conveniens illi fini, statim eligitur, nisi ex aliqua attentiori et maiori deliberatione impediatur."

25. Robert C. Roberts, "Thomas Aquinas on the Morality of the Emotions," *History of Philosophy Quarterly* 9, no. 3 (July 1992): 228.

26. Ibid., 302–3.

27. I.II 56.4 ad 3: "totus motus corporis refertur ad animam."

28. *In De ebdomadibus* 12, n.24: "Est autem participare quasi partem capere; et ideo quando aliquid particulariter recipit id quod ad alterum pertinet universaliter, [punctuation changed, following Wippel] dicitur participare illud."

29. *Contra Gentiles*, lib. 2 cap. 53 n.4: "Omne participans aliquid comparatur ad ipsum quod participatur ut potentia ad actum: per id enim quod participatur fit participans actu tale."

30. *De Veritate* 16.1: "natura inferior attingit in sui supremo ad aliquid quod est proprium superioris naturae, imperfecte illud participans."

31. *On the Virtues* 1.10 ad 3: "irascibilis autem et concupiscibilis sic accipiunt nomen rationis vel rationalis, in quantum participant aliqualiter ratione."

32. *Comm. Ethic.*, lib. 1 l. 20 n.10, n.12; *On the Virtues* 1.5 ad sc 1; I.II 74.2 ad 2.

33. *On the Virtues* 1.10 ad 3: "Hoc etiam quilibet experiri potest in seipso, applicando enim aliquas universales considerationes, mitigatur ira aut timor aut aliquid huiusmodi, vel etiam instigatur."

34. *De Veritate* 14.1 ad 9.

35. Pasnau, *Thomas Aquinas on Human Nature*, 274–78.

36. 56.4c: "irascibilis vel concupiscibilis potest esse subiectum virtutis humanae, sic enim est principium humani actus, inquantum participat rationem."

37. *Super Sent.*, lib. 3 d. 33 q. 2 a. 4 qc. 2 ad 1.

38. *On the Virtues* 1.4 ad 2: "actus virtutis non potest esse irascibilis vel concupiscibilis tantum, sine ratione. . . . Non ergo pro tanto dicitur esse virtus in irascibili vel concupiscibili, quasi per eas totus actus virtutis vel principalior pars expleatur; sed in quantum, per virtutis habitum, ultimum complementum bonitatis actui virtutis confertur."

39. 56.4 ad 3: "Sed irascibilis et concupiscibilis non ad nutum obediunt rationi, sed habent proprios motus suos, quibus interdum rationi repugnant, unde in eodem libro philosophus dicit quod ratio regit irascibilem et concupiscibilem principatu politico, quo scilicet reguntur liberi, qui habent in aliquibus propriam voluntatem. Et propter hoc etiam oportet in irascibili et concupiscibili esse aliquas virtutes, quibus bene disponantur ad actum."

40. I 81.3 ad 2: "per hoc quod sentimus vel imaginamur aliquod delectabile quod ratio vetat, vel triste quod ratio praecipit."

41. Miner, *Thomas Aquinas on the Passions*, 107.

42. Giuseppe Butera, "On Reason's Control of the Passions in Aquinas's Theory of Temperance," *Mediaeval Studies* 68, no. 1 (January 1, 2006): 152.

43. Steven J. Jensen, "Virtuous Deliberation and the Passions," *The Thomist* 77, no. 2 (2013): 204.

44. *Cursus Theologicus*, in I.II, Disp.15, Art.2, 9.

45. Ibid.

46. I.II 24.3 ad 1: "cum obnubilent iudicium rationis, ex quo dependet bonitas moralis actus."

47. 9.2: "secundum quod homo est in passione aliqua, videtur sibi aliquid conveniens, quod non videtur extra passionem existenti."

48. Pasnau, *Thomas Aquinas on Human Nature*, 263.

49. Ibid.

50. Butera, "On Reason's Control," 143.

51. *Super Sent.*, lib. 3 d. 23 q. 1 a. 1c.

52. See the helpful commentary in the Salamancans, *Cursus Theologicus*, Tract. 12, *De Virtutibus*, Disp.1, Dub.2, n.45 (6:218).

53. 1.9: "Unde, si recte consideretur, virtus appetitivae partis nihil est aliud quam quaedam dispositio, sive forma, sigillata et impressa in vi appetitiva a ratione."

54. *De Veritate* 26.6 ad 3: "Et inde est quod passio electionem praeveniens impedit actum virtutis, in quantum impedit iudicium rationis, quod necessarium est in eligendo; postquam vero puro iudicio rationis iam electio est perfecta, passio sequens plus prodest quam noceat; quia si in aliquo turbet iudicium rationis, facit tamen ad promptitudinem executionis."

55. Jensen, "Virtuous Deliberation and the Passions."

56. II.II 45.2: "Rectitudo autem iudicii potest contingere dupliciter, uno modo, secundum perfectum usum rationis; alio modo, propter connaturalitatem quandam ad ea de quibus iam est iudicandum. Sicut de his quae ad castitatem pertinent per rationis inquisitionem recte iudicat ille qui didicit scientiam moralem, sed per quandam connaturalitatem ad ipsa recte iudicat de eis ille qui habet habitum castitatis."

CHAPTER 9

Telic Virtue

Suggested reading: *Summa Theologiae* I.II 56.3, 57,
58.4, 61.1, 65.1; II.II 2.5, 4.4–5, 23.7, 45.2, 141.6

The four causes—formal, material, final, and efficient—consist of two pairs, each with its own characteristic role in virtue theory. Whereas the formal and material causes have to do with the *specification* of virtue, the final and efficient causes are principles of *execution* (compare I.II 9.1). Thus the discussion must move from the static, essentialist to the more dynamic, existentialist aspect of Aquinas's ethics.[1] What, then, is the final cause of virtue?

THE FINAL CAUSES

Since virtue is a good operative habit (I.II 55.2–3), on one level virtue's final cause is simply good operation. "The end of virtue, since it is an operative habit, is operation itself" (55.4c);[2] and "That to which virtue is ordained is a good act" (71.1).[3] Yet this idea just pushes the question back one stage: If the end of virtue is virtuous action, what is the final cause of virtuous operation?

We find a clue in ancient tradition. The monk John Cassian (ca. 360–435) reports a journey to the desert of Scete in search of instruction from the renowned anchorite abbot Moses. The holy abbot begins his teaching: "All arts and disciplines [he says] have a certain *scopos*, that is, target; and they also have a *telos*, that is, their own proper end."[4] This is the first piece of instruction found in the *Conferences*, the classic text compiling the wisdom of the desert fathers.

The distinction between the *scopos* and the *telos* of any art, science, or, indeed, of any virtue goes back to Peripatetic and Stoic ethics. Abbot Moses illustrates the distinction by means of a farmer who wishes to secure a good harvest and so earn his living (the farmer's *telos*) but who has little chance of achieving that goal without applying himself diligently to ploughing the earth, clearing it of weeds, sowing the crop, and so on (the farmer's *scopos*).

While a simple analogy, the insight has immense practical significance. The holy abbot is warning Cassian and his companions that it is not enough to desire the Kingdom of God, like a farmer who dearly wishes for a flourishing harvest and a barn full of grain. The monk must be focused on the more proximate goal or target of the monastic life (its *scopos*) if he is to hope to make any progress to the overall end (*telos*), just as the farmer must take action to achieve the end of a good harvest. A sports coach might say the same to an athlete: dreams of Olympic gold medals are worth little if there is no diligence in application to daily training.

Aquinas likewise distinguishes two final causes of virtue: the *overall end* and the more proximate goal or *target*. Let us begin with the former.

The Overall End

Virtue's ultimate final cause for Aquinas is the overall end of the whole of human life (*finis communis totius humanae vitae*), which he identifies with beatitude (I.II 2 pr). The basis for this thesis lies in the first question of the *Treatise on Morals*, where Aquinas shows that a condition of the possibility of human action is that it not only be done for an end but for some overall end (1.1–6). Admittedly, virtuous action requires only "virtual," not "actual" intention toward the true end, just as a person walks home in virtue of a first intention, and need not be consciously thinking always of the destination (see 1.3 ad 3). Nevertheless, the virtues in this conception are qualities that ensure our lives go well as a whole by orienting us to the real, as opposed to the merely apparent or illusory, end of life. "True virtue simply so-called is that which orders to a human's principal good" (II.II 23.7).[5] Virtues are principles of the good human actions by which we arrive at our last end (I.II 6pr, 49pr). Aquinas's virtue theory therefore presupposes the final-causal orientation of good human actions whereby we journey toward the final end. As he explains, "It is of the rationale of virtue that it incline a human being to the good" (II.II 141.1).[6]

Virtue's telic orientation is clarified by the contrast between moral and merely technical rationality—that is, between prudence and art (I.II 21.2 ad 2). By the term "art" (*ars*) Aquinas refers to both the servile and the liberal arts (57.3 ad 3). The servile arts are ordered toward completely external works, and include farming, weaving, being a smith or carpenter, and even military and naval warfare; the liberal arts are more of the interior life and closer to the speculative virtues; they include grammar, rhetoric, dialectic, arithmetic, geometry, and music. Aquinas distinguishes the teleology of technical and moral reason, art and virtue, as follows: "Reason stands otherwise in matters of art than in morals. For in technical matters, reason is ordered to a particular end, which is something thought up by reason; in moral matters, however, reason is ordered to the overall end of human life" (21.2 ad 2).[7] Art aims at a limited or particular end or good, moral virtue at what is good all things considered. This is why a terrorist pilot who flies a plane into a building may have perfected the art of flying but has badly failed in the moral task of living well. For, "In moral matters, where the ordering of reason to the overall end of human life is what matters, sin and evil are understood by deviation from the order of reason to the overall end of human life" (21.2 ad 2).[8]

The Target

Besides seeing virtue as oriented to the overall end of human life, does Aquinas acknowledge a target of each specific virtue—that is, a *scopos* as well as a *telos*? There is no doubt that he does, as he refers to the moral virtues as disposing a person well to "those things that are for the end"—that is, the more particular ends that are further referred to the ultimate end (for example, I.II 65.3 ad 1; II.II 23.7). Aquinas gives few clues as to how he conceives of the particular ends of the moral virtues, so a certain amount of speculative reconstruction is therefore necessary.[9]

The distinction between target and overall end is clearest in his discussion of temperance (II.II 141.6 ad 2). Aquinas compares temperance with a builder. The builder's end in building a house is to earn a living. Aquinas calls this overall goal "the agent's end" (*finis operantis*). The purpose of the act of building, however, is to produce a house. He calls this more proximate end or target "the action's end" (*finis operis*). The target and overall end are linked: the builder earns his living by the hard work of building. As with Abbot Moses's farmer, it is necessary to focus on the *scopos* to achieve the *telos*.

Aquinas applies this same connection to temperance: "We should consider that sometimes the agent's end and the act's end are distinct, just as it is clear that the end of building is a house, but the end of the builder is sometimes money. Thus, therefore, the end and rule of temperance itself is beatitude, but of the thing that it uses, the end and rule is the necessity of this life" (141.6 ad 2).[10] All moral virtues aim at the overall end of beatitude (131.1 ad 2); what is distinctive about temperance is that its target, in its proper sphere of emotional attraction, is what is needed (rather than what is wanted). Temperate eating, for example, is guided by what is needed for health and social life, not by transitory peckishness.

Evidence that this distinction applies to all the virtues can be found if we think about the object again. The twofold object of virtue is the material object (matter-about-which) and the formal rationale of the object (the mode). The mode is the method or manner of achieving a good. The mode, therefore, seems to presuppose some good that is to be achieved in some matter rather than itself being fully constitutive of that good. We need a more substantive, rather than purely formal, account of that good. Does one moderate one's appetite and eating habits for physical health or psychological well-being, or is this virtue for some more social or even spiritual good?

It helps to think in terms of at least a threefold object: the material object, the formal object that is obtained, and the formal object by which it is obtained. Applying this to virtue's object, we should expect a threefold analysis:

(1) The material object: the objective matter of a virtue—that is, the actions, passions, and objects that the virtue concerns, considered as conformable, with some difficulty, to the rational good;

(2) The object *that*: the target good at stake, to which the virtue is directed;

(3) The object *by which*: the mode of achieving the target in regard to the material object.

Each virtue will have its objective matter, its target, and its characteristic mode by which the target is attained. For example, temperance is about the concupiscible appetite for pleasant things; its target is what meets the need of human life; its mode is moderation.

When it comes to specifying a particular virtue, how important is it to identify its twofold end (its target and the overall end)? When a habit is rightly ordered to the overall end of human life, then it is specified as a moral virtue, as distinct from a vice (which is oriented to a bad end), from an "art" (which is oriented to some particular good), or an intellectual virtue (which is oriented to some aspect of the true). However, the overall end does not distinguish one moral virtue from any other, since it is a common end that they all share. The proximate end or target, however, will be specific to each particular moral virtue. For, as Aquinas observes, it is the proximate end that determines the species of an act, and therefore of a habit (I.II 1.3 ad 3).

What about the theological virtues? Since their object is God Himself (62.2), there is no distinction between the target and the overall end of faith, hope, and charity; rather, there is only a single end and object, namely, God Himself. This helps to make sense of Aquinas's claim that the theological virtues concern the end itself, whereas the moral virtues concern those things that are for the end (65.3 ad 1). The moral virtues have as their target a good that is not fully constitutive of the overall end but is ordered toward it; the theological virtues, on the other hand, have as their target some aspect of the divine good itself. For God can be the direct target of virtue in three ways: as the first truth revealed by God (the target of faith), as our highest good attainable by the help of God (the target of hope), or as the highest good lovable by the love of friendship (the target of charity). Since the target of the theological virtues is God, who is the overall end of human life, in these virtues there is no distinction between target and end (between *scopos* and *telos*).

THE "GOOD USE" THESIS

Virtue's final cause is morally good operation, which in turn has a twofold final cause in its target and overall end. In the causal definition of virtue, Aquinas adds an important qualification to the idea that virtue's end is good operation:

> Since virtue is an operative habit, its end is operation itself. But we should note that, among operative habits, some are *always* towards something *bad*, for example, vicious habits; some however are *sometimes* towards a *good*, and *sometimes* towards something *bad*, just as opinion disposes oneself towards true and false; virtue, however, is a habit *always* disposing towards *good*. And therefore, to distinguish virtue from those habits disposing oneself sometimes towards good, sometimes to evil, [virtue] is said to be [a habit] "which no one uses badly." (I.II 55.4c)[11]

The telic orientation of virtue to good operation, Aquinas claims, is of a peculiarly strong form: virtue *always* disposes to good operation. This can be called the "good use" thesis.[12] Positively, it states that a virtue *always* inclines to its own good use or exercise—that is, to good and virtuous acts; negatively, it states that a virtue can *never* be used or exercised badly.[13] The good use thesis is a way of saying that the telic orientation to good operation is essential to virtue.

There are antecedents to the good use thesis in Aristotle.[14] Aquinas, however, draws especially Augustine's discussion of virtue in *On Free Choice of the Will* (I.II 55.4sc). Augustine derives the good use thesis from the idea that virtue by definition involves right reason: "For no one uses prudence or fortitude or temperance badly, since in all of these, as in justice ... right reason is active, without which there can be no virtues. But no one can use right reason badly."[15] Virtue, then, is unlike free will, which, though good and comes from God, can be used badly.[16]

It may be objected that a virtuous act could be used for a bad end, as when someone gives to the poor in order to look good. However, Aquinas would reject this: "The will cannot be called good if a bad intention is the cause of willing. For he who wants to give alms out of vainglory, wants what of itself is good under the aspect of bad, and, therefore, it is bad insofar as it is willed by him" (I.II 19.7 ad 2).[17] While the deed itself is materially an act of mercy, formally speaking it is an act of vanity. The vainglorious end vitiates the virtue of the act. In general, a good act with an otherwise good object done for a bad end is overall vicious since "good is caused from an integral cause" (18.4 ad 3).[18] Since both virtue's target and its overall end are good, its act will also be good, as having a good object and end.

It is necessary to obviate a possible misunderstanding. When Aquinas claims that virtue disposes *always* to good operation, is he committing himself to the idea that a virtuous person simply cannot sin? That would be an excessively strong claim, and one that Aquinas himself would reject. As he says, "A habit in the soul does not produce its operation from necessity, but someone uses it when he wills. So someone can decline to use a habit, or act contrary to its act, at the same time that the habit exists in him" (74.1c).[19] Terence Irwin sees a contradiction here: if virtuous people do not always act virtuously, virtue cannot always be inclined to the good.[20] Cajetan anticipates this objection and solves it. The objection confuses the strong telic orientation of virtue toward right use with determinism: "When it is said that a [virtuous] habit imparts . . . right use, this is not to be understood except in the way a habit by its nature imparts [right use]. For a habit does not impart goodness by forcing to it, nor by subjecting a power to itself so entirely, even immovably, that it cannot go to the opposite, but it does so in the manner of an inclination" (in I.II 56.3). Virtues infallibly *incline* to their own good use; in no way does it follow that they infallibly *guarantee* their own good use, since inclinations are not always followed. The kind do not always act kindly, and sometimes can fail to show kindness when they should or even on occasion act cruelly. The virtuous person's fallibility in acting virtuously shows that sometimes even the virtuous person acts out of character, not that she does not possess that character.

The Scope of the "Good Use" Thesis

To which virtues does the good use thesis apply? What is its scope? It is not clear that it applies to all virtues in an unqualified way.

The good use thesis has to do with the way virtue is directed toward a virtuous act as its end. However, Aquinas notes that there are two forms that this directedness to good operation can take:

> A habit may be ordered to a good act in two ways. In one way, insofar as someone acquires through a habit of this kind *a faculty for a good act.* (For example, someone has a faculty to speak rightly through the habit of grammar, but grammar

however, does not bring it about that a human always speak rightly, for a grammarian can barbarize or commit a solecism; and the same kind of thing applies in the
other arts and sciences.) In the second way, some habit not only produces a faculty
of acting, but even brings it about that someone *rightly use that faculty*. (Justice,
for example, not only brings it about that a human be ready of will to doing just
things, but even brings it about that he operate justly.) (I.II 56.3c, emphasis added)[21]

Thus Aquinas affirms that the intellectual virtues (sciences and arts) bestow on
a person the faculty (*facultas*) for a good act, whereas the moral virtues bestow
right use. The former, he says, are virtues only in a qualified sense (*virtutes
secundum quid*), whereas the latter are unqualified virtues (*virtutes simpliciter
dicta*) (ibid.). The division of virtue into unqualified and qualified is what is
termed an "analogical" rather than "univocal" division: the common genus
"virtue" does not survive equally in both members of the division but is more
perfectly found in unqualified than in qualified virtue (61.1c).

How does this distinction affect the good use thesis? Yves Simon and Philippa
Foot interpret Aquinas as saying that art, as a qualified virtue, does not confer
right use: for example, the grammarian can use her habit of grammar to perform
a grammatical error, whereas a morally virtuous person cannot use her justice
or temperance to perform an unjust or intemperate act.[22] However, consider
the more decisive treatment by the Salamancans.[23] Despite Aquinas's comments
about the grammarian barbarizing and committing solecisms, they point out
that he soon after claims that someone possessing an art cannot use that art
against the art: "When someone having an art produces a bad piece of work,
this is not the work of the art, indeed it is against the art, just as when someone
lies while knowing the truth, he says what is against, rather than in accord with,
his knowledge" (57.3 ad 1).[24] Therefore Aquinas would disagree with Foot and
Simon: one cannot use a habit of grammar to perform a grammatical error.

It is difficult to understand what Aquinas is saying. If an art cannot be used
against itself, how can grammarians sometimes commit solecisms and barba-
risms and pianists sometimes play the wrong notes? Those possessing art do
sometimes commit mistakes, after all. This is sometimes done unintentionally,
but sometimes, it would seem, done intentionally, as when a grammarian deliberately barbarizes.

To answer this question it helps to distinguish between three different kinds
of mistake or error that someone possessing an art can commit. First, there are
errors of non-use. A teacher of English writes an email to a friend and cannot
be bothered to ensure her sentences are grammatically correct. Such errors are
indeed against the art *but do not involve the use of the art*. This kind of error,
therefore, does not pose any conceptual challenge. When a person commits an
error of non-use, the art is not used badly, it is simply not used.

The second kind of error are *artful errors*. For example, a grammarian illustrates a barbarism or solecism for her students, or the comic pianist Les Dawson hits exactly the wrong note for comic effect. This kind of error, the artful error, appears to confirm the argument of Foot and Simon and presents a counterexample to Aquinas's claim that an art can never be used to produce a bad work. A grammarian can sin, grammatically speaking; a pianist can intentionally play the wrong the note. However, as the Salamancans point out, Aquinas elsewhere points out that to evaluate a work of art, technically speaking, is to ask whether the product conforms to the idea that the artisan intended to realize in reality (21.2 ad 2). Error or success in execution of art is defined by reference to the intended product. To illustrate, Aquinas makes the surprising observation that a sin or error proper to an art can be committed in one of two ways: by producing a bad work while intending to produce a good one or by *producing a good work while intending to produce a bad one* (21.2 ad 2). If the comic pianist were to accidentally hit the right note, that would not be due to his artfulness as a piano player; it would, strictly speaking, be an error.

It follows that, contrary to Foot and Simon, artful errors are not errors against art but rather are successful exercises of it. If a grammarian produces a barbarism or solecism for the instruction of her students, the so-called error is not something hidden within the artist's action. Rather, it is what is artfully aimed at by the artist's action. Materially it is an error, but formally it is exactly right and artful; the grammarian has in a sense made no error, but got things exactly right.

What sense, then, can be made of the claim that arts, as virtues only in a qualified sense, can be used badly? It would seem that any use of the habit of grammar is by definition grammatical and therefore correct. The solution comes when we note that there are also *moral errors*—that is, sins in their fullest sense. A person uses her grammar to blaspheme or detract from someone's good name in perfectly good English. The error here is not in the art itself but in the use of the art for a bad end. The reason that the good use thesis does not apply strictly to qualified virtues such as the arts and sciences is that they can be used badly, morally speaking. The good use thesis, therefore, applies strictly to unqualified virtue: only unqualified virtues, such as the moral virtues, prudence, and the theological virtues, cannot be used badly in any way.[25]

This leads to a problem about the causal definition of virtue. If the qualified virtues, such as the arts and sciences, are virtues in some sense, then the good use thesis must apply to them in some qualified way. The thesis is a definitional one: it says that something cannot count as a virtue unless it is always oriented to the good, and it cannot be used badly.

Cajetan offers the solution. He shows that there is indeed a weaker sense in which the good use thesis applies, even to the qualified virtues (in I.II 55.4,

57.3). In a qualified sense of "bad use," not even arts and sciences can be used badly, since they cannot be used to produce a work contrary to the goodness proper to those habits: artful errors are not really errors against art. In the unqualified sense, however, arts and sciences can be used badly, in the sense of what Cajetan calls a "bad extrinsic end"—for example, when a grammarian uses her grammar to form a grammatically correct blasphemy or unjust insult.

So the good use thesis does apply in a *qualified* sense to the *qualified* virtues, but in an *unqualified* sense to the *unqualified* virtues. For the qualified virtues (arts and sciences) always incline to their own good use by the technical goodness proper to those habits; the unqualified virtues incline to their own good use simply or morally speaking.

The deep reason that unqualified virtue inclines to morally right use, and cannot be used badly, is precisely because this kind of virtue has a necessary connection to a rightly ordered will. Aquinas argues that since it is the will that applies powers and habits to acts, their use is principally and primarily an act of the will; it is the prime mover, as it were, of any operation (I.II 16.1). The production of right use, Aquinas infers, "belongs only to those habits that are related to the appetitive part of the soul, since it is the appetitive power of the soul that produces the use of all powers and habits" (57.1c).[26]

This helps to clarify further the contrast between qualified and unqualified virtue. Qualified virtue can be perfect in its own domain, whether or not its possessor has a rightly ordered will (57.4). As Aquinas explains regarding art, "It does not pertain to the praise of an artisan, insofar as he is an artisan, with what will he does his work; but how excellent is the work which he does" (57.3).[27] However, unqualified virtue "requires rectitude of appetite, for this kind of virtue not only produces a capacity for acting well, but also causes the very use of a good work" (61.1c).[28] Unqualified virtue—that is, virtue always inclining to right use morally speaking—cannot exist without a rightly disposed will. Consequently, while we need virtue in order to use art well, virtue does not need yet another virtue to be used well since, by perfecting the inclination of the will, it inclines to its own good use (57.3; 61).

THE PROBLEM OF THE COURAGEOUS NAZI

Many virtue theorists seem to deny or qualify the good use thesis since they often concede that a virtue can be used for a bad end. For further clarification, then, it helps to explore Aquinas's thesis through a "test case" first raised by Peter Geach: the "courageous" Nazi. Geach asks a challenging question: Did the young Germans who adopted the Nazi cause wholeheartedly, and were ready to sacrifice their lives for it, possess the virtue of courage? Geach responds: "There can be no virtue in courage, in the facing of sudden danger or the endurance of affliction, if the cause for which this is done is worthless or positively vicious. . . . Endurance or defiance of danger in pursuance of a wrong end is not virtuous and in my book is not courageous either."[29] For Geach, the morally bad exercise or use of a habit is never in any sense virtuous.

Other authors have not been so convinced that the Nazi's courage is not a virtue. Is the Nazi's courage a virtue in any sense, given that it can be used for a bad end? We will examine four different ways of looking at the problem to see how well Aquinas's good use thesis survives.

Germinal Virtue

The first approach is offered by Alasdair MacIntyre. He asks us to consider: "What would be involved, what was in fact involved, in the moral re-education of such a Nazi."[30] Such a person would have to unlearn many vices and learn many virtues. However, "it is crucial that he would not have to unlearn or relearn what he knew about avoiding both cowardice and intemperate rashness in the face of harm and danger."[31] MacIntyre claims, then, that since the young Nazi would not have to acquire courage in his postwar moral reformation (although he would have to acquire justice and other virtues), he does possess courage even before his conversion.

MacIntyre makes a contribution: there is something in the Nazi's character that endures his moral reformation. Yet the Thomistic viewpoint would question MacIntyre's concept of courage as a virtue since it does not recognize any final cause beyond the object or target of persevering in the face of risk. Aquinas insists that the virtue of fortitude has an essential relation to its further overall end: "It belongs properly and in itself to the object of fortitude to withstand the dangers of death and to attack the enemy with danger *on account of the common good*" (II.II 2.5c, emphasis added).[32] Enduring dangers for no good reason is not virtuous. The Nazi's courage seems not to count as the moral virtue of fortitude, because it lacks telic orientation to an overall good end.

How, though, do we incorporate MacIntyre's positive contribution, that the "courage" of the young Nazi persists through his moral reformation? A Thomistic approach can do this through Aquinas's concept of germinal virtue (*inchoatio virtutis*).[33] Germinal virtue is incomplete virtue; it is an inclination that falls short of the full nature of virtue but has the potential to grow into it as a child becomes an adult. It may arise as a gift of nature or by habituation (I.II 65.1c). In either case, germinal virtue differs from complete virtue (*virtus perfecta*) in that the latter is directed and informed by prudence.[34]

Aquinas observes that a germinal virtue can be morally problematic:

> A natural inclination to the good of virtue is a germinal virtue but not a complete virtue. For an inclination of this kind can be more dangerous the stronger it is, unless right reason is joined to it, through which a right choice of those things which are fitting for a due end is made, just as a running horse, if it be blind, falls harder and is more badly injured the faster it runs. (58.4 ad 3).[35]

Germinal virtue is not unqualified virtue since, lacking prudential direction to a due end, it does not dispose to its own right use. However, the analogy with the blind horse's swiftness suggests that a germinal virtue not merely falls short of perfect virtue but that it can also be a kind of vice. Ordinarily swiftness in a horse is an excellence, but when this excellence is combined with blindness, the result is worse overall than if the blind horse were slow. Similarly, a germinal virtue, when combined with certain character deficiencies, may lead to a result that is worse overall than if it were absent.

Something similar seems to hold of the Nazi's courage. It does place a person "closer" to full virtue in the MacIntyrean sense, in that, as a germinal virtue, it can grow into full virtue. This is why the Nazi has less work to do in order to reach full virtue than if he lacked this trait: not that he possesses the virtue of courage simply speaking but that he has the germinal virtue of courage. However, when combined with his injustice, it has the especially toxic result of a man being prepared to give his life for an unjust cause. The germinal virtue of courage in the Nazi is "more dangerous," like the swiftness of a blind horse.

Secondary Actional Virtue

Gregory A. Trianosky offers an approach that contrasts with MacIntyre's. Trianosky distinguishes *primary actional virtues* that involve a concern or motivation to act rightly, such as justice, from *secondary actional virtues* that "enable us better to carry through on our good motives (or which perhaps serve to augment their force)."[36] Self-control and courage, as secondary actional virtues, are not virtues of good motivation and do not aim at any particular good result. Rather, they serve the primary actional virtues and enable us to act rightly.

Trianosky's secondary actional virtues are exceptions to the good use thesis since they can serve whatever projects a person happens to have, even if they are evil. Trianosky has no hesitation in stating that courage and self-control "seem to be traits which can actually enable bad people to do worse things."[37] For Trianosky this ability to do worse things does not mean that they are not really virtues; it merely shows that virtues can be "subverted by the company they keep"—namely, by defects of character with which they coexist.[38] The Nazi may possess courage and self-control, and in him they can be virtues, but in this case they make their possessor worse, not better.[39] This would be a shock to Aquinas (and Aristotle), for whom "a virtue is what makes its possessor good, and his work good" (I.II 56.1 arg 2).[40] Trianosky's secondary actional virtue can make a morally bad person worse and his work even more evil.

Trianosky does, however, offer a way of making sense of his paradoxical claim. He proposes an interesting analogy: "A virtue is a state, disposition, relation, or quality with a certain power. Being a virtue is like being an explosive. The gunpowder in a certain keg may still *be* an explosive even if due to its dampened condition it cannot now *operate as* an explosive."[41] For Trianosky the courage of the Nazi is like damp gunpowder: it is still a virtue, but it cannot operate as a virtue while the Nazi possesses his other defects of character. It retains its "normative power" to contribute to the overall moral worth of the possessor and to contribute to the goodness of his actions, even though it may fail in this instance to do so.

There is something helpful in Trianosky's analogy: it makes a similar point as Aquinas's example of the swiftness of the blind horse. What is missing from Trianosky's viewpoint, however, is an adequate final causal analysis of virtue. He says that self-control and courage are not primary or motivational virtues; rather, they are secondary actional virtues that serve whatever motivations the agent happens to have. Aquinas makes a somewhat similar point when he claims that temperance and fortitude are "preservative" rather than "productive" of the rational good (II.II 123.12). However, there is a distinction: they are preservative *of the rational good*, not simply of whatever goals the person happens to have. To throw one's life away for no good reason is not an act of virtue, "To tolerate death is not praiseworthy in itself, but only insofar as it is ordered to some good that consists in an act of virtue, for example, to faith and the love of God" (124.3c).[42] Fortitude is oriented to the immediate object or target of enduring risks (*finis operis*) but only as conducive to some good further end (*finis operantis*). Aquinas is correct, therefore, that a good overall end belongs "properly and in itself to the object of fortitude" (2.5c).[43] Fortitude, as an unqualified virtue, is not merely a "secondary actional virtue."

The State of Virtue

A third approach can be based on Aquinas and Cajetan. Trianosky is right to raise the question of the coexistence of virtues with vices. Following in biblical tradition, Aquinas distinguishes between a living faith and a lifeless faith, or between "formed" and "formless" faith (II.II 4.4). The former, on Aquinas's account, is a faith animated by charity; the latter is a faith that continues to exist in someone who has lost charity due to sin. Aquinas claims that since charity pertains to the will, and faith primarily is situated in the intellect, a faith that becomes lifeless due to the loss of charity will remain the same habit (ibid.). If it is the same habit, then is it still a virtue? Aquinas asserts that it is not:

> Unformed faith is not a virtue, because even if it has the perfection of a due act of informed faith on the side of the intellect, it does not however have a due perfection on the part of the will. In the same way also, if temperance were in the concupiscible, and prudence were not in the rational [power], temperance would not be a virtue, as we have already seen. For both an act of reason and an act of the concupiscible is required for an act of temperance, just as an act of the will as well as an act of the intellect is required for the act of faith. (4.5c)[44]

Formed faith is a virtue and unformed faith is not a virtue, yet formed faith and unformed faith are one and the same habit, just as formed and unformed temperance are one and the same. Is it a problem that Aquinas seems to be saying that *being a virtue* is accidental to the habits of faith and temperance?

Cajetan suggests a promising solution: while *being a virtue* is essential to the habits of faith and temperance, what is accidental is *being in the state of virtue,* and therefore being a virtue in the unqualified sense (in I.II 65.1 n.4). Unformed faith and temperance in any given person are indeed virtues, but the person is not in the state of virtue because of the absence of charity (in the case of faith) or prudence (in the case of temperance). Only a virtue in the state of virtue deserves to be called an unqualified virtue since only then is the good use thesis strictly verified in its regard: "It is necessary that virtue properly and simply so-called is a principle of a virtuous work simply, and not in a qualified way; whereas virtue not in the state of virtue does not produce such a work, because it is defective, insofar as deprived of its proper state." (Cajetan, ibid.) Cajetan interprets Aquinas's claim that unformed faith or temperance are not virtues by saying they have the essence of virtue but are not in the state of virtue, and hence are not virtues *in the unqualified sense.*

Cajetan's distinction between the essence and state of virtue is helpful. To paraphrase Trianosky, "Being a virtue is like being an explosive. The gunpowder in a certain keg may still *be* an explosive even if due to its dampened condition it is not now in the *state* of being an explosive, nor does it *operate* as an explosive." The idea makes sense on the supposition that the virtues, in their perfect form, are an interconnected whole (II.II 65). For example, one may be disposed to drink temperately and lack any immoderate desire for intoxicating drink, yet fail to be temperate because one easily gives in to peer pressure. So one cannot be temperate in an unqualified sense unless one has the relevant virtues of standing firm in the face of unwelcome peer pressure. Temperance can be helped, or subverted, by the company it keeps.

How might this Cajetanian perspective relate to the question of the courageous Nazi? Courage can count as a virtue in the state of virtue only if it is oriented to an overall good end as provided by a motivational virtue such as justice, formed faith, or charity. It is possible the Nazi possesses not merely the germinal virtue of courage but also the virtue of courage itself in its essence; however, due to its coexistence with his folly and injustice, the Nazi's courage does not exist in the state of virtue nor does it operate as a virtue.

If so, it is not merely that courage exists without justice but that in the young Nazi it coexists with injustice. His courage does not merely lack the state of virtue; it exists in him *in the state of vice* because, as Trianosky rightly points out, it makes him worse overall and makes his acts more evil. Like swiftness in a blind horse, courage in a Nazi makes him and his evil works still more vicious.

Counterfeit Virtue

There is a fourth possible approach to understanding the Nazi's courage. In his discussion of charity, Aquinas speaks of *counterfeit* virtue (*falsa similitudo virtutis*) (II.II 23.7). Counterfeit virtue is a candidate when it comes to categorizing the Nazi's courage. Eugene F. Rogers also claims that "the Nazi counterfeits courage."[45]

There is a basis for this claim in Aquinas's text (23.7). He says that simply true virtue (*simpliciter vera virtus*) is that which directs to the principal good and the ultimate end of human life. Virtue that directs to a limited good without order to the final and complete good will be true but incomplete (*vera virtus, sed imperfecta*). Virtue that directs to a merely apparent good will be *counterfeit* virtue. Aquinas points to the counterfeit virtue of the miser who devises cunning schemes for gain, avoids self-indulgence because of its expense, and goes through fire and water to avoid poverty. The reason why the miser's "prudence," "temperance," and "fortitude" are counterfeit is that they are oriented to the wrong overall end. It may be that since the Nazi's courage is ordered to an illusory final good, the Nazi cause, this courage is a counterfeit virtue.

The Nazi's Vicious Courage

So how should we describe the young Nazi's courage: as a germinal virtue, as a virtue existing in the state of vice, or as a counterfeit virtue? To answer this question we need to be clear about the difference between germinal virtue, virtue not in the state of virtue, and counterfeit virtue. The three are similar in that they all lack a fixed order toward a true good. However, counterfeit virtues have an *intrinsic* negative teleology in that they are essentially directed toward a particular bad end. The miser, after all, possesses only the false similitudes of prudence, temperance, and fortitude since the strong overriding goal is toward possessing money at all costs. These similitudes are, therefore, strictly vices. Both virtues existing in the state of vice and germinal virtues have an *indeterminate* teleology to serve good or bad ends. This is why they are not virtues in the unqualified sense, as they can be used badly: they fail to satisfy the good use thesis and therefore the strict causal definition of virtue.

Aquinas does not give us a way of reading into the soul of a thinly characterized fictional character. He and Cajetan do, nevertheless, offer a way of understanding the possibilities. Note, however, that in all three cases the courage of the young Nazi possesses a telic orientation to an unjust end. His courage therefore comes out either as a vice or as a virtue (germinal or otherwise) existing in the state of a vice. Either it is corrupt of itself or it is corrupted by the company it keeps. Unqualified virtue—virtue in the state of virtue—is always oriented to a good overall end. The final cause of virtue is the good.

NOTES

1. Compare Jacques Maritain, *An Introduction to the Basic Problems of Moral Philosophy* (Albany, NY: Magi, 1990), 94.

2. 55.4c: "Finis autem virtutis, cum sit habitus operativus, est ipsa operatio."

3. 71.1: "Id autem ad quod virtus ordinatur, est actus bonus."

4. John Cassian, "Conference I, with the Abbot Moses," in *Conlationes 23*, vol. 13, I: *Corpus Scriptorum Ecclesiasticorum Latinorum*, ed. Michael Petschenig (Vindobonae, Austria: Apud C. Geroldi filium, 1886), 8n2.

5. II.II 23.7: "virtus vera simpliciter est illa quae ordinat ad principale bonum hominis."

6. II.II 141.1: "de ratione virtutis est ut inclinet hominem ad bonum."

7. 21.2 ad 2: "ratio aliter se habet in artificialibus et aliter in moralibus. In artificialibus enim ratio ordinatur ad finem particularem, quod est aliquid per rationem excogitatum. In moralibus autem ordinatur ad finem communem totius humanae vitae."

8. 21.2 ad 2: "Sed in moralibus, ubi attenditur ordo rationis ad finem communem humanae vitae, good definition of ordo rationis semper peccatum et malum attenditur per deviationem ab ordine rationis ad finem communem humanae vitae."

9. Dominic Farrell, *The Ends of the Moral Virtues and the First Principles of Practical Reason in Thomas Aquinas* (Rome: Gregorian Biblical Bookshop, 2012), chap. 3.

10. 141.6 ad 2: "Considerandum est autem quod quandoque aliud est finis operantis, et aliud finis operis, sicut patet quod aedificationis finis est domus, sed aedificatoris finis quandoque est lucrum. Sic igitur temperantiae ipsius finis et regula est beatitudo, sed eius rei qua utitur, finis et regula est necessitas humanae vitae."

11. I.II 55.4c: "Finis autem virtutis, cum sit habitus operativus, est ipsa operatio. Sed notandum quod habituum operativorum aliqui sunt semper ad malum, sicut habitus vitiosi; aliqui vero quandoque ad bonum, et quandoque ad malum, sicut opinio se habet ad verum et ad falsum; virtus autem est habitus semper se habens ad bonum. Et ideo, ut discernatur virtus ab his quae semper se habent ad malum, dicitur, qua recte vivitur, ut autem discernatur ab his quae se habent quandoque ad bonum, quandoque ad malum, dicitur, qua nullus male utitur."

12. For statements of this thesis see I.II 55.4, 56.3, 57.1; 3 ad 1–2, 57.4, and 61.1. Chadwick Ray refers to it as the "no-bad-use thesis," which emphasizes the negative rather than the positive aspect. See Ray, "A Fact about the Virtues," *The Thomist* 54, no. 3 (1990): 429–51.

13. To clarify, Aquinas concedes that someone may badly use virtue *as an object*, for example, by taking undue pride in virtue, but he insists that one cannot badly use it *as the principle of a bad action*, since then the act of a virtue would itself be an evil; see I.II 55.4 ad 5, and compare *Super Sent.*, lib. 2 d. 27 q. 1 a. 2 ad 5.

14. Aristotle, *The Art of Rhetoric*, trans. Hugh Lawson-Tancred (London: Penguin, 1991), 69 [1355b].

15. *De Libero Arbitrio* II.18.50: "Nam neque prudentia neque fortitudine neque temperantia male quis utitur; etiam in his enim omnibus . . . recta ratio uiget, sine qua uirtutes esse non possunt. Recta autem ratione male tui nemo potest."

16. *De Libero Arbitrio* II.19.53.

17. I.II 19.7 ad 2: "voluntas non potest dici bona, si sit intentio mala causa volendi. Qui enim vult dare eleemosynam propter inanem gloriam consequendam, vult id quod de se est bonum, sub ratione mali, et ideo, prout est volitum ab ipso, est malum."

18. 18.4 ad 3: "bonum autem causatur ex integra causa."

19. 74.1c: "habitus in anima non ex necessitate producit suam operationem, sed homo utitur eo cum voluerit. Unde simul habitu in homine existente, potest non uti habitu aut agere contrarium actum. Et sic potest habens virtutem procedere ad actum peccati."

20. Terence Irwin, *The Development of Ethics: A Historical and Critical Study,* vol. 1: *From Socrates to the Reformation* (Oxford: Oxford University Press, 2007), 541.

21. I.II 56.3c: "Dupliciter autem habitus aliquis ordinatur ad bonum actum. Uno modo, inquantum per huiusmodi habitum acquiritur homini facultas ad bonum actum, sicut per habitum grammaticae habet homo facultatem recte loquendi. Non tamen grammatica facit ut homo semper recte loquatur, potest enim grammaticus barbarizare aut soloecismum facere. Et eadem ratio est in aliis scientiis et artibus. Alio modo, aliquis habitus non solum facit facultatem agendi, sed etiam facit quod aliquis recte facultate utatur, sicut iustitia non solum facit quod homo sit promptae voluntatis ad iusta operandum, sed etiam facit ut iuste operetur."

22. Philippa Foot, *Virtues and Vices and Other Essays in Moral Philosophy* (New York: Clarendon, 2002), 8–9; and Yves R. M. Simon, *The Definition of Moral Virtue* (New York: Fordham University Press, 1986), 69.

23. *Cursus Theologicus*, Tract. 12, *De Virtutibus*, in I.II 56.3, nn.1–2 (6:231–32).

24. 57.3 ad 1: "cum aliquis habens artem operatur malum artificium, hoc non est opus artis, immo est contra artem, sicut etiam cum aliquis sciens verum mentitur, hoc quod dicit non est secundum scientiam, sed contra scientiam."

25. There is an apparent exception in the case of (unformed) faith that arises from the fact that it is in the first place a speculative or intellectual virtue. See II.II 47.13 ad 1.

26. 57.1c: "pertinet solum ad illos habitus qui respiciunt partem appetitivam, eo quod vis appetitiva animae est quae facit uti omnibus potentiis et habitibus."

27. 57.3: "Non enim pertinet ad laudem artificis, inquantum artifex est, qua voluntate opus faciat; sed quale sit opus quod facit."

28. 61.1c: "quae requirit rectitudinem appetitus, huiusmodi enim virtus non solum facit facultatem bene agendi, sed ipsum etiam usum boni operis causat."

29. Peter Thomas Geach, *The Virtues*, Stanton Lectures 1973–74 (Cambridge: Cambridge University Press, 1977), 160.

30. Alasdair MacIntyre, *After Virtue*, 3rd ed. (Notre Dame, IN: University of Notre Dame Press, 2007), 180.

31. Ibid.

32. II.II 2.5c: "ad obiectum fortitudinis proprie et per se pertinet sustinere pericula mortis et aggredi hostes cum periculo propter bonum commune."

33. I.II 49.1 ad 3; 58.4 ad 3; 65.1, 2, 4; *On the Virtues* 1.8c.

34. When Aquinas refers to *virtus perfecta* it is not of virtue that lacks no degree of excellence but rather virtue that possesses all the components of virtue in the full sense, such as orientation to good use: *completa virtus,* as he sometimes calls it (*On the Virtues* 1.10 ad 1).

35. 58.4 ad 3: "naturalis inclinatio ad bonum virtutis, est quaedam inchoatio virtutis, non autem est virtus perfecta. Huiusmodi enim inclinatio, quanto est fortior, tanto potest esse periculosior, nisi recta ratio adiungatur, per quam fiat recta electio eorum quae conveniunt ad debitum finem, sicut equus currens, si sit caecus, tanto fortius impingit et laeditur, quanto fortius currit."

36. Gregory W. Trianosky, "Virtue, Action, and the Good Life: Toward a Theory of the Virtues," *Pacific Philosophical Quarterly* 68, no. 2 (June 1987): 128.

37. Ibid., 130.

38. Ibid.

39. Ibid., 132–33.

40. I.II 56.1 arg 2: "virtus est quae bonum facit habentem, et opus eius bonum reddit."

41. Trianosky, "Virtue, Action, and the Good Life," 132.

42. 124.3c: "tolerare mortem non est laudabile secundum se, sed solum secundum quod ordinatur ad aliquod bonum quod consistit in actu virtutis, puta ad fidem et dilectionem Dei."

43. 2.5c: "ad obiectum fortitudinis proprie et per se pertinet."

44. 4.5c: "Fides autem informis non est virtus, quia etsi habeat perfectionem debitam actus fidei informis ex parte intellectus, non tamen habet perfectionem debitam ex parte voluntatis. Sicut etiam si temperantia esset in concupiscibili et prudentia non esset in rationali, temperantia non esset virtus, ut supra dictum est, quia ad actum temperantiae requiritur et actus rationis et actus concupiscibilis, sicut ad actum fidei requiritur actus voluntatis et actus intellectus."

45. Eugene F. Rogers, "How the Virtues of an Interpreter Presuppose and Perfect Hermeneutics: The Case of Thomas Aquinas," *Journal of Religion* 76, no. 1 (January 1996): 77–78.

CHAPTER 10

Graced Virtue

Suggested reading: *Summa Theologiae* I.II 51, 52, 62, 63, 65.1–2; II.II 23.6–8, 47.11, 81.1; *On the Virtues* 1.8–11

When Aquinas finally comes to the last of virtue's causes—the efficient or agent cause—he corrects Peter Lombard's definition once again: "The efficient cause of infused virtue, about which the [Augustinian] definition is given, is God. This is why it is said, 'which God works in us without us.' If this particular element were taken out, the remainder of the definition would be common to all virtues, both acquired and infused" (I.II 55.4c).[1] In this dual recognition of virtue acquired by human action and virtue infused by God, we encounter the most controversial aspect of Aquinas's virtue theory. Is this another example of a harmonious synthesis of Aristotelian and Augustinian perspectives for which Aquinas is so well known, or is it not rather an undesirable dichotomy between human and divine agency? It is important to establish what Aquinas claims about virtue's efficient cause before proposing a rethinking of virtue's infusion; interpretation needs to precede critical evaluation.

It will help to clarify some terms. Aquinas initially acknowledges two ways efficient causation operates positively in regard to virtue: by *generating* or by *increasing* it (51 pr). To generate a virtue is to cause it to come into being; virtues already generated can then be augmented. Elsewhere Aquinas implies that moral virtue is not only generated and increased but also *maintained* in existence (53.3; 109.10c). Negatively, a virtue can be *decreased* or even go out of being altogether—that is, *corrupted*.

Aquinas distinguishes two ways in which a habit can increase: either *extensively* or *intensively* (51.2; 66.1; II.II 24.5). A habit increases extensively when it extends to more objects, as when a grammarian learns about some new aspect of grammar; a habit increases intensively when it is possessed more perfectly by its bearer, as when a person becomes still more temperate concerning matters she was already somewhat temperate about.

Aquinas unexpectedly claims a virtue by definition has maximum extension, and so cannot increase extensively (*On the Virtues* 1.11 ad 15). "Whoever has some virtue, for example, temperance, has this as regards all things to which temperance extends itself" (66.1).[2] This is not clearly convincing. If the nature of virtue as a maximum rules out extensive increase, it should also rule out intensive increase (an unacceptable result, which Aquinas himself rules out, since we can certainly become more just or temperate). The rejection of extensive increase also seems to run counter to experience: I may be temperate with most foods, but not salted peanuts; with time I may conquer this deficiency. The core question, however, is this: What brings about the generation, increase, and maintenance of a virtue? Let us begin with the human causes.

BECOMING VIRTUOUS THROUGH ACTION

Aquinas begins his discussion of virtue's efficient cause by asking, "Whether virtue is in us by nature?" (I.II 63.1; cf. *On the Virtues* 1.8). If virtue is in us by nature, there is no need of an efficient cause. Complete virtue (*virtus perfecta*) is not from nature; if it were, every human would be virtuous from birth. However, while virtue in its completed form is not *from* nature, it is nevertheless *according to* nature: "For, as the Philosopher says (*Physics* 7.17), 'virtue is a certain disposition of the perfect, where "perfect" refers to what is disposed according to nature'" (110.3c).[3]

We therefore naturally possess virtue only according to "germ" (*inchaotio*) (63.1, 65.1; *On the Virtues* 1.8). This germ of virtue in human nature is twofold: either it lies in the nature of the human species (in the natural inclination of the will toward the good, the natural obedience of the sensitive appetite to reason, and *synderesis*) or in the nature of an individual (in that one individual may have a temperament inclining her to one or another virtue).

If moral virtues are not in us by nature except germinally, how are they generated in us? The fundamental principle is this: "similar acts cause similar habits" (*similes actus similes habitus causant*) (52.3c). Just as a person becomes a good builder by frequently building well, and a person becomes a bad builder by frequently building badly, so we become just or temperate from doing just or temperate deeds. Human action can be the efficient cause of at least some virtues (63.2c).

Aquinas makes two qualifications to the claim that human action causes moral virtue. First, just as many drops of water are required to wear away the stone, many acts are required to cause moral virtue (52.3). This is evidently an experiential truth, but Aquinas wants to offer a fuller explanation. A virtue, like any operative habit, is a quasi-nature (56.5) because it gives a certain reliable inclination toward some one operation (justice toward just acts, temperance toward temperate acts, and so on). However, the appetitive power that moral virtue perfects is "inclined in diverse ways, to many things" (51.3).[4] This is why it takes many acts for reason to "conquer" the appetitive power and change it from being *ad multa* to *ad unum* (ibid.). Second, a virtue will increase by repeated action only if these acts are equal or greater in "intensity" (*intensio*) to that of the respective virtue (52.3). Intensity here is a technical term: it does not mean emotional intensity but rather the degree to which a form is possessed. A person does not grow further in virtue if she performs only marginally virtuous acts. The idea that virtue is acquired by habituation is, however, easily misunderstood.

Reasoned Habituation

Just as a habit does not incline to unthinking, nonvoluntary action, so neither can it be acquired by action of this kind. If a habit is a principle of human act (*actus humanus*), not the mere act of a human (*actus hominis*), then it can be acquired only by the former, not the latter. Since human action is deliberate action, reason and will are necessarily involved in the acquisition of moral virtue.

The role of reason is clarified if we examine what we may term "the problem of causal circularity." How can virtuous actions cause virtue if we are not already virtuous (*On the Virtues* 1.9 arg 13)? Aquinas's core solution is to distinguish two principles within the human soul. As long as the agent is conceived of as non-complex, there will remain the paradox of an agent causing itself to possess what it does not have. However, the paradox is dissolved if one of the principles (namely, reason) is characterized as active, emitting, more perfect, and forming, and the other principle (namely, the appetitive power) is characterized as passive, receiving, less perfect, and being formed. As Aquinas states, "An agent, insofar as it is acting, does not receive anything. But insofar as it acts having been moved by another, thus it receives something from the moving [cause], and it is in this way a habit is caused" (51.2 ad 1; cf. ad 2).[5]

For Aquinas, then, it is an incomplete account of the acquisition of moral virtue to say that virtue is acquired by acts. Rather, it is acquired by appetitive acts *as moved by reason*: "The virtue of man directed to the good that is measured according to the rule of human reason, can be caused by human acts, *insofar as acts of this kind proceed from reason*" (63.3, emphasis added).[6] Virtue is generated and increased only by reasoned habituation, not by mindless repetition.

Facility as the Sign of Virtue

Aquinas offers the following nuance to the claim that virtuous acts cause virtues:

> Virtue is generated from acts that are in some way virtuous and in some way not virtuous. For acts preceding virtue are indeed virtuous as far as *that which is done*, namely, insofar as a man does brave and just works; not, however, as regards *the manner of acting*. For, before an acquired habit of virtue, a man does not do the works of virtue in the manner in which a virtuous person acts, namely, promptly without hesitation, and delightedly without difficulty. (*On the Virtues* 1.9 ad 13, emphasis added)[7]

Even the nonvirtuous person can perform acts that are virtuous in *substance*; only the virtuous can perform acts that are virtuous also in *manner*. To act virtuously in the manner of virtue (*modus virtutis*) one must employ the four general modes of virtue: to act knowingly (prudence); to act from choice, not mere passion (temperance); to act for a due end (justice); and to act firmly and immovably (fortitude) (I.II 61.4 arg 3, ad 3; 96.3 ad 2; 100.9).

A person who lacks the habit of a virtue cannot yet perform virtuous acts in the manner of virtue, since the last condition presupposes the firm possession of the habit; she can, however, perform acts that are virtuous in substance or species in that they fulfil the other requirements—namely, acting prudently and choosing with an intention of a due end. A person becomes virtuous by actions that are virtuous in substance; once the virtue is acquired, the actions that flow from virtue are virtuous in manner as well as in substance.

The sign or mark of virtue (*signum virtutis*) is, therefore, that virtuous action is done delightedly and without difficulty and promptly and without hesitation (*On the Virtues* 1.9). This facility in virtuous action is a sign that the habit is possessed firmly and immovably.

Aquinas's account of how appetitive virtue is acquired by rational agency can be summarized as follows: Human nature contains certain "germs" of virtue: the naturally known principles of practical reason, the natural appetite of the will for the rational good, and the natural aptitude of the sensitive appetite to obey reason. Individuals also may possess inclinations of temperament toward specific virtues. Repetition of action according to reason is required to bring these germs to sprout into virtue. Through this reasoned habituation the form of reason impresses itself on the appetite, which thereby acquires a quasi-natural inclination to operate according to reason. The sign that such a second nature has been acquired is the facility of virtuous action.

BECOMING VIRTUOUS THROUGH GRACE

Aquinas claims that, in addition to virtues acquired through human agency, there are virtues "infused" by God. Here even questions of interpretation are contested.

The Idea of Infusion

Today we easily accept the idea that virtue is acquired by human effort, and we ask for explanation of how virtue can be infused by God. In Aquinas's day it was the other way around. As István P. Bejczy shows, the challenge for Aquinas and other thirteenth-century theologians was not so much to explain the category of infused virtue as that of acquired virtue, since to acknowledge true and complete virtue outside of grace was to risk the Pelagian heresy that eternal life can be merited by one's own unaided natural powers.[8]

What does it mean to say virtues are "infused" (*infunditur*) by God alone (I.II 62.1)? The image has scriptural roots.[9] Aquinas quotes the following texts: "The Lord fills him with the spirit of wisdom and understanding" (Ecclesiasticus 15:5); "She teaches sobriety and justice, prudence and virtue." (Wisdom 8:7); and "The love of God is poured forth in our hearts through the Holy Spirit, which is given to us" (Romans 5:5). Infusion, pouring out, inflowing, filling: these metaphorical terms with scriptural origins identify virtue as originating in God's free giving.

Aquinas also brings another terminology to hand, that of "divine virtue" (*virtus divina*) versus "human virtue" (*virtus humana*): "Human virtue, which disposes to an act fitting to human nature, is distinguished from divine or heroic virtue, which disposes to an act fitting to a certain superior nature" (54.3).[10] This latter distinction is based more on formal and final than efficient causality: human virtue corresponds to a nature oriented to natural happiness, while divine virtue corresponds to a nature ordered to the supernatural happiness of the next life. In the same way we might follow later Thomists and refer to "natural" versus "supernatural" virtue.[11] Natural virtues (not Aquinas's terminology) tend to beatitude within the natural order, whereas supernatural virtues tend to supernatural beatitude.

Infusion can also be understood in terms of the Augustinian definition: infused virtues are qualities God works in us "without us" (*sine nobis*). For Aquinas this part of the definition applies only to the infused virtues, not to acquired virtues (55.4c). The infused virtues "are infused by God alone" (62.1).[12]

This *sine nobis* clause is problematic. If God infuses virtue in us without us, are we entirely passive in its generation? Aquinas replies, "Infused virtue is caused in us by God without us acting, not however without us consenting. And thus we are to understand the words, 'which God works in us without us'" (55.4 ad 6).[13] Here is yet another qualification of Peter Lombard's definition. God works virtue in us without our acting (*sine nobis agentibus*) but not without us consenting (*non sine nobis consentientibus*). Elsewhere Aquinas insists, "In the infusion of charity, a motion of freewill is required" (II.II 24.10 ad 3).[14] Although God does not need our cooperation to infuse virtue, He also does not violently force it on us without our consent: virtue's infusion is noncoercive.

The contrast between the causes of acquired virtue and infused virtue should therefore not be overestimated. Just as infused virtue requires human consent, so does acquired virtue's generation have a divine cause: "A man can have no good unless God gives it; but certain [goods] are had from God without our cooperating (for example, those [virtues] which are infused), and some with us cooperating (for example, the acquired [virtues])."[15] *Both* infused *and* acquired virtue are caused by God; furthermore, *neither* infused *nor* acquired virtue are attained without free will. The difference lies in this: God causes acquired virtue through the medium of human action—that is, with our cooperation—whereas God causes infused virtue without the mediation of our action, although not without our consent.

Aquinas also explains virtue's infusion through the idea of habitual grace. He notes that Lombard thought that grace and virtue were the same in essence, although different in rationale (110.3). "Grace" signifies what makes a human pleasing to God (*gratum)* or what is given freely by God (*gratis*); "virtue" signifies what perfects for acting well. However, Aquinas insists on a real as well as a conceptual difference: grace is a habit in the essence of the soul, whereas virtue is in the powers of the soul (110.4c; cf. III 62.2c).[16] If grace perfects the essence of the soul, and virtue perfects the powers of the soul, then how are they related? Aquinas states: "Just as from the soul's essence flow its powers, the principles of deeds, so also from grace itself flow the virtues in the powers of the soul, by which powers are moved to act" (I.II 110.4 ad 1).[17] Grace is virtue's "principle and root" (110.3c and ad 3). Virtue's infusion, then, is its flowing from habitual grace.

Increasing Infused Virtues

If God alone generates infused virtues, is God alone likewise the cause of their increase? Like acts produce like habits, so it may seem that our actions can play a direct role here. Aquinas at one point says that "acts that are produced by an infused habit ... confirm a pre-existing habit" (I.II 51.4 ad 3).[18] He even goes so far as to say that a preexistent habit is "increased" by acts of infused virtue

(*On the Virtues* 1.10 ad 10). Yet Aquinas's full view seems to be that "charity and the other infused virtues are not increased actively by actions, but only dispositively and meritoriously" (*On the Virtues* 1.11 ad 14).[19] Actions increase virtue *actively* when they are the direct cause of increase, as with acquired virtue. What does Aquinas mean by actions increasing infused virtue *dispositively* and *meritoriously*?

By acts of charity we *merit* an increase in charity, Aquinas says, although it is only God who causes that increase (cf. II.II 24.6 ad 1). This is a way of preserving infused virtue as an unexacted gift. For human merit does not imply that God, morally speaking, has no choice but to reward: we cannot force God's hand. Rather, it implies that we become more fit to receive the gift through living well, also through God's gift.

What does it mean that charitable acts increase charity *dispositively*? The concept of dispositive causation comes from Avicenna. As Aquinas explains: "A disposing [cause], however, does not induce the ultimate form that perfects something, but only prepares the matter for that form; just as he who hews timbers and stones is said to make a house. This is not properly called an efficient [cause], since that which he makes is not a house except in potentiality."[20] Acts of infused virtue prepare us to receive an increase of them from their divine source, but they do not directly cause the virtue to increase (*On the Virtues* 1.11c). This is not to lapse into quietism: in his discussion of the increase of charity, Aquinas says that though acts of charity increase charity only dispositively, nevertheless a person may strive (*conetur*) to progress in this virtue (II.II 24.6). Yet God's action alone directly causes the increase. By performing acts of a virtue we may hew the timber but not build the house.

Aquinas asserts that it is necessary to restrict the causal role of habituation in the increase of infused virtue by assigning it only dispositive causality, in order to recognize the graced origin of infused virtue's increase: "Just as acquired virtues are increased by the acts through which they are caused, so the infused virtues are increased through the action of God, by which they are caused" (*On the Virtues* 1.11c).[21] God alone is the *per se* efficient cause of the increase, as well as the generation, of infused virtue.

Do Infused Virtues Exist?

Is there sound reason for positing infused virtues? Church teaching, both before and after Aquinas, is relevant to this question. In 1201 Pope Innocent III recognized three theological opinions on the infusion of the theological virtues at infant baptism, without adjudicating between them: first, since babies cannot consent, the virtues are not infused at baptism; second, although baptism forgives sins, no grace and hence no virtues are conferred; and third, the virtues are infused as habits, although infants are unable to exercise them until the age of discretion. Pope Clement V, at the Council of Vienne (1311–1312), saw the third opinion as the more probable opinion.[22] In the Decree on Justification, the Council of Trent states: "A human being, in the said justification, receives together with the remission of sins all these [gifts], namely, faith, hope and charity, infused together through Jesus Christ, to whom he is grafted."[23] John Poinsot argues on this basis that "the existence of infused virtues can in no way be denied, since it is evident from the Council of Trent."[24]

Aquinas's own primary argument is causal: "Because habits must be proportionate to that [end] to which man is disposed by them, therefore it is necessary that those habits disposing to such an end [that is, ultimate and complete beatitude] exceed the capacity of human nature [to produce]. Whence such habits can never exist in man except by divine infusion, just as is the case with all gratuitous virtues" (I.II 51.4; cf. 62.1, *On the Virtues* 1.10).[25] The *efficient* cause of virtue that directs us to the *final* cause of the vision of God can only be God Himself since there are no germs in our created nature that can germinate of themselves in a disposition to such an exalted end.

MORAL VIRTUE: INFUSED AND ACQUIRED

Having outlined Aquinas's account of virtue's efficient cause, we now turn to the problematic idea of infused *moral* virtue and its relationship to acquired moral virtue. For it is not merely that Aquinas recognizes faith, hope, and charity, the theological virtues infused by God, in addition to the acquired moral virtues (I.II 62.1). He also posits infused moral virtues. These are virtues at the service of the theological virtues in directing the whole of our lives to God (63.3). The interpretation of this category is contested.

The Necessity of Infused Moral Virtue

Aquinas argues for the necessity of this third kind of virtue by distinguishing its role from that of the theological and the acquired moral virtues. First, then, Aquinas resists the Augustinian view that the cardinal virtues are facets of charity (I.II 62.2 arg 3, ad 3). While the infused moral virtues derive their intrinsic finality to perfect beatitude from charity (65.2), they are distinct from the theological virtues: "The theological virtues sufficiently ordain us to a supernatural end, according to a certain germ, namely, to the extent [that they ordain us] immediately to God himself. But it is necessary that the soul be perfected through other infused virtues concerning other matters, in order, however, to God" (63 ad 3).[26] To be fully directed to God involves not merely relating to Him *immediately* but also *mediately*—that is, by living prudently, justly, bravely, and temperately in the ordinary moral matters of life for the sake of God and our supernatural beatitude in Him. We need the theological virtues to orient us directly to the supernatural end, whereas we need other virtues to order the means to that end, literally, "those things that are for the end" (*ea quae sunt ad finem*) (61.1 arg 2, ad 2; II.II 161.5). The infused moral virtues do not target God Himself (this is the role of the theological virtues); they do orient our more proximate aims to the ultimate aim of happiness with God.

It is important not to misinterpret Aquinas here. He is not saying that prudent, just, brave, and temperate action has value only as a mere means. Since the formal object of any moral virtue is always some particular species of moral goodness, its target always has some moral goodness or "honesty" (*honestas*). This target is no less a good in itself for being ordered to a further end. As the Salamancans put it: "The objects of the moral virtues are not related to the object of charity as 'means' properly and strictly so-called . . . but as ends intermediate to the ultimate end, in which, beside the goodness of an actual relation to the ultimate end itself, there exists a characteristic honesty and conformity of matter with the rule of reason."[27] Yet for Aquinas the infused moral virtues are distinct from the theological virtues because, while both share the same overall end, they differ in their matter and consequently their target. The theological virtues' target is God Himself; the target of infused moral virtues is the more proximate ends of the moral life. The two sets of virtue are therefore distinct.

Aquinas distinguishes infused moral virtue not only from theological but also from acquired moral virtue: the infused and acquired moral virtues "differ in species" (*differunt specie*) (I.II 63.4). It is not the efficient or material causes that account for the difference. It is possible that God miraculously infuses a human virtue (63.4 ad 3). Furthermore, the two kinds of moral virtue share the same matter. For example, "infused and acquired temperance agree in matter, for each is about the pleasurable things of touch" (*On the Virtues* 1.10 ad 8).[28] Aquinas's argument for specific difference is that a difference in final cause leads to a difference in formal cause.

For example, take temperance: "For infused temperance looks for the mean according to the reasons of the divine law, which are taken from order to the ultimate end; whereas acquired temperance takes the mean according to inferior reasons, in order to the good of the present life" (*On the Virtues* 1.10 ad 8).[29] Since the formal cause (mean or mode) indicates a way of achieving the good in a specific matter, a difference in final cause indicates a difference in formal cause: "For example, in the consumption of foods, the mode is established by human reason that one not harm the health of the body, nor impede the act of reason, whereas according to the rule of the divine law, it is required that 'a human castigate his body, and bring it into servitude' (1 Corinthians 9:27)" (I.II 63.4).[30] The supernatural motive leads to a more exacting standard for the restraint of temperance. As the Salamancans point out, then, "Many infused virtues have the same matter as the acquired, but they respect it under a different formal rationale, and from a distinct and supernatural motive."[31]

A key objection can be raised. The specification of an act or a habit is derived from its object or target (*finis operis*) rather than from its overall end (*finis operantis*). Why should a difference in ultimate end indicate a difference in species between acquired and infused moral virtues? Aquinas replies: "The ultimate end does not specify in morals except insofar as there is a due proportion to the ultimate end in the proximate end. For what is for the end must be proportioned to the end" (*On the Virtues* 1.10 ad 9).[32] While the overall end of a virtue does not directly distinguish it from other virtues, it does so indirectly, by influencing the virtue's target. The target is prudentially determined precisely by proportion to the ultimate end, so a difference in overall end leads to a difference in target and therefore in species.

Aquinas also argues from two kinds of citizenship: of the earthly city and of the heavenly city. Aristotle had noted that the citizens of different political systems will have different virtues insofar as the *telos* of each polis differs. Aquinas similarly contrasts the moral virtues required for the civil good versus those ordered to the good of eternal glory. Whereas the acquired moral virtues dispose us to be good citizens of the earthly city, the infused moral virtues dispose us to be "fellow-citizens with the saints, and [citizens] of the household of God (Ephesians 2:19)" (I.II 63.4; cf. *On the Virtues* 1.9).[33] Here again the infused moral virtues are needed because the life of grace introduces a new order of final causality into the life of virtue.

The Question of "Pagan Virtue"

How are infused moral virtue and acquired moral virtue related? Is it possible to possess one set of virtues without the other, or can they coexist within a single person? Aquinas thinks infused moral virtue can exist without its acquired counterpart (see chap. 11). First let us focus on the opposite question, whether acquired virtue can exist without infused virtue. This debate is currently conducted under the rubric of Aquinas's view of "pagan virtue," an unfortunate term, given that it is an inauspicious way for Christians to talk of the moral character non-Christians today, and is not Aquinas's own phrase.

There is evidence that, for Aquinas, acquired virtue without charity is a possibility, indeed a reality evidenced in the lives of some pagans or nonbelievers.

He claims that human (as opposed to divine) virtues can be caused in us by habituation: "A virtue of a human ordained to a good that is modified according to the rule of human reason, can be caused by human acts, insofar as acts of this kind proceed from reason, under whose power and rule such a good stands" (I.II 63.2).[34] He repeats this when he discusses whether moral virtues can exist without charity: "Moral virtues, insofar as they are operative of the good in order to some end that does not exceed the natural capacity of man, can be acquired through human works. And thus they can be acquired without charity, just as they were in many gentiles" (65.2).[35] Aquinas therefore seems to modify the strong Augustinian position, according to which the "virtue" of the pagans is not true virtue. As Brian Shanley comments, it is reasonable to suppose that when Aquinas says virtues can be caused by human acts, he is not referring to humans in the hypothetical state of "pure nature" but rather in the "existential state" of fallen nature: humans really can become virtuous by their natural agency.[36]

However, Aquinas quickly goes on to relativize acquired moral virtue in those lacking grace. Moral virtue is imperfect if it is not oriented to the supernatural end of human life: "Only infused virtues are perfect, and are virtues simply so called, for they ordain a human well to the ultimate end simply. Other virtues, however, namely the acquired virtues, are virtues in some way, not however simply, for they ordain a human well in respect of the ultimate end in some genus, not however in respect of the ultimate end simply" (65.2).[37] Acquired moral virtue, unlike infused moral virtue, is only virtue *in some way*. It is therefore imperfect virtue since it involves an orientation to the overall end of human life "in some genus"—that is, to the imperfect beatitude that is the ultimate end in the natural order.

Aquinas also seems to say that virtue in a person lacking charity and grace but oriented to a particular good, such as the good of the city, is true but imperfect virtue unless oriented to supernatural beatitude:

> True virtue simply [speaking] is that which orders to a human's principal good. . . . And in this sense there can be no true virtue without charity. But if virtue is taken insofar as it exists in order to some particular end, in this way it can be said that there is some virtue without charity, insofar as it is ordered to some particular good. . . . If, however, that particular good be a true good, for example, preservation of the city, or something of this kind, it will indeed be true virtue, but imperfect, unless it be referred to a final and perfect good. (II.II 23.7c)[38]

Once again, Aquinas seems to acknowledge that the virtue possessed by a pagan (and therefore acquired not through grace but human action) is truly virtue, albeit lacking in the perfection of virtues directed to a supernatural end.

Thomas M. Osborne Jr. claims that the acquired virtues as they exist in a person lacking the infused virtues are imperfect, not merely in the sense that they do not direct to the end simply speaking but also in the sense that they must exist in a state of disconnection from prudence. His Augustinian interpretation seems to reduce the pagan's virtue to mere germinal virtue: "Although Thomas thinks that pagans without charity can have true virtues, he does not think that they can lead morally virtuous lives. By 'true virtues' he means only habits or dispositions for performing good actions. Without charity someone can perform good actions, but he can never be good."[39] Osborne supports this viewpoint by showing that Aquinas, at least in his later writings, takes the Augustinian anti-Pelagian stance: in the state of fallen nature, human beings are morally deficient without the help of healing grace (e.g., I.II 109.4). In particular, while Gentiles can know through natural reason of the duty to love God above all, they cannot fulfil this obligation without supernatural assistance. Because of the effects of the fall, a person without grace can avoid any particular mortal sin but cannot avoid mortally sinning at some point (109.8).[40] So, while acquired virtue would have been possible in a state of pure or integral nature—perfect and connected within its own natural order—acquired virtue is not possible in the state of fallen nature without grace.

While Osborne refers to his view as the "traditional" view, it is notable that it is not the same as Cajetan's (in I.II 65.2; 63.3 n.2; in II.II 23.7). Cajetan worries that this kind of reading of the text will "excite laughter among the philosophers and the wise of this world" (in II.II 23.7). He insists, "In reality there can indeed be true virtues absolutely considered in a human without charity, and perfect with the perfection required for human virtue." Is this not a straight contradiction of Aquinas (I.II 65.2; II.II 4.7c, 23.7c)? Cajetan distinguishes the theologian's and the philosopher's perspective. For the theologian, who knows about supernatural beatitude, acquired virtue is "perfect in genus but not simply." In contrast, "The philosopher, who constitutes the good human in order to the natural ultimate end, and does not know the superior end, says that human virtues without faith and charity are true and perfect virtues simply." There is no contradiction here, Cajetan claims, because each correctly judges from within his own perspective and order: the one supernatural, the other natural. Because of a lack of charity, an act lacking due ordination to the ultimate end can still be *morally* good, even if it is not good *simply* (in II.II 23.7). Cajetan would say, against Osborne, that even a pagan without charity could be morally good, although not able to merit eternal life. Given that Aquinas expressly says that the acquired moral virtues existed in many Gentiles, Cajetan infers that this applies to humans in the state of fallen nature (in I.II 65.2). He further insists that, while Aquinas says a human cannot avoid mortal sin without grace, it still stands that he may have acquired virtues. A single act of mortal sin does not remove an acquired habit, and "there are certain mortal sins of another order from vices contrary to the acquired virtues, namely, that that are contrary to the precepts of the acts of the theological virtues" (in I.II 63.3 n.2). For Cajetan, then, a pagan can be morally good within the natural order.

In light of Henri de Lubac's famous criticism, theologians today will worry that Cajetan's viewpoint here reflects a "two-tier" theology that unduly separates nature from grace and philosophy from theology. Cajetan, so the argument goes, remains within the confines of an Aristotelian conception of nature and fails to acknowledge that, for Aquinas, there is a natural desire for supernatural beatitude.[41] There are not two ends of human life, a natural and supernatural one; there is only a supernatural one. Yet a more thoroughly theological argument defense of pagan virtue can be offered, as has been shown in detail by David Decosimo, for whom the acquired moral virtues, in their connected state, "were attained by pagans and are attainable by postlapsarian humanity."[42] Decosimo claims that Aquinas acknowledges and "welcomes" pagan virtue precisely for theological reasons. His ethics is a "work of charity" because Aquinas "*enacts* the very welcome of the pagan and his virtue that he commends."[43] Decosimo also entertains the thought (contra Osborne) that for Aquinas the pagan is capable of at least an imperfect form of the virtue of religion, which recognizes the need to worship the creator.[44]

We may once again be in the realm of "incommensurable readings" of Aquinas. Decosimo's argument that Aquinas is exercising charity in welcoming the virtues of "outsiders," and thereby recognizing the way God's goodness can be manifested outside the boundaries we construct, has much to recommend it. Aquinas's claim that the acquired moral virtues existed "in many gentiles," combined with his extended treatment of the acquisition of virtue by human action and his high regard for Aristotle and the other ancient philosophers, all argue in favor of a strong affirmation of the possibility of non-Christian virtue.

THE COEXISTENCE THESIS

Aquinas claims that infused and acquired moral virtue are not "connected": acquired moral virtues may exist without their infused counterparts, and vice versa. We now consider the possibility that both infused and acquired moral virtue can coexist in the same person. This possibility has recently been questioned. For example, William Mattison states forthrightly, "My thesis is that Christians cannot possess acquired cardinal virtues."[45] Can there be any prospect, then, for the integration of infused and acquired moral virtue in a single person?

Commanding and Eliciting

It helps to begin by considering the way Aquinas thinks that different virtues (and their acts) can inform each other. The metaphor of "command" is used by Aquinas to account for actions that express one virtue but are motivated by a different virtue. Take, for example, the virtue of religion (*religio*), the virtue of offering due reverence to God through sacrifice, adoration, and so on (II.II 81ff.).[46] Aquinas believes religion is a virtue directed toward God alone (I.II 81.1), yet he has to explain a scriptural text that apparently sees religion as expressed in acts of mercy or temperance: "Religion pure and undefiled in the face of God and the Father is this: to visit orphans and widows in their tribulation, and to keep oneself unstained from this world" (James 1:27; II.II 81.1 arg 1).[47] How can God-regarding religion be expressed in neighbor-regarding mercy and self-regarding temperance?

Aquinas's solution is to make a distinction between the acts a virtue "commands" through the medium of another virtue and the acts a virtue "elicits" of itself: "Nothing prevents the act that is proper to one virtue as eliciting, to be attributed to another virtue as commanding and ordaining it to its end" (II.II 32.1 ad 2).[48] The acts a virtue elicits are its proper and immediate acts (81.1 ad 1). That is, they are the acts it characteristically disposes a person toward (proper acts) and which it produces without the mediation of any other virtue (immediate acts). The acts a virtue commands are the acts it disposes a person to through the mediation of another virtue, by ordaining the elicited act of that virtue to its own end. Visiting the widow and the orphan is an act of the virtue of mercy as eliciting; if done not only to relieve the suffering but in so doing also to honor God, it is an act of religion as commanding (81.1 ad 1).

Some might object that to speak of one virtue as commanding another is to enter "homunculus territory," as though virtues could behave like agents themselves, commanding and obeying on their own. However, the metaphor is merely a way of saying that a single action may express one virtue and yet be motivated by another.

Causally, the relationship between commanding and eliciting virtue is one of form to matter. In the realm of moral acts and habits, the proximate final cause and the objective cause coincide since moral acts are specified by their targets (4.3). It follows that one habit's act has the potential to receive the form of another habit when performed for that habit's target: "For the act of one vice, as ordained to the end of another vice, receives its form: for example, someone who thieves in order to fornicate, is materially a thief, but formally intemperate" (*On the Virtues* 2.3).[49] What applies to vices also holds for virtues (81.1 ad 2; 85.3; 147.2 ad 2).

This form-matter relationship applies not only to the acts of the virtues but to the virtues themselves. We see this in Aquinas's explanation of his thesis that charity is the form of the virtues: "Through charity the acts of all the other virtues are ordained to the ultimate end. And therefore it gives the form to the acts of all the other virtues. And in this sense it is called the form of the virtues, for these are called 'virtues' in relation to formed acts" (23.8).[50] For example, a temperate person who loves God performs acts that receive the additional form of charity. Hence, just as an accident further perfects a substance, the commanding virtue (charity) informs the eliciting virtue (temperance).

Distinction and Union

The commanding-eliciting distinction helps to see how infused and acquired moral virtue may coexist in a unity by Aquinas's reckoning: the former are related to the latter as commanding virtues to eliciting virtues, and therefore as form to matter.

While the *intrinsic finality* of acquired moral virtue is toward some particular good, in the person with charity it acquires an *extrinsic finality* toward perfect beatitude, just as mercy has an intrinsic finality toward the good of one's neighbor but through the command of religion may acquire an extrinsic finality toward honoring God. Thus Aquinas says that virtue ordained to some particular good (rather than the universal good of perfect beatitude) is true virtue but imperfect, *unless it be referred to the final and perfect good* (I.II 23.7). Its orientation to ultimate end derives from the commanding virtue of charity.

Aquinas sees a hierarchical relationship of command, not just between, say, charity and prudence or justice and fortitude, but also between different kinds of prudence or fortitude. Aquinas notes that habits, as telic dispositions, are diversified in species according to diversity of ends (II.II 47.11). Thus he distinguishes three kinds of prudence: "One is prudence simply so-called, which is ordained to one's own good; another is domestic prudence, which is ordained to the common good of the household or family; and the third is political prudence, which is ordained to the common good of the city or kingdom" (ibid.).[51] Aquinas points out, however, that the individual's good is ordained to the political good (II.II 47.11 arg 3, ad 3). So there is also a relationship of command and obedience between the different kinds of prudence: "The habit that is ordained to the ultimate end is more principal, and commands the other habits" (47.11 ad 3).[52] Political prudence commands domestic prudence, which in turn commands self-regarding prudence.

Since the virtue ordained to the more ultimate end commands the other virtues, it makes sense that a prudence oriented not just to the common good of the earthly city but to God's kingdom itself is at the highest point of this hierarchy. If so, then the prudence ordained to the universal good of perfect beatitude commands all three forms of acquired prudence: infused moral virtue commands acquired moral virtue and perfects it as form perfects matter.

This picture is most strongly suggested by a text from *On the Virtues*. Aquinas raises an Occam's razor–like objection to positing the very existence of infused virtue: acquired moral virtue, when informed by grace, can be meritorious and therefore orient us to perfect beatitude without further need of infused virtue (1.10 arg 4). Aquinas replies:

> Since no merit may exist without charity, the act of acquired virtue cannot be meritorious without charity. However, with charity, the other virtues are infused at the same time; whence the act of acquired virtue cannot be meritorious unless by the mediation of infused virtue. For virtue ordained to an inferior end does not produce an act ordained to a superior end, unless by the mediation of a superior virtue, just as the fortitude that is the virtue of a human insofar as he is human does not ordain its act to the political good, unless by the mediation of the fortitude that is the virtue of a human insofar as he is a citizen. (*On the Virtues* 1.10 ad 4)[53]

A reasonable interpretation of this passage is that Aquinas envisages the possibility of charity making the act of acquired virtue meritorious by the mediation of infused (moral) virtue. He explains this in terms of superior (commanding) virtues ordering inferior (eliciting) virtues to their own end: the act of individual fortitude can be commanded by political fortitude and so be ordained to this higher, more universal good. Similarly, it is reasonable to infer that a fortitude ordained to the absolutely universal good (namely, God) would command both of these human fortitudes.

This view preserves the distinction between infused moral virtue and acquired moral virtue while unifying them in a single integral whole. The two virtues differ because of their *intrinsic finalities*. The acquired moral virtues are intrinsically oriented to particular goods, the infused moral virtues to perfect beatitude. However, under the command of the infused moral virtues their acquired counterparts acquire a new *extrinsic finality* to perfect beatitude. The infused moral virtues therefore perfect the acquired moral virtues just as form perfects matter: by raising their finality to a new level.

Differing Readings

William Mattison argues to the contrary: that the infused and acquired virtues cannot coexist in a person and that the virtuous Christian possesses only infused moral virtues. His argument is both interpretive and systematic. His first argument is based on the idea that the virtuous Christian has only one last end, namely supernatural beatitude. The acquired virtues are directed toward natural happiness as the last end. Since the Christian's last end is not natural happiness, for Mattison she cannot possess the acquired virtues, since that would corrupt her telic orientation toward supernatural beatitude as her only last end.[54]

Mattison's argument does not distinguish intrinsic and extrinsic finality. But because the intrinsic finality of the acquired virtues is toward natural happiness or some particular good, their extrinsic finality, in the person possessing charity and the infused moral virtues, is supernatural beatitude. The acquired virtues are indeed directed to natural happiness as the last end *in the person lacking grace*; but in the graced person this end becomes intermediate to the last end of supernatural beatitude. The end of natural beatitude is, after all, an end with its own goodness that can therefore be further oriented to supernatural beatitude. When Aquinas says that virtue oriented to a particular good will be true but imperfect virtue unless it is referred to the final and perfect good (II.II 27.3), it is natural to interpret him as saying that an acquired virtue can be referred to the final good as its extrinsic end by charity and the other infused virtues.

Mattison insists that "If an act is ordered toward supernatural happiness, it is no longer an act of an acquired cardinal virtue."[55] However, a single act can be expressive of a commanding as well as an eliciting virtue. There is no reason why an act ordered toward supernatural happiness cannot be an act of infused virtue as commanding and acquired virtue as eliciting. As Renée Mirkes explains, "In the Christian moral life, a perfect moral act directed to a single material object but performed from two ordered motives, natural and supernatural, is able to realize a created good that is a means to attaining the absolutely ultimate end."[56]

Mattison's second argument points out that the means of acquired and of infused moral virtue differ since they are based on two distinct rules, those of human reason and of divine wisdom. But then a Christian possessing both kinds of virtue "would have to perform actions concerning the very same activity based upon two distinct rules, namely, the rule of human reason and divine rule."[57] This argument unduly dichotomizes the twofold rule of the human will (*duplex regula*), which is not two rules but a single double-sided rule. Aquinas states: "Good and evil in human acts is considered according to whether the act is concordant with reason informed by divine law, whether naturally, or by doctrine, or by infusion."[58] Human reason has an "obediential potency" to being informed by divine reason. As we have seen, Aquinas thinks a prudence oriented to more encompassing goods can command the act of a prudence oriented to more particular goods, as when political prudence commands domestic or self-regarding prudence. In this case, Aquinas envisages no conflict in rule or mean. Similarly, when an acquired virtue is under the command of an infused virtue, there is no conflict in rule or mean. The mean of acquired moral virtue unconnected with infused virtue differs from the mean of infused moral virtue, but when it is connected to infused prudence informing acquired prudence it does not, due to its "obediential potency" to be conformed to a higher prudence.

In the *Commentary on the Sentences,* Aquinas argues for a difference of species between infused and acquired virtue: "Two forms of the same species cannot be in one subject. But infused virtue exists simultaneously with acquired virtue, as is clear in an adult who, having acquired virtue, comes to Baptism, and who receives the infused virtues not less than an infant."[59] Interpretively, this text has to be treated with some care, as it is one of his early texts and comes in a *sed contra.* Nevertheless, the argument is plausible. Baptism may wipe away sin but not virtue; an adult convert therefore does not lose the moral virtues acquired before faith any more than she loses the intellectual virtues. Christians may possess acquired moral virtues.

While this reading differs from Mattison's, I share his systematic concern that the Christian life is not split into distinct compartments of human agency and God's gracious action. It is necessary to turn, then, to the aspects of Aquinas's account of virtue's infusion that may need rethinking.

NOTES

1. I.II 55.4c: "Causa autem efficiens virtutis infusae, de qua definitio datur, Deus est. Propter quod dicitur, quam Deus in nobis sine nobis operatur. Quae quidem particula si auferatur, reliquum definitionis erit commune omnibus virtutibus, et acquisitis et infusis."

2. 66.1: "Quicumque autem habet aliquam virtutem, puta temperantiam, habet ipsam quantum ad omnia ad quae se temperantia extendit."

3. 110.3c: "Quia ut philosophus dicit, in VII Physic., virtus est quaedam dispositio perfecti, dico autem perfectum, quod est dispositum secundum naturam."

4. 51.3: "appetitiva potentia se habet diversimode et ad multa."

5. 51.2 ad 1: "agens, inquantum est agens, non recipit aliquid. Sed inquantum agit motum ab alio, sic recipit aliquid a movente, et sic causatur habitus."

6. 63.3: "Virtus igitur hominis ordinata ad bonum quod modificatur secundum regulam rationis humanae, potest ex actibus humanis causari, inquantum huiusmodi actus procedunt a ratione."

7. *On the Virtues* 1.9 ad 13: "virtus generatur ex actibus quodammodo virtuosis et quodammodo non virtuosis. Actus enim praecedentes virtutem, sunt quidem virtuosi quantum ad id quod agitur, in quantum scilicet homo agit fortia et iusta; non autem

quantum ad modum agendi: quia ante habitum virtutis acquisitum non agit homo opera virtutis eo modo quo virtuosus agit, scilicet prompte absque dubitatione et delectabiliter absque difficultate."

8. István Pieter Bejczy, "The Problem of Natural Virtue," in *Virtue and Ethics in the Twelfth Century*, ed. Richard Newhauser and István Pieter Bejczy (Leiden: Brill, 2005), 133–54; *The Cardinal Virtues in the Middle Ages: A Study in Moral Thought from the Fourth to the Fourteenth Century* (Leiden: Brill, 2011), 182–221.

9. I.II 51.4sc; 63.3sc; II.II 24.2sc; *On the Virtues* 1.10c. Renée Mirkes, "Aquinas on the Unity of Perfect Moral Virtue and Its Significance for the Nature-Grace Question" (PhD dissertation, Marquette University, 1995), 127.

10. 54.3: "virtus humana, quae disponit ad actum convenientem naturae humanae, distinguitur a divina virtute vel heroica, quae disponit ad actum convenientem cuidam superiori naturae."

11. John Harvey, "The Nature of the Infused Moral Virtues," in *Proceedings of the Tenth Annual Convention of the Catholic Theological Society of America* 10 (1955): 174–75. Aquinas uses the term "supernatural virtues" in I.II 63.3 arg 2.

12. 62.1: "a solo Deo nobis infunduntur."

13. 55.4 ad 6: "virtus infusa causatur in nobis a Deo sine nobis agentibus, non tamen sine nobis consentientibus. Et sic est intelligendum quod dicitur, quam Deus in nobis sine nobis operatur."

14. II.II 24.10 ad 3: "in infusione caritatis requiritur motus liberi arbitrii."

15. *Super Sent.*, lib. 3 d. 33 q. 1 a. 2 qc. 2 ad 1: "nullum bonum potest homo habere, nisi Deus det; sed quaedam habentur a Deo non cooperantibus nobis, sicut ea quae sunt infusa; et quaedam nobis cooperantibus, sicut acquisita."

16. On the distinction between the essence and the powers of the soul, see Pasnau, *Thomas Aquinas on Human Nature: A Philosophical Study of Summa Theologiae 1a, 75–89* (Cambridge: Cambridge University Press, 2002), 151–57.

17. I.II 110.4 ad 1: "sicut ab essentia animae effluunt eius potentiae, quae sunt operum principia; ita etiam ab ipsa gratia effluunt virtutes in potentias animae, per quas potentiae moventur ad actus."

18. I.II 51.4 ad 3: "actus qui producuntur ex habitu infuso . . . confirmant habitum praeexistentem."

19. *On the Virtues* 1.11 ad 14: "caritas et aliae virtutes infusae non augentur active ex actibus, sed tantum dispositive et meritorie."

20. *Comm. Metaph.*, lib. 5 l. 2 n.5: "Disponens autem quod non inducit ultimam formam perfectivam, sed tantummodo praeparat materiam ad formam; sicut ille, qui dolat ligna et lapides, dicitur domum facere. Et haec non proprie dicitur efficiens domus; quia id, quod ipse facit, non est domus nisi in potentiam."

21. *On the Virtues* 1.11c: "Unde sicut virtutes acquisitae augentur ex actibus per quos causantur, ita virtutes infusae augentur per actionem Dei, a quo causantur."

22. Florence Caffrey Bourg, "God Working in Us without Us? A Fresh Look at Formation of Virtue," Yamauchi Lecture Series, Loyola University, New Orleans, November 7, 2004, 9, http://cas.loyno.edu/sites/cas.loyno.edu/files/god-working-in-us-without-us.pdf.

23. *Conc. Trident.*, Sess. 6, cap. 7.

24. *Cursus Theologicus*, in I.II, Disp.16, Art.3.

25. I.II 51.4: "quia habitus oportet esse proportionatos ei ad quod homo disponitur secundum ipsos, ideo necesse est quod etiam habitus ad huiusmodi finem disponentes, excedant facultatem humanae naturae. Unde tales habitus nunquam possunt homini inesse nisi ex infusione divina, sicut est de omnibus gratuitis virtutibus."

26. 63 ad 3: "virtutes theologicae sufficienter nos ordinant in finem supernaturalem, secundum quandam inchoationem, quantum scilicet ad ipsum Deum immediate. Sed oportet quod per alias virtutes infusas perficiatur anima circa alias res, in ordine tamen ad Deum."

27. *Cursus Theologicus*, Tract. 12, *De Virtutibus*, Disp.3, Dub.1, n.15 (6:339–40).

28. *On the Virtues* 1.10 ad 8: "temperantia infusa et acquisita conveniunt in materia, utraque enim est circa delectabilia tactus."

29. *On the Virtues* 1.10 ad 8: "Nam temperantia infusa exquirit medium secundum rationes legis divinae, quae accipiuntur ex ordine ad ultimum finem; temperantia autem acquisita accipit medium secundum inferiores rationes, in ordine ad bonum praesentis vitae."

30. I.II 63.4: "Puta in sumptione ciborum, ratione humana modus statuitur ut non noceat valetudini corporis, nec impediat rationis actum, secundum autem regulam legis divinae, requiritur quod homo castiget corpus suum, et in servitutem redigat, per abstinentiam cibi et potus, et aliorum huiusmodi."

31. *Cursus Theologicus*, Tract. 13, *De Vitiis et Pecacatis*, Disp.1, Dub.2, n.10 (7:15).

32. *On the Virtues* 1.10 ad 9: "ultimus finis non dat speciem in moralibus nisi quatenus in fine proximo est debita proportio ad ultimum finem; oportet enim ea quae sunt ad finem, esse proportionata fini."

33. I.II 63.4: "cives sanctorum et domestici Dei."

34. I.II 63.2: "Virtus igitur hominis ordinata ad bonum quod modificatur secundum regulam rationis humanae, potest ex actibus humanis causari, inquantum huiusmodi actus procedunt a ratione, sub cuius potestate et regula tale bonum consistit."

35. 65.2: "virtutes morales prout sunt operativae boni in ordine ad finem qui non excedit facultatem naturalem hominis, possunt per opera humana acquiri. Et sic acquisitae sine caritate esse possunt, sicut fuerunt in multis gentilibus."

36. Brian J. Shanley, "Aquinas on Pagan Virtue," *The Thomist* 63, no. 4 (1999): 556.

37. 65.2: "virtutes infusae sunt perfectae, et simpliciter dicendae virtutes, quia bene ordinant hominem ad finem ultimum simpliciter. Aliae vero virtutes, scilicet acquisitae, sunt secundum quid virtutes, non autem simpliciter, ordinant enim hominem bene respectu finis ultimi in aliquo genere, non autem respectu finis ultimi simpliciter."

38. II.II 23.7c: "virtus vera simpliciter est illa quae ordinat ad principale bonum hominis, sicut etiam philosophus, in VII Physic., dicit quod virtus est dispositio perfecti ad optimum. Et sic nulla vera virtus potest esse sine caritate. Sed si accipiatur virtus secundum quod est in ordine ad aliquem finem particularem, sic potest aliqua virtus dici sine caritate, inquantum ordinatur ad aliquod particulare bonum. [. . .] Si vero illud bonum particulare sit verum bonum, puta conservatio civitatis vel aliquid huiusmodi, erit quidem vera virtus, sed imperfecta, nisi referatur ad finale et perfectum bonum."

39. Thomas M. Osborne Jr., "The Augustinianism of Thomas Aquinas's Moral Theory," *The Thomist* 67, no. 2 (2003): 301.

40. Ibid., 283–89.

41. Denis J. M. Bradley, *Aquinas on the Twofold Human Good: Reason and Human Happiness in Aquinas's Moral Science* (Washington, DC: Catholic University of America Press, 1997).

42. David Decosimo, *Ethics as a Work of Charity: Thomas Aquinas and Pagan Virtue* (Stanford, CA: Stanford University Press, 2014), 154.

43. Ibid., 253.

44. Ibid., 247–48.

45. William C. Mattison III, "Can Christians Possess the Acquired Cardinal Virtues?," *Theological Studies* 72, no. 3 (2011): 559. See also two works by Angela McKay Knobel: "Can Aquinas's Infused and Acquired Virtues Coexist in the Christian Life?," *Studies in Christian Ethics* 23, no. 4 (2010): 381; and "Relating Aquinas's Infused and Acquired Virtues: Some Problematic Texts for a Common Interpretation," *Nova et Vetera (English Edition)* 9, no. 2 (Spring 2011): 411–31.

46. For an account of this virtue see Nicholas Austin, "Thomas Aquinas on the Virtue of Religion," in *"Ahme Nach, Was Du Vollziehst" Positionsbestimmungen Zum Verhältnis von Liturgie Und Ethik*, ed. Martin Stuflesser and Stephan Winter (Regensburg: Pustet, 2009), 85–99.

47. II.II 81.1 arg 1: "religio munda et immaculata apud Deum et patrem haec est, visitare pupillos et viduas in tribulatione eorum, et immaculatum se custodire ab hoc saeculo."

48. II.II 32.1 ad 2: "nihil prohibet actum qui est proprie unius virtutis elicitive, attribui alteri virtuti sicut imperanti et ordinanti ad suum finem."

49. *On the Virtues* 2.3: "Actus enim unius vitii, secundum quod ordinatur ad finem alterius vitii, recipit formam eius; utpote qui furatur ut fornicetur, materialiter quidem fur est, formaliter vero intemperatus."

50. 23.8: "per caritatem ordinantur actus omnium aliarum virtutum ad ultimum finem. Et secundum hoc ipsa dat formam actibus omnium aliarum virtutum. Et pro tanto dicitur esse forma virtutum, nam et ipsae virtutes dicuntur in ordine ad actus formatos." For more on the development in Aquinas's thought about how to explain charity as the form of the virtues see Michael S. Sherwin, *By Knowledge and By Love: Charity and Knowledge in the Moral Theology of St. Thomas Aquinas* (Washington, DC: Catholic University of America Press, 2005), 192–202.

51. II.II 47.11: "una sit prudentia simpliciter dicta, quae ordinatur ad bonum proprium; alia autem oeconomica, quae ordinatur ad bonum commune domus vel familiae; et tertia politica, quae ordinatur ad bonum commune civitatis vel regni."

52. 47.11 ad 3: "habitus qui ordinatur ad finem ultimum sit principalior, et imperet aliis habitibus."

53. *On the Virtues* 1.10 ad 4: "cum nullum meritum sit sine caritate, actus virtutis acquisitae, non potest esse meritorius sine caritate. Cum caritate autem simul infunduntur aliae virtutes; unde actus virtutis acquisitae non potest esse meritorius nisi mediante virtute infusa. Nam virtus ordinata in finem inferiorem non facit actus ordinatum ad

finem superiorem, nisi mediante virtute superiori; sicut fortitudo, quae est virtus hominis qua homo, non ordinat actum suum ad bonum politicum, nisi mediante fortitudine
quae est virtus hominis in quantum est civis."

54. Mattison, "Can Christians Possess?," 560–65.

55. Ibid., 568.

56. Renée Mirkes, "Aquinas on the Unity," 204.

57. Mattison, "Can Christians Possess?," 565–66.

58. *De Malo* 2.4c: "bonum et malum in actibus humanis consideratur secundum
quod actus concordat rationi informatae lege divina, vel naturaliter, vel per doctrinam,
vel per infusionem."

59. *Super Sent.* lib. 3 d. 33 q. 1 a. 2 qc. 4 s.c. 2:"duae formae ejusdem speciei non
possunt esse in uno subjecto. Sed virtus infusa est simul cum virtute acquisita, ut patet
in adulto qui habens virtutem acquisitam ad Baptismum accedit, qui non minus recipit
de infusis quam puer."

CHAPTER 11

Rethinking Infusion

Suggested reading: *Summa Theologiae* I.II 5.5, 65.3,
68.1, 110.2; II.II 24.6, 24.12; III 62.1, 69.6.

Virtue's infusion by God is integral to Aquinas's theological ethics and is, in light of contemporary virtue theories, something distinctive and surprising. For some the infusion of virtue promises a welcome paradigm shift in virtue theory; for others the idea is disconcertingly problematic. An attempt will be made to do justice to both intuitions by identifying a core idea to be valued and associated ideas that today need critical examination. A causal approach can help in the rethinking of theological controversies that have, in the Thomistic tradition, proved remarkably resistant to resolution.

INFUSION AS GIFT

"Infusion" (*infusio*) is a useful metaphor, but a limited one. The image is of pouring liquid into a container.[1] Bernard of Clairvaux uses the idea to contrast the way a good angel can urge us to good things but only God can directly produce good things in us: "The Angel is in us, suggesting good things to us, but not placing them in [the soul]. It is in us, encouraging us to the good, not creating the good. God is in us in such a way that He affects [the soul], and infuses it [with what is good]. Or, rather, He Himself is infused and makes it participate in Himself."[2] The metaphor succeeds in conveying the idea that virtues are sheer gift from God; in other respects it is a limited image, as virtue is not much like a pourable liquid.

That gifting is at the heart of Aquinas's idea is confirmed by his attempt to distinguish the seven "gifts" of the Holy Spirit from the moral and theological virtues (I.II 68.1; see also 55 pr). Aquinas finds this in the Vulgate Bible: "And the spirit of the Lord will rest on him: the spirit of wisdom and understanding, the spirit of counsel and fortitude, the spirit of knowledge and piety. And he shall be filled with the fear of the Lord" (Isaiah 11:1–2). The Latin Fathers, such as Augustine of Hippo and Pope Gregory the Great, saw these seven "gifts" or "spirits" or "virtues" as special qualities given to Christ and the Church's members by the Holy Spirit.

Although sharing names with some of the virtues, Aquinas distinguishes the gifts from the moral, intellectual, and theological virtues. How to accomplish this? It is not enough to say that the "gifts" are given freely by God, whereas the virtues are not: "Nothing prohibits that which arises from another as a gift to be perfective of someone for acting well, especially since, as we have seen, certain virtues are infused in us from God. Whence, employing this method, gift cannot be distinguished from virtue" (I.II 68.1c).[3] The term "gift" refers to the causal origin of something. The gifts of the Holy Spirit are gifts, but then so are the infused moral and theological virtues. Perhaps the only reason Aquinas customarily uses the language of "infused" virtues rather than "gifted" virtues is simply that he does not want to confuse the theological and moral virtues with the seven gifts found in the Book of Isaiah.

Aquinas does sometimes refer to supernatural virtue as gifted virtue (*virtus gratuita*), and he talks of gifted prudence, fortitude, temperance, hope, and charity.[4] *Gratuita* is contrasted with *naturalia* (the natural) to refer to the sheer gift of what comes with supernatural grace, without denying that even natural things are gifts of God's love. For, "All gifts, both natural and gratuitous, are given to us by God through love, which is the first gift."[5] The core insight of the idea of virtue's infusion is simply that the virtues that lead us to God are themselves free gifts of a gracious God. Infused virtue is gifted virtue.

Aquinas observes that a person's excellence "he does not have from himself, but this is, as it were, something divinely inspired in him. And therefore, for this reason, the honor is due principally, not to him, but God" (II.II 131.1).[6] To view God, not our own effort, as virtue's origin effects a welcome Copernican revolution. As Robert Adams observes, "We may well have a richer as well as less self-centered view of virtue if we regard it largely as a gift."[7] The recognition of virtue as primarily gift is a decentering one, assigning praise to the divine source of all that is good in us.

The Augustinian interpretation of Aquinas acknowledges a genuine paradigm shift from Aristotle. According to Alasdair MacIntyre, Aquinas's recognition that we are *dependent* rational animals contrasts sharply with Aristotle's ideal of self-sufficiency. This contrast is especially noteworthy, as MacIntyre suggests, when Aquinas's ethical vision is compared to Aristotle's "magnanimous man."[8] Aquinas does not reject magnanimity as a virtue; nevertheless, his own account puts Aristotle into dialectical tension with Christian humility (II.II 129, 3 arg 4, ad 4; 161.1; 2 arg 3, ad 3; 4 arg 3, ad 3). This means that Aquinas must do some creative accounting to reconcile Aristotle's claim that the magnanimous man "needs nothing" with an anthropology that recognizes not only relationality but even dependence as part of what it means to be human: "For every human, in the first place indeed, needs divine help, but secondly, even human help, because a human is naturally a social animal, since he is not sufficient of himself for life" (II.II 129.6 ad 1).[9] The paradigm shift is masked only by Aquinas's charitable mode of interpretation that refuses to contradict Aristotle outright. Aquinas saves Aristotle's text by distinguishing between an unhelpful neediness from which the virtuous are free, and the need that every human—including the virtuous—has of divine and human help (*auxilium*). A human needs divine help "in the first place indeed" (*primo quidem*). Within this new paradigm we cannot attain the end without ongoing divine help (I.II 5.5), and the virtues that lead us to this end depend on God's ongoing giving as the illumination of the air depends on the sun (II.II 24.12c).

FACILITY

While the core idea of virtue's infusion, that the supernatural virtues are gifts from God, is theologically indispensable, associated claims in Aquinas's account are worthy of critical examination. The first is the idea that the infusion of moral virtue does not confer the same kind of facility as acquired moral virtue bestows. Since the exercise of virtue is characterized by ease, delight, and promptness, facility in virtuous action is therefore the sign of virtue (*signum virtutis*) in that indicates that it is performed from a well-rooted habit. This is not merely a philosophical claim. The graced life of Christian existence should be characterized by a sweetness and promptness in performing those actions that lead to eternal beatitude (I.II 110.2). Indeed, it is axiomatic for Aquinas that "it is not fitting that God should provide less for those he loves that they may possess the supernatural good, than for creatures whom he loves that they possess a natural good" (110.2).[10] It would be incongruous if God had so arranged things that the joy characteristic of natural virtue is lacking in supernatural virtue.

The claim that infused moral virtue does not confer facility in the same way as acquired virtue arises from an empirical observation combined with a thesis about virtue. The empirical evidence is that the newly converted often find it difficult and painful to act prudently, justly, bravely, or temperately even when they succeed in doing so; the thesis is that the moral virtues are infused along with grace at the moment of baptism. It follows from these that it can be difficult and painful to exercise infused moral virtue (65.3 ad 2; *On the Virtues* 1.10 ad 14–16).[11]

Michael S. Sherwin helpfully illustrates the idea with the case of Matthew Talbot, an Irish laborer and alcoholic who underwent a conversion, gave up drink, and dedicated his life to prayer and service of the poor.[12] While he "radically reoriented his life towards God," it remained true that "he still retained, especially in the beginning, a strong desire (and inclination) to continue drinking and to return to his former way of life."[13] In Aquinas's viewpoint, Sherwin suggests, Talbot has the infused virtue of temperance but finds it difficult to act temperately.

Aquinas therefore seems caught in a bind. If new converts find morally virtuous action difficult, and moral virtues are infused with grace, then either we question virtue's infusion at baptism or we have to account for the anomaly of moral virtues that lack the facility ordinarily characteristic of virtue:

> He who has virtue, does the works of virtue with facility, and they are pleasing to him for their own sake, whence also "the sign of a habit is the delight that arises in the work," as is said in the *Nicomachean Ethics* II. But many have charity, free from mortal sin, who nevertheless suffer difficulty in the works of the virtues, nor are these works pleasing to them for their own sake, but only insofar as they are referred to charity. (I.II 65.3 arg 2)[14]

Aquinas replies that the infused moral virtues do possess a facility, but of a different kind. Let us examine his account in his three major theological treatments of virtue.

The fundamental position is laid down in the *Commentary on the Sentences*, where Aquinas distinguishes two kinds of facility that we may term *habituated facility* and *agonistic facility*.[15] Habituated facility arises from preceding habit or custom; it is characteristic of acquired moral virtue. Agonistic facility belongs to infused moral virtue from its generation; it arises from a strong attachment to virtue's object. For Aquinas the latter kind of facility is compatible with difficulty in acting virtuously due to the hangover from a previous life of sin—that is, the "habits of vices" that have been impeded or diminished but not totally taken away.[16] This is "agonistic" facility because it involves countering strong contrary dispositions.

The two types of facility can be illustrated by adapting an example proposed by Louis Billot (1846–1931):[17] Bob finds it difficult to take his cholesterol medication because he is not yet accustomed to it, but he does so reliably because of his intense desire to avoid a heart attack. Bill, on the other hand, is used to the same medication regime and because it has become easy for him, he reliably keeps to it, although having a less intense desire to be well than Bob. The two men have contrasting kinds of facility in obeying their doctors' instructions: the first arises from a strong adherence to good health, the second simply from the accustomed ease with which medication is taken. Bob's facility is analogous to the agonistic facility of infused moral virtue, whereas Bill's corresponds to the habituated facility of acquired moral virtue. In the case of Matt Talbot, Sherwin suggests, "At the moment of his conversion, the infused virtues empowered him to live soberly, even as he continued to feel a burning desire to drink."[18]

In *On the Virtues* Aquinas defends this viewpoint by observing that there is at least one case of virtuous operation that is not delightful—namely, brave action (1.10 ad 15). If it is not necessarily delightful to act from fortitude when risking one's life on the battlefield, for example, then surely the lack of delight in acting according to newly infused virtue is not contrary to virtue's nature. In the *Summa Theologiae* Aquinas points out that often someone may possess a habit and yet not experience delight and complacency in its act due to an extrinsic obstacle (I.II 65.3 ad 2). A scientist may have difficulty in understanding because he is sleepy or physically sick. Aquinas concludes, "And similarly, the habits of infused moral virtues sometimes suffer difficulty in operating, due to certain contrary dispositions remaining from preceding acts."[19]

The analogies Aquinas offers to demonstrate that agonistic facility is sufficient for virtue are not convincing. The exercise of fortitude lacks delight because of an external threat it is virtuous to fear: the danger of injury or death. In contrast, the obstacle to enjoyment in exercising newly generated infused virtue is an acquired interior disposition contrary to virtue (65.3 ad 2). Similarly, sleepiness or sickness is, as Aquinas notes, a supervenient external impediment (ibid.); the inclination to sin, on the other hand, is something disordered within a person's soul. It does not make obvious sense to say that one has a virtue while suffering strong interior inclinations in the opposite direction. The ascription of agonistic facility to temperance is especially problematic: temperance collapses into continence, or the ability to act virtuously despite strong appetitive inclinations to the contrary.

Aquinas's distinction between the agonistic facility proper to newly infused moral virtue and the habitual facility proper to acquired virtue is unhelpful. Since facility involving promptness, ease, and joy is the sign of virtue, the lack of such facility in the new convert is not a sign that infused moral virtue lacks such facility. Rather, it is a sign that she does not possess infused virtue in its complete form. If a person finds difficulty and pain in exercising moral virtue, then, lacking that facility (the sign of virtue), it is more reasonable to conclude she is not yet, simply speaking, morally virtuous. In the case of Matt Talbot, it is more plausible to say not that he possesses infused temperance yet still experiences the inclination to sin but rather that he possesses continence or self-control.

GRADUALNESS

The problem of facility indicates the need for a more developmental perspective. Aquinas, however, claims that the supernatural virtues are all infused simultaneously with the grace of justification at the moment of repentance, which "opens the door to the virtues" (III 85.6 ad 3).[20] Referring to faith, hope, and charity, Aquinas says, "[These] habits are infused at the same time" (*habitus simul infunduntur*) (I.II 62.4c). Nor is this a matter of the theological virtues alone: "The moral virtues are infused simultaneously with charity" (65.3).[21] For Aquinas the normal locus for the infusion of the virtues is baptism: "By Baptism, a person receives grace and the virtues" (III 69.4).[22]

Why is it necessary that all the virtues be infused simultaneously? Aquinas argues: "Charity is generated simultaneously with the other virtues, not because it is indistinguishable from them, but because the works of God are perfect. Hence, when charity is infused, he infuses all those things that are necessary for salvation" (*On the Virtues* 2.5 ad 11).[23] To say that God does not give all the virtues simultaneously would be a slight on the perfection and love of God.

Aquinas recognizes that the simultaneity thesis is difficult to reconcile with human experience. There is the case of the new convert who finds it difficult to act virtuously. Another apparent counterexample is the newly baptized infant, who has grace yet is unable to exercise prudence (II.II 47.14 arg 3). Aquinas concedes that the infant will lack acquired prudence since she lacks the requisite experience, time, and opportunity for exercise. He claims, however, that since the virtues flow from grace, baptized infants do possess infused prudence, at least in habit if not in act (*secundum habitum, sed non secundum actum*) (ad 3). Elsewhere, he explains this view as follows:

> Some of the ancients thought that infants were not given grace and the virtues in Baptism. . . . The reason for their error was that they did not know how to distinguish between habit and act. And so, seeing infants incapable of acts of the virtues, they believed that they have no virtues at all after Baptism. But this impotency of operating does not happen to infants because of the lack of habits, but from a bodily impediment, just as people sleeping, although they may have the habits of virtues, are nevertheless impeded from acts because of sleep. (III 69.6c)[24]

The distinction between possessing a virtue *in habit* and having it *in act* does make sense. A person who is sleeping has no opportunity to exercise her virtue but would characteristically do so if awake and the opportunity presented itself. However, Aquinas's comparison with the sleeping adult is unconvincing since the "impediment" to acting virtuously is much more fundamental for a baby than for an adult.[25] To say that a baby possesses prudence in habit rather than in act is to imply the baby *would* characteristically exercise prudence under certain circumstances. But in what circumstances *could* a baby do so? Presumably only in circumstances in which it ceases to be a baby and acquires a different set of capabilities.

Does nothing change with baptism? A newly baptized baby is now explicitly part of the Christian community that mediates God's grace and so is on the path toward infused virtue. Or the baby possesses virtue *in germ* rather than *in habit*. (On the idea of germinal virtue, see chap. 9.) Something similar could be said of the newly converted Christian: Matt Talbot has a new commitment and relationship to God and so will have a new motivation to be prudent, just, brave, and temperate, but it is premature to say that he is such already.

The idea that the virtues arrive all at once in the soul by infusion, as if a light switch has been turned on, does not correspond to a meaningful narrative of the ordinary process of moral development.[26] Baptism is not like Robert Nozick's "transformation machine" that makes us instantly virtuous.[27] Baptized infants are not yet prudent, just, or temperate. Once baptized, adults still struggle, still fall, and take time to attain to the virtues. The simultaneity thesis, as Aquinas states it, fails to do justice to the gradualness of spiritual growth.

The simultaneity thesis can be rethought and made more consistent with the ordinary narrative of spiritual growth if we attend to Cajetan's neglected but intriguing interpretation (in I.II 62.4). Cajetan thinks that someone persisting in mortal sin after baptism could well have received faith and hope but still lacks charity: the mortally sinful acts of the convert prevent the generation of charity in the soul by infusion. Whatever we make of the plausibility of this case, it nevertheless provides Cajetan the occasion for making a valuable distinction between the *infusion* of the virtues, which in the strict and formal sense is an activity of God, and their *reception*, which is something that may happen in the soul as a consequence of God's action but only on condition that the person is appropriately disposed. Cajetan therefore restates the simultaneity thesis this way: the habits of theological virtues are infused at the same time "*on the part of the one infusing and by the rationale of infusion,* although the opposite may happen *from the disposition of the one receiving*" (emphasis added). In other words, infusion *as infusion* of all the virtues happens simultaneously since God does not hold back on His gifts; yet one or other of the virtues may fail to be generated or increased because of a person's lack of openness to this infusion.

Cajetan's distinction between infusion and reception is not without its basis in Aquinas's thinking:

Charity, since it is an infused habit, depends on the action of the one doing the infusing, namely, God, who stands to charity's infusion and preservation as the

sun does to the air's illumination. . . . And therefore, just as the light would immediately cease in the air were some obstacle to the sun's illuminating, so also charity would cease at once to be in the soul, through some obstacle being placed to
the inflowing of charity into the soul. (II.II 24.12c)[28]

God's action is ongoing, like the illumination of the sun, even when the disposition of the recipient prevents it from working its proper effect—that is, the
generation and maintenance of charity and the other virtues in the soul. Aquinas thinks of this in unduly binary terms: either a person is open to infusion or
she is not, and the virtues are generated or they are not. A person can "open the
door to the virtues" to a greater or lesser degree, hence the generation of virtue
can be gradual, beginning with germinal virtue, and eventually being perfected
in complete virtue.

Aquinas does offer two reasons for saying that the virtues are infused at
the moment of baptism, even in infants (III 69.6c). The first is that children, as
members of Christ's body, must receive from the head "an influx of grace and
virtue" (*influx gratiae et virtutis*). However, the gradual generation of infused
virtue is no slight on God's goodness or Christ's efficacy. As the sun continues
to shine whether the shutters are open or not, so God continues actively to
offer the gift of the supernatural virtues to all through Christ; due to immatu-
rity or sin the person may be indisposed to receive this infusion fully.

The second reason Aquinas gives for infusion at the moment of baptism is
that infants who die after being baptized would not arrive at eternal life if they
did not possess the virtues at least in habit (ibid.). However, on the story of
gradual generation, baptized infants possess, in addition to grace, the germinal
supernatural virtue that is fitting for their stage in life and which marks the
beginning of eternal life.

Cajetan's distinction between infusion and reception opens a way to a more
plausible developmental account of virtue's infusion that respects the theological concerns.[29] As William McDonough puts it, "Though grace effects a complete new beginning in an instant, its work through the whole of the human
person is not instantaneous."[30] When we note that, for Aquinas, the theological
virtues of faith and hope may exist in an imperfect and germinal state (I.II
65.4), there seems no obstacle to understanding infusion as the gift of God,
and, on our part, as a gradual process.

MEDIATION

According to Aquinas, the infused virtues are "caused immediately by God"
(*immediate a Deo causari*) (I.II 63.3 ad 1). In contrast to the acquired virtues,

God generates, increases, and maintains the supernatural virtues without mediation of human action or other secondary causes. The most that human agency can contribute is consent and, in the case of infused virtue's increase, dispositive and meritorious causation, but not cooperation. This is the third thesis associated with Aquinas's account of infusion that can fruitfully be examined critically.

Aquinas's theology of grace might suggest a more positive role for human cooperation in the generation, increase, and maintenance of infused virtue.[31] Aquinas opposes an occasionalist view of causation, according to which, for example, "It is not fire that heats, but God in the fire" (I 105.5).[32] On the contrary, God works in things without thereby taking away their own agency; indeed, their active power is due to God Himself (ibid.). Actions issue simultaneously from created beings (as secondary causes) and from God (the primary cause) (I 105.5 ad 1). On this "concurrentist" understanding, grace and free human action are seen as complementary rather than competitive. The claim that God infuses virtue immediately may seem to run against the grain of Aquinas's theology of grace by taking away human agency in becoming more virtuous. Yet the more we attribute to our own agency, the greater the danger we undermine the core insight of the doctrine of infusion: that the virtues are more gifts than attainments.

There are other reasons for questioning the immediacy of infusion. Human beings in some way contribute to their own justification and sanctification. Aquinas quotes Augustine: "He who created you without you will not justify you without you" (I.II 55.4 arg 6).[33] Again, tensions exist: to ascribe too much to human agency risks a Pelagian eclipse of the primacy of God's grace in our justification and sanctification.

Florence Caffrey Bourg brings out a more practical consideration: "There is a tension between that part of the developing theological tradition which considers Christian families or domestic churches as schools of virtue, and that part of the tradition which has insisted that the supernatural virtues are caused by God alone through sacraments of baptism and penance."[34] Bourg is dissatisfied with the idea that our contribution to the cultivation of virtue lies purely in dispositive causation, since this perspective fails to do justice to the rich variety of ways God's grace can be mediated to us through community and sacrament. She proposes a rethinking of the causal role of human agency in the attainment of evangelical virtue: "Human agency may be understood as a secondary, instrumental, ministerial, or mediating cause enlisted by God in formation of supernatural virtue—comparable to the role Aquinas assigns to sacraments and their ministers as causes of grace."[35] Bourg's practical perspective urges us to see the extent to which human agency can be said to cooperate in the attainment of supernatural virtue. She proposes that our causal contribution to the generation and increase of infused virtue goes beyond mere dispositive causation and genuinely "mediates" God's grace. How tenable is this viewpoint?

The central theological challenge is being able to hold a tension. The first pole of this tension is the core insight in the doctrine of supernatural virtue's infusion: that such virtue is gratuitous since we can only be oriented to, and begin to participate in, eternal life by the sheer gift of a gracious God; the second is that God's gift is mediated in manifold ways—through creation, the Church, and even human agency—since, as the doctrine of the Incarnation most clearly shows, God chooses not to bypass the created world or human freedom in communicating His grace. How may we describe the relation between grace and human agency in virtue's infusion without either undermining the giftedness or underestimating the agency? Progress can come from examining two parallel cases in which secondary causes mediate grace or infusion in more than a merely dispositive way.

The first analogy concerns the causality of the sacraments and their ministers, as Bourg suggests. In the early text of the *Commentary on the Sentences*, Aquinas says it is necessary to say that the sacraments are in some way the cause of grace, but he shows a concern to discern what this causal role is.[36] He makes two distinctions. One is between the principal agent (*agens principale*), who is the first mover, and the instrumental agent (*agens instrumentale*), which is a moved mover. By assigning sacrament to the category of instrumental cause, Aquinas preserves the theological insight that God alone is the origin of grace: the water of baptism, for example, causes grace only because it is used for that effect by God. So a sacrament is an instrumental cause of grace.

However, Aquinas makes an important further distinction between two kinds of instrumental cause: disposing (*disponens*) and completing (*perficiens*). The latter causes a form but the former only directly causes the *disposition* or readiness for that form. A saw used to produce a stool is an example of a perfecting instrumental cause: the saw produces an effect that goes beyond what it can produce of itself, as with all instrumental causes, but when it is used by the principal agent it really does bring about the stool, making it a *completing* instrumental cause. A disposing instrumental cause, in contrast, merely produces the material on which the principal agent can freely bestow the form. The example Aquinas gives is of the begetting of a human child: the material elements provide the substratum into which God infuses the immortal human soul.

Which kind of instrumental cause is a sacrament? Crucially, in this early text, Aquinas says it is a merely disposing rather than perfecting instrumental cause of grace. In this way he is able to preserve the gratuity of grace, as it is God Himself who completes its conferral. Yet, since disposing causes produce only a readiness for a form, Aquinas thereby limits the extent to which a sacrament can truly be said to mediate grace.

Reginald M. Lynch, following Cajetan, argues for a development in Aquinas's view that goes beyond the cautious teaching of the *Commentary* and assigns completing instrumental causality to the sacraments.[37] In the *Summa Theologiae* Aquinas repeats the basic point that God is the principal agent of grace: "The principal [agent] operates in the power of its form, to which its effect is made to be like, just as fire by its heat heats. And in this manner [of causation] nothing can cause grace except God, because grace is nothing other than a certain participated likeness of the divine nature" (III 62.1).[38] However, he says that just as an axe is a secondary and instrumental cause of the building of a couch, so the sacraments cause grace by divine institution (ibid.). While Aquinas does not use the language of completing instrumental causation, the analogy with the axe and couch implies that the sacraments are not merely disposing causes of grace. Nor does this violate God's sovereignty in producing grace, since the instrumental cause acts not in virtue of its own form but by the motion originating in the principal agent, God. "And so the effect is not made to resemble the instrument, but the principal agent" (ibid.).[39]

As Lynch highlights, Cajetan illustrates this idea with the image of a musician playing a harp (in III 62.4 n.4). In disposing causality, there are two steps: the instrument first produces an effect that is then perfected by the principal agent. The completing cause, in contrast, participates much more integrally in bringing about the effect. Even though the principal and the completing cause both operate, there is only one motion or one event. Of itself the harp can produce only sounds; in the hands of a musician it really does produce music, not merely sounds that then can be made into music. When played in this way the harp is the subject not merely of a "motion" but of an "empowered motion" (*motus virtuosus*).[40] Similarly, in Cajetan's interpretation, a sacrament can be a completing cause of grace through an empowered motion without thereby undermining the understood principle that, in a sense, nothing can cause grace except God. Only God can cause a human to participate in his own life and form. Could the same not be said about human agency in generating supernatural virtue? In this case our own virtuous acts would be a harp, as it were, by which God effects a "music" of which we are not capable on our own: the generation and increase of supernatural virtue. A distinction between the infusion and acquisition would be preserved since in the former human agency generates and increases virtue only in virtue of a graced empowerment; the virtues therefore remain sheer gift rather than acquisition.

Another analogy lies in the begetting of the child. Pope Pius XII states, "The Catholic faith obliges us to hold that souls are immediately created by God."[41] Karl Rahner, in a well-known discussion, points out that it is also true that parents really do beget their own children. How do we reconcile these two truths? Rahner says: "The statement that God directly [immediately] creates the soul of a human being does not imply any denial of the statement that the parents procreate the human being in his unity. It makes the statement more precise by indicating that this procreation belongs to that kind of created efficient causality in which the agent by virtue of divine causality essentially exceeds the limits set by his own essence."[42] Rahner is expressing something that parents say they themselves experience: no matter how important their role, they intuitively recognize that the new person is not something they themselves could produce or make of themselves. This new human being is both their child and a sheer gift of God. A Thomistic approach that attempts to rethink our role in virtue's "immediate" infusion would have to say something similar: that whatever the role of human agency in increasing supernatural virtue, it accomplishes this only by mediating a gracious gift that transcends its proper effectiveness. In this way it may be possible to assign a greater causal role to human action in the attainment of infused virtue without undermining its giftedness. While our own agency might be said not only to dispose to but really to generate supernatural virtue through divine help, as the harp produces music in the hands of the musician, it remains that gratuitous virtue comes to us *primo quidem et principaliter, per gratiae donum*: in the very first place and principally by the gift of grace (II.II 161.6 ad 2).

MORAL VIRTUE

Another element of Aquinas's account of infused virtue, and theologically the most controversial, is his claim that infused and acquired moral virtue "differ in species" (I.II 63.4). This generates two problems, one intrapersonal (explaining the relationship of infused and acquired prudence, justice, fortitude, and temperance within the same person) and the other interpersonal (understanding the kind of moral virtue, and possibly also theological virtue, possessed by non-Christians).

Adams, in a different context, rightly warns of the danger of using virtue language to make interpersonal comparisons between groups of people: "It would be hard to defend talk of virtues and vices if that must mean dividing humanity into purely good guys and unmitigatedly bad guys. That aggravates conflict, and also dulls moral discernment. I think it is virtually always factually unjustified."[43] It is reasonable to think that Aquinas understands that "pagans" are capable of connected, acquired moral virtue (virtue that is perfect and unqualified virtue within the natural order). Nevertheless, his recognition of pagan moral goodness is highly qualified; he claims that in the state of fallen nature, no one can avoid mortal sin without grace. Cajetan points out that a single act of mortal sin is not inconsistent with the habitual possession of moral virtue, and so a pagan could still be morally good (in I.II 65.2). While Cajetan is more generous than Osborne in recognizing the connected virtue of the pagan, the "pagan" may not find much consolation in the thought that she may be morally virtuous but cannot avoid mortal sin, and so, unless she converts to Christianity, is damned anyway.

In this area it is important to acknowledge the gap between Aquinas's (or Cajetan's) day and our own. In today's pluralist world, the question of how Christians should relate to people of other faiths and those who have none becomes more urgent. The Church teaches that grace is present in the hearts of all people of good will and the Holy Spirit works "in a manner known only to God" (*Gaudium et Spes* 22). Are we then to countenance the possibility of infused virtue, even beyond the realms of explicit Christian faith? Theologians range from a strong affirmation (William McDonough) to an affirmation that acknowledges theological difficulties (Jean Porter) to a cautious consideration (Michael Sherwin).[44] It would not be tenable to hold a position that automatically excludes the majority of the human race from the possibility of salvation, since that is not to honor the goodness of the God we know.

What about the intrapersonal question of the relationship between infused moral virtue and its acquired counterparts? There are three main positions on this tangled issue. The first is ascribed to Aquinas: that the two sets of moral virtue can exist in graced union; the infused moral virtues relate to the acquired moral virtues as commanding to eliciting, and so as form to matter. While this may be a plausible interpretation, and the one that became the traditional Thomistic viewpoint, it risks duplicating virtues beyond necessity, as Aquinas himself worries (I.II 63.3 arg 1, arg 2). The second is Mattison's interpretation, that the Christian possesses only the infused moral virtues. While this eliminates the two-tier structure within a single Christian, the dividing line problematically is shifted from an intrapersonal to an interpersonal one: Christians are separated from the rest of humanity by a different set of moral virtues. Plus there is another problem. It is axiomatic for Thomism that grace perfects nature without destroying it (*gratia perficit naturam, non tollit*).[45] Mattison faces the difficulty of explaining the *non tollit* of the axiom: the acquired moral virtues are not perfected but rather they are replaced with a whole new set of virtues.

The third is the Scotist solution, according to which it suffices for Christian prudence, justice, fortitude, and temperance that the acquired moral virtues fall under the command and direction of the theological virtues; there is no need for a distinct species of moral virtue infused by God.[46] Is this not more promising? After all, a moral virtue is specified by its formal object or target (*finis operis*) rather than its overall end (*finis operantis*) (60.1 ad 3). Yet to ditch infused moral virtue without speaking to the core issue that the concept was meant to address may be to employ Occam's razor too enthusiastically. For McKay Knobel it would be to propose "a relatively unimaginative appropriation of the Aristotelian theory of virtue, with faith, hope and love spliced somewhat awkwardly on top."[47] Thomists have always rightly seen the Scotist view as problematic. A difference in overall end indicates a difference in target since prudence determines the target precisely by due proportion to the overall end (*On the Virtues* 1.10 ad 9). It is difficult to see how the end can fail, at least indirectly, to be specifying and distinguishing. Indeed, "It is from the end that it is necessary to take the rationales of what is ordered to the end" (I.II pr).[48] The Scotist solution glosses over the difference made to the more proximate aims of the moral life when oriented by a revealed vision of its ultimate end.

Can causal analysis shed light on this contested question? First, it helps to question the problematic vocabulary of "infused" and "acquired" moral virtue. Aquinas acknowledges that God could infuse a virtue directed only to finite goods, just as He may miraculously produce health without its normal secondary natural causes: "Sometimes, to show his power, [God] infuses in a human even those habits which can be caused by a natural power," as when He gave knowledge of tongues to the apostles (I.II 51.4; cf. 63.4).[49] We may conceive of a kind of virtue that cuts across Aquinas's distinction: a moral virtue that is infused yet is, of itself, only directed to a natural end. The reason for this confusion is that "infused" and "acquired" point not to the formal cause of certain virtues but rather to their efficient cause, which is extrinsic and accidental to the nature of a virtue in a way that the formal and final causes are not. The efficient cause does not enter into the formal definition of a virtue, since the efficient cause as such explains what brings a virtue into *existence* rather than saying anything about its *essence* (see chaps. 2 and 5).

Cajetan sees the problem and attempts to improve on Aquinas's vocabulary by distinguishing virtue infused *per se*—that is, virtue of such a nature that it can be generated only by God's immediate action—from virtue infused *per accidens*, which is the kind of virtue that is normally acquired by human action but in this case happens to have been generated by God's immediate intervention (in I.II 63.4). Cajetan's terminology seems to work for theological virtue since, as Aquinas argues, a virtue that is intrinsically and essentially directed to a supernatural object and end must have a supernatural cause (I.II 51.4, 62.1; *On the Virtues* 1.10). Yet it remains to be shown that moral virtues directed to a supernatural end need to be so directed essentially and intrinsically.

We seem caught in a dilemma. Either moral virtue within the Christian is *intrinsically* ordered to the supernatural end, in which case we seem to have an essential difference in target and therefore species, or moral virtue is *extrinsically* ordered to a supernatural end by the command of the theological virtues, in which case we lack a virtue with a supernatural target. Either position has its weaknesses.

A tentatively proposed fourth approach, which mediates between the Thomistic and Scotist solutions and has not yet been considered, is that moral virtue is neither intrinsically nor merely extrinsically related to a supernatural end; it is only "conditionally" and "obliquely" related so. This distinction can be derived from the Salamancans' discussion of the virtue of fortitude.[50]

The Salamancans discuss how to define the target of fortitude. One might say that the proximate end of fortitude is to stand firm even when in mortal danger. But this is not a morally good target (*finis operis*) unless it is referred further to some further good (*finis operantis*). To voluntarily risk death without adequate reason is not an act of virtue. As Aquinas says, "To suffer death is not praiseworthy in itself, but only insofar as it is ordered to some good, which lies in an act of virtue, for example, to faith, and to the love of God" (II. II 124.3).[51] It is necessary to define the proper object of fortitude, not simply as standing firm in mortal danger but rather, as the Salamancans say, "to face danger according to reason insofar as there is need." Note, however, that this way of defining the proper object of fortitude, and hence the virtue of fortitude itself, does not intrinsically and directly include any particular good remote end in the definition or specification of fortitude; it only defines it obliquely or "as a condition":

> To face danger even unto death, which is the principal object of fortitude, speaks no goodness unless it is added that it be in order to a higher end, for example, of faith, of justice, of charity, and so on. And so if someone were to expose himself to danger without such an end, he would sin. However, this end does not concur to constituting a good object for fortitude directly and as a formal rationale, but only as a condition.[52]

In other words, the Salamancans offer a somewhat indeterminate definition of the proper object of fortitude since they recognize that true bravery can be motivated by any number of different worthy ends. This partly defined, partly vague proper object of fortitude—any good worth dying for—is "determined" or "specified" differently in differing circumstances.

How might this apply to the question of infused and acquired moral virtue? The dilemma is whether to acknowledge that a difference in overall end signals a difference in object and target. If it does, we face the problem of the superfluous duplication of supernatural and natural virtues. If it doesn't, we fail to recognize the difference that the ultimate end of eternal life makes to the more proximate goals of the moral life. However, the Salamancans' account of fortitude brings an alternative into view: the proper object of moral virtue is defined with a certain amount of indeterminacy; the object can be constituted in view of different remote ends. For example, it is essential to fortitude that there be some further good that motivates one to stand firm in mortal danger; what that further good is, provided it be some good greater than the preservation of a single human life, is accidental to fortitude's proper object. As Aquinas himself says, "That the brave person acts bravely for the good of fortitude, this is not a circumstance [of the brave act]; but [it is a circumstance] that he act for the liberation of the city, or for the Christian people, or something of this kind" (I.II 7.3 ad 3).[53] It seems to follow that pagan and Christian fortitude differ, and yet are not different *in species*. The brave pagan is ready to die for the good of the city; the brave Christian is ready also to die for Christ. These are not virtues differing in species, since they share the same proper object or target: to face the danger of death for some greater good according to reason. The Occam's razor objection has no unnecessary duplication to eliminate. However, this proper object gets "determined" or "specified" differently for pagans and Christians, and so the objection to the Scotist solution—that it fails to recognize the difference an overall end makes to the proximate ends of the moral life—also finds no purchase here.

The alternative view, generalized from the example of fortitude, is that a moral virtue's specifying target is somewhat indeterminate and capable of being filled out either naturally or supernaturally. A moral virtue is related to a natural or supernatural end neither intrinsically and directly (as for the traditional Thomist position) nor extrinsically (as for the Scotists) but only "as a condition." For example, natural and supernatural temperance do not differ in species, since they both consist in moderating emotional attractions for the sake of bodily, relational, and moral goods. But these goods get specified differently by unaided human reason and reason informed by faith.

What does this fourth possibility imply about moral virtue's efficient cause? Such virtue, in this view, is indeterminate between infusion and acquisition: it can be either acquired by human action or infused by grace (with or without mediation of the completing instrumentality of human action), or both. The efficient cause is accidental. This seems more consonant with ordinary experience, which indicates that acting prudently, bravely, temperately, or justly increases our inclination toward prudent, brave, temperate, and just acts, for the Christian as well as for others. At the same time, these dispositions are undoubtedly increased in us by the Holy Spirit, as when a martyr finds, by grace, a more than human bravery.

The advantage of this tentative solution is that it preserves distinction while avoiding dichotomy. Thus it is in overall continuity with Aquinas's own trajectory in the context of the discussion of his day. If it is inadequate, a fifth approach is always possible: to allow that the mysterious relation between human agency and God's grace in the attainment of moral virtue eludes us still.

LOVE

James Keenan has highlighted the need to rethink a classicist understanding of virtue in the light of a more relational anthropology.[54] Nel Noddings claims that we do not grow into virtue in isolation. Virtue, she says, "is built up in relation. It reaches out to the other and grows in response to the other."[55] These insights may require not so much a rethinking of Aquinas as rethinking of our interpretation of him. Could it be said that infused virtue is virtue that is built up in relation to, and in response to, God? Andrew Pinsent has suggested that the key to this kind of "paradigm shift" lies in Aquinas's account of the seven gifts of the Holy Spirit.[56]

Aquinas distinguishes the seven gifts from the moral and theological virtues. While the gifts are virtues in a broad sense, they also are distinctive in that they perfect a human "insofar as he is moved by God" (68.1 ad 1).[57] As "spirits" bestowed by God they enable us to be "inspired" or moved by God more promptly (68.1c). In sum, "the gifts are certain perfections of a human, by which a human is disposed to this: that he follows the divine impulse well" (68.2c).[58]

Causally, what is the difference between the virtues and gifts? Aquinas does not see the matter of the gifts as distinctive (68.1 arg 2, ad 2). Pinsent says that since the gifts and virtues share the same matter, they must share the same form.[59] This cannot be right, since if gifts and virtues have the same form and matter, then they are the same habits. Cajetan is more precise: "Although gifts are not about any other objects, they are about them by a different mode: for they are about them in such a way that their acts originate from the impulse of the Holy Spirit" (in 68.1 n.2). While their subject, material object, target, end, and agent will be the same, generically speaking, their mode differs. The gifts, Aquinas says, surpass the virtues in their modus operandi insofar as they are moved by God (68.2 ad 1). The key to understanding the gifts, then, is to unpack the gift's characteristic mode.

The gift's mode is not the same as that of a moral virtue (the mode of reason) but is a receptivity to the movements of a divine and interior impulse (*instinctus*): "Even the Philosopher recognizes, in the chapter 'On Good Fortune' [*Eudemian Ethics* VII, 8], that those who are moved by a divine impulse do not need to be counselled by human reason, but that they follow an interior impulse, because they are moved by a principle better than human reason" (68.1c).[60] The question is how to understand this "impulse" and "movement."

This is where Pinsent can help us. He points out that we are in danger of being misled by the modern mechanistic connotations of "impulse" and "movement": the movement essential to the gifts is not a coercive push. Rather, Aquinas conceives of this movement as happening in an intensely personal context by which a person learns to participate in God's stance toward an object. For example: "By the gift of piety, we are moved to regard other persons as God regards them, namely as potential or actual children, and thereby our brothers and sisters." . . . By the gift of counsel, we are 'directed as though counseled by God,' implying that we take on God's stance towards possible courses of action."[61] Similar analyses can be given of the other gifts. Pinsent concludes, then, that the "movement" characteristic of the gifts is a kind of "joint attention" in which we learn to share in God's stance toward some object.[62]

How does this perspective of "second-person relatedness with God" and "joint attention" enable us to understand the infusion of virtue? Joint attention, or sharing the stance of another, is possible only in the context of personal relationship. Employing joint attention as a "metaphor" by which to interpret Aquinas, Pinsent argues that the theological virtues, which unite us with God, precede the gifts and enable us to be moved through joint attention; these in turn precede the infused moral virtues, which are understood as "virtues of shared stance."[63] Indeed, Aquinas claims that in the order of perfection, the theological virtues come first, followed by the gifts, followed by the infused moral virtues (68.8 ad 2).

Pinsent makes two contributions: he accents the second-personal perspective in Aquinas's account of the virtues and he offers an illuminating account of the gifts as virtues of shared stance. However, he overstates the degree to which "joint attention" provides an interpretation of Aquinas on virtue's infusion. While it makes sense to see the gifts as flowing from the theological virtues, it is less clear that Aquinas thinks the infused moral virtues flow from the gifts. While the gifts precede the infused moral virtues in the order of perfection, in the order of generation the opposite is the case: "The moral and intellectual virtues precede the gifts, because by being well disposed in his own reason, a human is disposed to being well disposed in order to God" (68.8 ad 2).[64] There is a problem in seeing the moral virtues purely as virtues of shared stance, as doing so underestimates the role of human agency in their attainment. Furthermore, since gifts flow from the theological virtues, we still need an account of the former's infusion.

The interpretive key to a more relational Thomistic account of infused virtue in general lies not so much in contemporary research on joint attention as on the primacy of the virtue of charity within theological ethics.[65] For Aquinas charity is understood in terms of the mutual communication of friendship: "Charity signifies, not only the love of God, but even a certain friendship towards him, which indeed adds to love a mutual return with a certain mutual communication" (65.5).[66] There is, however, an asymmetry in this mutual communication since we are drawn into it only by God's loving initiative. God's love for us comes first; only then are we empowered to love Him in return. As Aquinas explains, charity is a love founded on God's communication (II.II 23.1c). Unlike human friendship, charity "is not founded on human virtue, but on divine goodness" (23.3 ad 1).[67] This is indisputable Christian doctrine and experience: God loved us while we were sinners, and God's gracious love comes first, empowering us to love. As Aquinas puts it, "All gifts, both natural and gratuitous, are given to us by God through love, which is the first gift."[68]

Charity, generated in response to God's communication, in turn is the context in which the other supernatural virtues and gifts are generated and increased, as Pinsent himself observes. Indeed, all the virtues are in some way dependent on charity (II.II 23.4 ad 1). Just as the moral virtues are connected through prudence (I.II 65.1), so all the infused virtues are connected through charity (65.2, 4). Charity orients a person to the virtues' ultimate end in God.

Virtue is built up in relationship. As David Decosimo puts it, even to have the capacity for virtue is "to have others do for oneself and on one's behalf that for which one can take no credit."[69] The supernatural virtues are generated and increased in us when we are transformed by the friendship God draws us into. This is what virtue's "infusion" is at its heart: becoming more like God in response to God's loving self-communication. As Aquinas claims about our good works, so it is in regard to our virtue: all of it is from God, *totum est a Deo*.[70] All is gift.

NOTES

1. Roy J. Deferrari, *A Lexicon of Saint Thomas Aquinas* (Baltimore, MD: Catholic University of America Press, 1948), 555.

2. Bernard of Clairvaux, "De consideratione," in *Patrologia Latina*, ed. J. P. Migne, vol. 182, book 5 (Paris: Migne, 1862), 12:795. I owe this reference to Terence O'Reilly.

3. I.II 68.1c: "Nihil autem prohibet illud quod est ab alio ut donum, esse perfectivum alicuius ad bene operandum, praesertim cum supra dixerimus quod virtutes quaedam nobis sunt infusae a Deo. Unde secundum hoc, donum a virtute distingui non potest."

4. For example, II.II 47.14 ad 3; 124.2 ad 1; *De Veritate*, q. 14 a. 2 arg 3; q. 17 a. 2 ad 8.; *On the Virtues*, q. 5 a. 4 ad 2.

5. *Super Sent.*, lib. 1 d. 18 q. 1 a. 3 ad 4: "omnia dona et naturalia et gratuita, dentur nobis a Deo per amorem, qui est primum donum."

6. II.II 131.1: "non habet homo a seipso, sed est quasi quiddam divinum in eo. Et ideo ex hoc non debetur principaliter sibi honor, sed Deo."

7. Robert Merrihew Adams, *A Theory of Virtue: Excellence in Being for the Good* (New York: Oxford University Press, 2006), 165.

8. Alasdair MacIntyre, *Dependent Rational Animals: Why Human Beings Need the Virtues* (London: Duckworth, 1999), xi.

9. II.II 129.6 ad 1: "Indiget enim omnis homo, primo quidem, divino auxilio, secundario autem etiam auxilio humano, quia homo est naturaliter animal sociale, eo quod sibi non sufficit ad vitam."

10. 110.2: "non est conveniens quod Deus minus provideat his quos diligit ad supernaturale bonum habendum, quam creaturis quas diligit ad bonum naturale habendum."

11. *Super Sent.*, lib. 4 d. 14 q. 2 a. 2 ad 4, 5.

12. Michael S. Sherwin, "Infused Virtue and the Effects of Acquired Vice: A Test Case for the Thomistic Theory of Infused Cardinal Virtues," *The Thomist* 73 (2009): 36.

13. Ibid., 37.

14. I.II 65.3 arg 2: "qui habet habitum virtutis, de facili operatur ea quae sunt virtutis, et ei secundum se placent, unde et 'signum habitus est delectatio quae fit in opere,' ut dicitur in II Ethic. Sed multi habent caritatem, absque peccato mortali existentes, qui tamen difficultatem in operibus virtutum patiuntur, neque eis secundum se placent, sed solum secundum quod referuntur ad caritatem."

15. *Super Sent.*, lib. 4 d. 14 q. 2 a. 2 ad 5.

16. Ibid., ad 4.

17. Louis Billot, *De Virtutibus Infusis* (Roma: Gregoriana, 1905); Prolegomenon (I–II, QQ. 49–61, para. 2, 2), 35.

18. Sherwin, "Infused Virtue," 51.

19. I.II 65.3 ad 2: "Et similiter habitus moralium virtutum infusarum patiuntur interdum difficultatem in operando, propter aliquas dispositiones contrarias ex praecedentibus actibus relictas."

20. III 85.6 ad 3: "poenitentia aperit aditum virtutibus."

21. 65.3: "cum caritate simul infunduntur omnes virtutes morales."

22. III 69.4: "per Baptismum aliquis consequitur gratiam et virtutes."

23. *On the Virtues* 2.5 ad 11: "caritas simul habet generationem cum aliis virtutibus, non quia sit indistincta ab aliis, sed quia Dei perfecta sunt opera; unde infundens caritatem simul infundit omnia illa quae sunt necessaria ad salutem."

24. III 69.6c: "quidam antiqui posuerunt quod pueris in Baptismo non dantur gratia et virtutes. . . . Causa autem erroris fuit quia nescierunt distinguere inter habitum et actum. Et sic, videntes pueros inhabiles ad actus virtutum, crediderunt eos post Baptismum nullatenus virtutem habere. Sed ista impotentia operandi non accidit pueris ex defectu habituum, sed ex impedimento corporali, sicut etiam dormientes, quamvis habeant habitus virtutum, impediuntur tamen ab actibus propter somnum."

25. Florence Caffrey Bourg, "God Working in Us without Us? A Fresh Look at Formation of Virtue," Yamauchi Lecture Series, Loyola University, New Orleans, November 7, 2004, 13.

26. See Nicholas Austin, "Spirituality and Virtue in Christian Formation: A Conversation between Thomistic and Ignatian Traditions," *New Blackfriars* 97, no. 1068 (March 2016): 202–17.

27. Robert Nozick, *Anarchy, State, and Utopia* (New York: Basic, 1974), 44. See the discussion in Linda T. Zagzebski, *Virtues of the Mind: An Inquiry into the Nature of Virtue and the Ethical Foundations of Knowledge* (Cambridge: Cambridge University Press, 1996), 116–25.

28. II.II 24.12c: "Sed caritas, cum sit habitus infusus, dependet ex actione Dei infundentis, qui sic se habet in infusione et conservatione caritatis sicut sol in illuminatione aeris, ut dictum est. Et ideo, sicut lumen statim cessaret esse in aere quod aliquod obstaculum poneretur illuminationi solis, ita etiam caritas statim deficit esse in anima quod aliquod obstaculum ponitur influentiae caritatis a Deo in animam."

29. "Rather than the rapidity of acquisition, or even the mode, 'infusion' points to the source from whence the theological virtues come, namely by a special act of God which brings us into relation with God, not only forming but utterly transforming our character." Stanley Hauerwas and Charles Robert Pinches, *Christians among the Virtues: Theological Conversations with Ancient and Modern Ethics* (Notre Dame, IN: University of Notre Dame Press, 1997), 68–69.

30. William McDonough, "'Caritas' as the 'Prae-Ambulum' of All Virtue: Eberhard Schockenhoff on the Theological-Anthropological Significance and the Contemporary Interreligious Relevance of Thomas Aquinas's Teaching on the 'Virtutes Morales Infusae,'" *Journal of the Society of Christian Ethics* 27, no. 2 (2007): 105.

31. Nicholas Austin, "Is the Concept of Infused Moral Virtue Really Necessary?" (Licentiate Thesis, Boston College School of Theology and Ministry, 2010).

32. I 105.5: "ignis calefaceret, sed Deus in igne."

33. I.II 55.4 arg 6: "qui creavit te sine te, non iustificabit te sine te."

34. Bourg, "God Working in Us," 5.

35. Bourg, "God Working in Us," 8–9.

36. *Super Sent.*, lib. 4 d. 1 q. 1 a. 4 qc. 1c.

37. Reginald Lynch, "Cajetan's Harp: Sacraments and the Life of Grace in Light of Perfective Instrumentality," *The Thomist* 78, no. 1 (2014): 65–106.

38. III 62.1: "Principalis quidem operatur per virtutem suae formae, cui assimilatur effectus, sicut ignis suo calore calefacit. Et hoc modo non potest causare gratiam nisi Deus, quia gratia nihil est aliud quam quaedam participata similitudo divinae naturae."

39. III 62.1: "Unde effectus non assimilatur instrumento, sed principali agenti."

40. Lynch translates *motus virtuosus* as "artistic motion"; I prefer "empowered motion." See Lynch, "Cajetan's Harp," 89n74.

41. Pius XII, *Humani Generis,* August 12, 1956, 36. English translation available on the Vatican website: http://w2.vatican.va/content/vatican/en.html.

42. Karl Rahner, *Hominisation: The Evolutionary Origin of Man as a Theological Problem* (London: Burns & Oates, 1965), 99.

43. Adams, *Theory of Virtue*, 231.

44. McDonough, "'Caritas' as the 'Prae-Ambulum'"; Jean Porter, *Nature as Reason: A Thomistic Theory of the Natural Law* (Grand Rapids, MI: Eerdmans, 2005), 396–98; and Michael Sherwin, *By Knowledge and By Love: Charity and Knowledge in the Moral Theology of St. Thomas Aquinas* (Washington, DC: Catholic University of America Press, 2005), 233–35.

45. See, e.g., I.1.8 ad 2: "Cum enim gratia non tollat naturam, sed perficiat." Also *Super De Trinitate*, pars 1 q. 2 a. 3 co. 1.

46. On Scotus's view, see Bonnie Kent, "Rethinking Moral Dispositions: Scotus on the Virtues" in *The Cambridge Companion to Duns Scotus*, ed. Thomas Williams (Cambridge: Cambridge University Press, 2006), 352–76.

47. Angela McKay Knobel, "The Infused and Acquired Virtues in Aquinas' Moral Philosophy" (PhD dissertation, University of Notre Dame, 2004), 2.

48. I.II pr: "ex fine enim oportet accipere rationes eorum quae ordinantur ad finem."

49. I.II 51.4: "quandoque, ad ostendendam suam virtutem, infundit homini illos etiam habitus qui naturali virtute possunt causari."

50. *Cursus Theologicus*, Tract. 11, *De Bonitate et Malitia Humanorum Actuum*, Disp.3, Dub.1, nn.14–17 (6:70–72); Tract. 13, *De Vitiis et Peccatis*, Disp.9, Dub.4, n.64 (7:280).

51. II.II 124.3: "Quia tolerare mortem non est laudabile secundum se, sed solum secundum quod ordinatur ad aliquod bonum quod consistit in actu virtutis, puta ad fidem et dilectionem Dei."

52. *Cursus Theologicus*, Tract. 11, *De Bonitate et Malitia Humanorum Actuum*, Disp.3, Dub.1, n.15 (6:70).

53. I.II 7.3 ad 3: "quod fortis fortiter agat propter bonum fortitudinis, non est circumstantia; sed si fortiter agat propter liberationem civitatis, vel populi Christiani, vel aliquid huiusmodi."

54. James F. Keenan, "Proposing Cardinal Virtues," *Theological Studies* 56, no. 4 (December 1995): 709–29, esp. 722–23.

55. Nel Noddings, *Caring: A Feminine Approach to Ethics and Moral Education* (Berkeley: University of California Press, 1984), 80–81.

56. See also Eleonore Stump, "The Non-Aristotelian Character of Aquinas's Ethics: Aquinas on the Passions," in *Faith, Rationality, and the Passions*, ed. Sarah Coakley (Oxford: Wiley-Blackwell, 2012), 91–106.

57. 68.1 ad 1: "inquantum est a Deo motus."

58. 68.2c: "dona sunt quaedam hominis perfectiones, quibus homo disponitur ad hoc quod bene sequatur instinctum divinum."

59. Andrew Pinsent, "Aquinas: Infused Virtues," in *The Routledge Companion to Virtue Ethics*, ed. Michael Slote and Lorraine Besser-Jones (New York: Routledge, 2015), 148.

60. 68.1c: "Et philosophus etiam dicit, in cap. de bona fortuna, quod his qui moventur per instinctum divinum, non expedit consiliari secundum rationem humanam, sed quod sequantur interiorem instinctum, quia moventur a meliori principio quam sit ratio humana."

61. Andrew Pinsent, "Aquinas and the Second Person in the Formation of Virtues," in *Aquinas, Education, and the East*, ed. T. Brian Mooney and Mark Nowacki (New York: Springer, 2013), 52.

62. Ibid., 54.

63. Andrew Pinsent, *The Second-Person Perspective in Aquinas's Ethics: Virtues and Gifts* (New York: Routledge, 2011), 67, 69, 77, and 83.

64. 68.8 ad 2: "virtutes morales et intellectuales praecedunt dona, quia per hoc quod homo bene se habet circa rationem propriam, disponitur ad hoc quod se bene habeat in ordine ad Deum."

65. See Matthew B. O'Brien, review of "The Second-Person Perspective in Aquinas's Ethics: Virtues and Gifts," by Andrew Pinsent, *Notre Dame Philosophical Reviews* (December 2010).

66. 65.5: "caritas non solum significat amorem Dei, sed etiam amicitiam quandam ad ipsum; quae quidem super amorem addit mutuam redamationem cum quadam mutua communicatione."

67. 23.3 ad 1: "non fundatur principaliter super virtute humana, sed super bonitate divina."

68. *Super Sent.*, lib. 1 d. 18 q. 1 a. 3 ad 4: "Omnia dona et naturalia et gratuita, dentur nobis a Deo per amorem, qui est primum donum."

69. David Decosimo, *Ethics as a Work of Charity: Thomas Aquinas and Pagan Virtue* (Stanford, CA: Stanford University Press, 2014), 269.

70. *Super Io.*, cap. 3 l. 3. See also ibid., 252.

APPENDIX

Virtue Defined

The interpretive argument proposed herein is that the article defining virtue (I.II 55.4) is intensely "holographic" in that, from this fragment of Aquinas's causal virtue theory, an image of the whole emerges. The following is an exegesis of the causal definition of virtue found in that holographic text.

A virtue is:

(1) an operative habit agreeing with human nature or supernature and therefore with the twofold rule of divine and human reason / *formal cause*

in that it

    (1a) concerns some sphere of human passions and operations (and their objects) capable of rational direction / *material object*

    (1b) and targets some aspect of the moral good in regard to that sphere / *formal object that is attained*

    (1c) attaining that target according to some characteristic mode / *formal object by which the target good is attained*

    (1d) participating in the goodness of God in a manner fitting to a human being / *exemplar cause*;

(2) inhering in the powers of the soul that are rational either essentially or by participation / *subjective material cause*;

(3) always oriented toward morally good operation / *immediate final cause*

and thereby to

    (3a) some morally good target (*finis operis*) [=1b] / *proximate final cause*

    (3b) and thence to the overall end of human life (*finis operantis*) / *remote final cause*;

(4) and generated and increased either by infusion or by repeated human action / *efficient or agent cause*

SELECTED BIBLIOGRAPHY

Adams, Robert Merrihew. *A Theory of Virtue: Excellence in Being for the Good*. New York: Oxford University Press, 2006.

Annas, Julia. "Being Virtuous and Doing the Right Thing." *Proceedings and Addresses of the American Philosophical Association* 78, no. 2 (November 1, 2004): 61–75.

———. *Intelligent Virtue*. Oxford: Oxford University Press, 2011.

———. "Virtue Ethics." In *The Oxford Handbook of Ethical Theory*, edited by David Copp, 515–36. Oxford: Oxford University Press, 2006.

Anscombe, G. E. M. "Modern Moral Philosophy." *Philosophy* 33, no. 124 (1958): 1–19.

Aquinas, Thomas. *Commentary on Aristotle's Nicomachean Ethics*. Translated by Rev. C. I. Litzinger. South Bend, IN: Dumb Ox, 1993.

———. *Disputed Questions on the Virtues*. Edited by E. M. Atkins and Thomas Williams. Cambridge, UK: Cambridge University Press, 2005.

———. *Corpus Thomisticum. S. Thomae de Aquino Opera Omnia*. Edited by Enrique Alarcón. Pamplona, 2000. Online at http://www.corpusthomisticum.org/iopera.html.

———. *Disputed Questions on Virtue*. Edited by Jeffrey Hause and Claudia Eisen Murphy. Indianapolis, IN: Hackett, 2010.

———. *Summa Theologica*. Translated by Fathers of the English Domican Province. New York: Benzinger Brothers, 1947.

Ariew, André. "Teleology." In *The Cambridge Companion to the Philosophy of Biology*, edited by David L. Hull and Michael Ruse, 160–81. Cambridge, UK: Cambridge University Press, 2007.

Aristotle. *The Art of Rhetoric*. Translated by Hugh Lawson-Tancred. London: Penguin, 1991.

Austin, Nicholas. "Is the Concept of Infused Moral Virtue Really Necessary?" Licentiate thesis, Boston College School of Theology and Ministry, 2010.

———. "Spirituality and Virtue in Christian Formation: A Conversation between Thomistic and Ignatian Traditions." *New Blackfriars* 97, no. 1068 (March 2016): 202–17.

———. "Thomas Aquinas on the Four Causes of Temperance." PhD diss., Boston College, 2010.

———. "Thomas Aquinas on the Virtue of Religion." In *"Ahme Nach, Was Du Vollziehst": Positionsbestimmungen Zum Verhältnis von Liturgie Und Ethik*, edited by Martin Stuflesser and Stephan Winter, 85–99. Regensburg: Pustet, 2009.

Beebee, Helen, Christopher Hitchcock, and Peter Menzies, eds. *The Oxford Handbook of Causation*. Oxford: Oxford University Press, 2009.

Behe, Michael J. *The Edge of Evolution: The Search for the Limits of Darwinism*. New York: Simon and Schuster, 2008.

Bejczy, István Pieter. *The Cardinal Virtues in the Middle Ages: A Study in Moral Thought from the Fourth to the Fourteenth Century*. Leiden: Brill, 2011.

———. "The Problem of Natural Virtue." In *Virtue and Ethics in the Twelfth Century*, edited by Richard Newhauser and István Pieter Bejczy, 133–54. Leiden: Brill, 2005.

Bernard of Clairvaux. "De Consideratione." In *Patrologia Latina*, edited by J. P. Migne, 182: 727–808. Paris: Migne, 1862.

Billot, Louis. *De Virtutibus Infusis*. Rome: Gregoriana, 1905.

Bourg, Florence Caffrey. "God Working in Us without Us? A Fresh Look at Formation of Virtue." Yamauchi Lecture Series, Loyola University, New Orleans, November 7, 2004, http://cas.loyno.edu/sites/cas.loyno.edu/files/god-working-in-us-without-us.pdf.

Bourke, Vernon Joseph. *Ethics: A Textbook in Moral Philosophy*. New York: Macmillan, 1966.

Bradley, Denis J. M. *Aquinas on the Twofold Human Good: Reason and Human Happiness in Aquinas's Moral Science*. Washington, DC: Catholic University of America Press, 1997.

Brentano, Franz. *Psychology from an Empirical Standpoint*. New York: Routledge, 2014.

Brock, Stephen L. "Intentional Being, Natural Being, and the First-Person Perspective in Thomas Aquinas." *The Thomist* 77 (2013): 103–33.

Bushlack, Thomas J. *Politics for a Pilgrim Church: A Thomistic Theory of Civic Virtue*. Grand Rapids, MI: Eerdmans, 2015.

Butera, Giuseppe. "On Reason's Control of the Passions in Aquinas's Theory of Temperance." *Mediaeval Studies* 68, no. 1 (January 1, 2006): 133–60.

Cajetan (Tommaso de Vio). "Commentary on the Summa Theologiae." In *Sancti Thomae de Aquinas Opera Omnia Iussu Impensaque Leonis XIII* (Leonine), vols. 4–12. Rome: Editori di San Tommaso, 1882.

Carr, Mark F. *Passionate Deliberation: Emotion, Temperance, and the Care Ethic in Clinical Moral Deliberation*. Boston: Kluwer Academic, 2001.

Cassian, John. *Conlationes 24*. Edited by Michael Petschenig. Vol. 13.1, *Corpus Scriptorum Ecclesiasticorum Latinorum*. Vindobonae, Austria: Apud C. Geroldi filium, 1886.

Cates, Diana Fritz. *Aquinas on the Emotions*. Washington, DC: Georgetown University Press, 2009.

Clark, Patrick M. "The Case for an Exemplarist Approach to Virtue in Catholic Moral Theology." *Journal of Moral Theology* 3, no. 1 (2014): 54–82.

Clatterbaugh, Kenneth. *The Causation Debate in Modern Philosophy, 1637–1739*. New York: Routledge, 1999.

Cloutier, David, and William C. Mattison III. "Review Essay: The Resurgence of Virtue in Recent Moral Theology." *Journal of Moral Theology* 3, no. 1 (January 2014): 228–59.

Cuypers, Stefaan E. "Thomistic Agent-Causalism." In *Mind, Metaphysics, and Value in the Thomistic and Analytic Traditions*, edited by John Haldane, 90–108. Notre Dame, IN: University of Notre Dame Press, 2002.

Davidson, Donald. *Essays on Actions and Events*. Oxford: Oxford University Press, 2001.

Dawkins, Richard. *The Blind Watchmaker: Why the Evidence of Evolution Reveals a Universe without Design*. New York: Norton, 1996.

———. *River Out of Eden: A Darwinian View of Life*. New York: Basic, 1995.

Dean, Jeremy. *Making Habits, Breaking Habits: Why We Do Things, Why We Don't, and How to Make Any Change Stick*. Philadelphia: Da Capo, 2013.

De Anna, Gabriele. "Causal Relations: A Thomistic Account." In *Analytical Thomism: Traditions in Dialogue*, edited by Craig Paterson and Matthew S. Pugh, 79–100. Aldershot, UK: Ashgate, 2006.

Decosimo, David. *Ethics as a Work of Charity: Thomas Aquinas and Pagan Virtue*. Stanford, CA: Stanford University Press, 2014.

Deely, John. *Purely Objective Reality*. Berlin: Walter de Gruyter, 2009.

———. "Quid Sit Postmodernismus?" In *Postmodernism and Christian Philosophy*, edited by Roman T Ciapalo, 68–96. Mishawaka, IN: American Maritain Association, 1997.

Deferrari, Roy J. *A Lexicon of Saint Thomas Aquinas*. Baltimore, MD: Catholic University of America Press, 1948.

Dembski, William A. *The Design Revolution: Answering the Toughest Questions about Intelligent Design*. Downers Grove, IL: InterVarsity Press, 2004.

Dewan, Lawrence. "'Obiectum': Notes on the Invention of a Word." In *Wisdom, Law, and Virtue: Essays in Thomistic Ethics*, 403–43. New York: Fordham University Press, 2007.

DeYoung, Rebecca Konyndyk, Colleen McCluskey, and Christina Van Dyke. *Aquinas's Ethics: Metaphysical Foundations, Moral Theory, and Theological Context*. Notre Dame, IN: University of Notre Dame Press, 2009.

Dodds, Michael J. *Unlocking Divine Action*. Washington, DC: Catholic University of America Press, 2012.

Doolan, Gregory T. *Aquinas on the Divine Ideas as Exemplar Causes*. Washington, DC: Catholic University of America Press, 2008.

Doris, John M. *Lack of Character: Personality and Moral Behavior*. Cambridge, UK: Cambridge University Press, 2002.

Driver, Julia. "The Virtues and Human Nature." In *How Should One Live? Essays on the Virtues*, edited by Roger Crisp, 111–29. Oxford: Oxford University Press, 1996.

Duhigg, Charles. *The Power of Habit: Why We Do What We Do in Life and Business*. London: William Heinemann, 2012.

Eschmann, Ignatius Theodore. *Ethics of St. Thomas Aquinas*. Edited by Edward A. Synan. Toronto: Pontifical Institute of Mediaeval Studies, 1997.

Farrell, Dominic. *The Ends of the Moral Virtues and the First Principles of Practical Reason in Thomas Aquinas*. Rome: Gregorian Biblical Bookshop, 2012.

Feser, Edward. *Scholastic Metaphysics: A Contemporary Introduction*. Heusenstamm: Editiones Scholasticae, 2014.

———. "Teleology: A Shopper's Guide." *Philosophia Christi* 12, no. 1 (2010): 142–59.

Finnis, John. *Aquinas: Moral, Political, and Legal Theory*. Oxford: Oxford University Press, 1998.

Foot, Philippa. *Natural Goodness*. Oxford: Oxford University Press, 2001.

———. *Virtues and Vices and Other Essays in Moral Philosophy*. New York: Clarendon, 2002.

Gallagher, David M. "Aquinas on Goodness and Moral Goodness." In *Thomas Aquinas and His Legacy*, 37–60. Washington, DC: Catholic University of America Press, 1994.

———. *Thomas Aquinas and His Legacy*. Washington, DC: Catholic University of America Press, 1994.

Garcia, Jorge L. A. "The Right and the Good." *Philosophia* 21, no. 3 (1992): 235–56.

Geach, Peter Thomas. *The Virtues*. The Stanton Lectures, 1973–74. Cambridge, UK: Cambridge University Press, 1977.

Gilby, Thomas. *St. Thomas Aquinas: Summa Theologiae*. Vol. 43 (2a2ae), *Temperance*. Cambridge, UK: Cambridge University Press, 2006.

Glowala, Michał. "What Kind of Power Is a Virtue? John of St. Thomas OP on Causality of Virtues and Vices." *Studia Neoaristotelica* 9, no. 1 (2012): 25–27.

Gondreau, Paul. *The Passions of Christ's Soul in the Theology of St. Thomas Aquinas*. Scranton, PA: University of Scranton Press, 2002.

Haldane, John. "Analytical Thomism: How We Got Here, Why It Is Worth Remaining and Where We May Go Next." Afterword in *Analytical Thomism: Traditions in Dialogue*, edited by Craig Paterson and Matthew S. Pugh, 303–10. Aldershot, UK: Ashgate, 2006.

Hall, Pamela M. *Narrative and the Natural Law: An Interpretation of Thomistic Ethics*. Notre Dame, IN: University of Notre Dame, 1994.

Harman, Gilbert. "Moral Philosophy Meets Social Psychology: Virtue Ethics and the Fundamental Attribution Error." *Proceedings of the Aristotelian Society* 99 (January 1, 1999): 315–31.

Harmon, Thomas P. "The Sacramental Consummation of the Moral Life according to St. Thomas Aquinas." *New Blackfriars* 91, no. 1034 (2010): 465–80.

Hartman, Laura Marie. "An Ethics of Consumption: Christianity, Economy, and Ecology." PhD diss., University of Virginia, 2008.

Harvey, John. "The Nature of the Infused Moral Virtues." In *Proceedings of the Tenth Annual Convention of the Catholic Theological Society of America* 10 (1955): 172–221.

Hauerwas, Stanley, and Charles Robert Pinches. *Christians among the Virtues: Theological Conversations with Ancient and Modern Ethics*. Notre Dame, IN: University of Notre Dame Press, 1997.

Hoffman, Paul. "Does Efficient Causation Presuppose Final Causation? Aquinas vs. Early Modern Mechanism." In *Metaphysics and the Good: Themes from the*

Philosophy of Robert Merrihew Adams, edited by Samuel Newlands and Larry M. Jorgensen, 295–312. Oxford: Oxford University Press, 2009.

Hursthouse, Rosalind. "The Central Doctrine of the Mean." In *The Blackwell Guide to Aristotle's Nicomachean Ethics*, edited by Richard Kraut, 96–115. Oxford: Blackwell, 2006.

———. "A False Doctrine of the Mean." *Proceedings of the Aristotelian Society* 81 (1980): 57–72.

———. *On Virtue Ethics*. Oxford: Oxford University Press, 1999.

Inagaki, Bernard. "Habitus and Natura in Aquinas." In *Studies in Medieval Philosophy*, edited by John F. Wippel, 159–75. Washington, DC: Catholic University of America Press, 1987.

Irwin, Terence. *The Development of Ethics: A Historical and Critical Study*. Vol. 1, *From Socrates to the Reformation*. Oxford: Oxford University Press, 2007.

James, William. *The Principles of Psychology*. Vol. 1. New York: Cosimo, 2007.

———. *Talks to Teachers on Psychology: And to Students on Some of Life's Ideals*. Rockville, MD: Arc Manor, 2008.

Jensen, Steven J. "Virtuous Deliberation and the Passions." *The Thomist* 77, no. 2 (2013): 193–227.

Jordan, Mark D. *Rewritten Theology: Aquinas after His Readers*. Oxford: Blackwell, 2005.

———. "Theology and Philosophy." In *The Cambridge Companion to Aquinas*, edited by Norman Kretzmann and Eleonore Stump, 232–51. New York: Cambridge University Press, 1993.

Kamtekar, Rachana. "Situationism and Virtue Ethics on the Content of Our Character." *Ethics* 114, no. 3 (April 1, 2004): 458–91.

Keenan, James F. "Proposing Cardinal Virtues." *Theological Studies* 56, no. 4 (December 1995): 709–29.

Kent, Bonnie. "Habits and Virtues (Ia IIae, qq.49–70)." In *The Ethics of Aquinas*, edited by Stephen J. Pope, 116–30. Moral Traditions Series. Washington, DC: Georgetown University Press, 2002.

———. "Rethinking Moral Dispositions: Scotus on the Virtues." In *The Cambridge Companion to Duns Scotus*, edited by Thomas Williams, 352–76. Cambridge, UK: Cambridge University Press, 2006.

Kerr, Fergus. *After Aquinas: Versions of Thomism*. Malden, MA: Blackwell, 2002.

King, Peter. "Aquinas on the Passions." In *Thomas Aquinas: Contemporary Philosophical Perspectives*, edited by Brian Davies, 353–84. New York: Oxford University Press, 1998.

Klubertanz, G. P. *Habits and Virtues*. New York: Appleton-Century-Crofts, 1965.

Knobel, Angela McKay. "Can Aquinas's Infused and Acquired Virtues Coexist in the Christian Life?" *Studies in Christian Ethics* 23, no. 4 (2010): 381.

———. "The Infused and Acquired Virtues in Aquinas' Moral Philosophy." PhD diss., University of Notre Dame, 2004.

———. "Relating Aquinas's Infused and Acquired Virtues: Some Problematic Texts for a Common Interpretation." *Nova et Vetera* 9, no. 2 (Spring 2011): 411–31. English edition.

———. "Synderesis, Law, and Virtue." In *The Normativity of the Natural: Human Goods, Human Virtues, and Human Flourishing*, edited by Mark J. Cherry, 33–44. Austin, TX: Springer, 2009.

Kossell, Clifford G., SJ. "Natural Law and Human Law (Ia IIae, Qq. 90–97)." In *The Ethics of Aquinas*, edited by Stephen J. Pope, 169–93. Washington, DC: Georgetown University Press, 2002.

Lawler, Michael G., and Todd A. Salzman. "Virtue Ethics: Natural and Christian." *Theological Studies* 74, no. 2 (2013): 442–73.

Leget, Carlo. *Living with God: Thomas Aquinas on the Relation between Life on Earth and "Life" after Death*. Leuven: Peeters, 1997.

Lewis, David. "Causation." *The Journal of Philosophy* 70, no. 17 (1973): 556–67.

Lombard, Peter. *Sententiae in IV Libris Distinctae*. 3rd ed. Rome: Editiones Collegii S. Bonaventurae, 1971.

Lombardo, Nicholas E. *The Logic of Desire: Aquinas on Emotion*. Washington, DC: Catholic University of America Press, 2010.

Lynch, Reginald. "Cajetan's Harp: Sacraments and the Life of Grace in Light of Perfective Instrumentality." *The Thomist* 78, no. 1 (2014): 65–106.

MacIntyre, Alasdair. *After Virtue*. 3rd ed. Notre Dame, IN: University of Notre Dame Press, 2007.

———. *Dependent Rational Animals: Why Human Beings Need the Virtues*. London: Duckworth, 1999.

Mackie, John L. "Causes and Conditions." *American Philosophical Quarterly* 2, no. 4 (1965): 245–64.

Mahoney, John. *The Making of Moral Theology: A Study of the Roman Catholic Tradition*. The Martin D'Arcy Memorial Lectures, 1981–82. Oxford: Clarendon, 1987.

Maritain, Jacques. *Distinguish to Unite, Or, The Degrees of Knowledge*. The Collected Works of Jacques Maritain, vol. 7. Notre Dame, IN: University of Notre Dame Press, 1995.

———. *An Introduction to the Basic Problems of Moral Philosophy*. Albany, NY: Magi, 1990.

———. *Science and Wisdom*. Translated by Bernard Wall. London: Geoffrey Bles–Centenary, 1954.

Martin, Christopher F. J. *Thomas Aquinas: God and Explanations*. Edinburgh: Edinburgh University Press, 1997.

Mattison, William C., III. "Can Christians Possess the Acquired Cardinal Virtues?" *Theological Studies* 72, no. 3 (2011): 558–85.

———. "Thomas's Categorizations of Virtue: Historical Background and Contemporary Significance." *The Thomist* 74, no. 2 (2010): 189–235.

Maurer, Armand A. "Darwin, Thomists, and Secondary Causality." *The Review of Metaphysics* 57, no. 3 (2004): 491–514.

———. *The Division and Methods of the Sciences*. Toronto: Pontifical Institute of Mediaeval Studies, 1986.

Mayr, Ernst. *Toward a New Philosophy of Biology: Observations of an Evolutionist*. Cambridge, MA: Harvard University Press, 1988.

McDonough, William. "'Caritas' as the 'Prae-Ambulum' of All Virtue: Eberhard Schockenhoff on the Theological-Anthropological Significance and the Contemporary Interreligious Relevance of Thomas Aquinas's Teaching on the 'Virtutes Morales Infusae.'" *Journal of the Society of Christian Ethics* 27, no. 2 (2007): 97–126.

Miner, Robert. *Thomas Aquinas on the Passions: A Study of Summa Theologiae, 1a2ae 22–48.* Cambridge, UK: Cambridge University Press, 2009.

Mirkes, Renée. "Aquinas on the Unity of Perfect Moral Virtue and Its Significance for the Nature-Grace Question." PhD diss., Marquette University, 1995.

Moser, Robbie. "Thomas Aquinas, Esse Intentionale, and the Cognitive as Such." *Review of Metaphysics* 64, no. 4 (June 2011): 763–88.

Nelson, Daniel Mark. *The Priority of Prudence.* University Park: Pennsylvania State University Press, 1992.

Niemiec, Ryan M., and Jeremy Clyman. "Temperance: The Quiet Virtue Finds a Home." *PsychCritiques* 54 (November 18, 2009), n.p.

Noddings, Nel. *Caring: A Feminine Approach to Ethics and Moral Education.* Berkeley: University of California Press, 1984.

North, Helen. *Sophrosyne: Self-Knowledge and Self-Restraint in Greek Literature.* Ithaca, NY: Cornell University Press, 1966.

Nozick, Robert. *Anarchy, State, and Utopia.* New York: Basic, 1974.

Nussbaum, Martha C. "Non-Relative Virtues: An Aristotelian Approach." In *Moral Relativism: A Reader,* edited by Paul K. Moser and Thomas L. Carson, 199–225. New York: Oxford University Press, 2001.

O'Brien, Matthew B. Review of "The Second-Person Perspective in Aquinas's Ethics: Virtues and Gifts," by Andrew Pinsent. *Notre Dame Philosophical Reviews* (December 2010).

O'Brien, T. C. *Summa Theologiae,* Vol. 14 (Ia.103–109), *Divine Government.* Cambridge, UK: Cambridge University Press, 2006.

Oderberg, David S. "On the Cardinality of the Cardinal Virtues." *International Journal of Philosophical Studies* 7, no. 3 (1999): 305–22.

———. "Teleology: Inorganic and Organic." In *Contemporary Perspectives on Natural Law: Natural Law as a Limiting Concept,* edited by Ana Marta González, 259–79. Aldershot, UK: Ashgate, 2008.

Oliver, Simon. "Teleology Revived? Cooperation and the Ends of Nature." *Studies in Christian Ethics* 26, no. 2 (May 1, 2013): 158–65.

O'Meara, Thomas F. "Jean-Pierre Torrell's Research on Thomas Aquinas." *Theological Studies* 62, no. 4 (December 1, 2001): 787–801.

Osborne, Thomas M., Jr. "The Augustinianism of Thomas Aquinas's Moral Theory." *The Thomist* 67, no. 2 (2003): 279–305.

Osler, Margaret J. "Renaissance Humanism, Lingering Aristotelianism, and the New Natural Philosophy: Gassendi on Final Causes." In *Humanism and Early Modern Philosophy,* edited by Jill Kraye and Martin William Francis Stone, 193–208. London: Routledge, 2000.

Pasnau, Robert. Review of "The Ethics of Aquinas," edited by Stephen J. Pope. *Notre Dame Philosophical Reviews* (January 2003).

———. *Thomas Aquinas on Human Nature: A Philosophical Study of Summa Theologiae 1a, 75–89*. Cambridge, UK: Cambridge University Press, 2002.

Pasnau, Robert, and Christopher John Shields. *The Philosophy of Aquinas*. Oxford: Westview, 2004.

Peters, Julia. "On Automaticity as a Constituent of Virtue." *Ethical Theory and Moral Practice* 18, no. 1 (February 2015): 165–75.

Pieper, Josef. *The Four Cardinal Virtues: Prudence, Justice, Fortitude, Temperance*. Notre Dame, IN: University of Notre Dame Press, 1966.

Pilsner, Joseph. *The Specification of Human Actions in St. Thomas Aquinas*. Oxford: Oxford University Press, 2006.

Pinckaers, Servais. "Virtue Is Not a Habit." *Cross Currents* 12 (1962): 65–81.

Pinsent, Andrew. "Aquinas: Infused Virtues." In *The Routledge Companion to Virtue Ethics*, edited by Michael Slote and Lorraine Besser-Jones, 141–54. New York: Routledge, 2015.

———. "Aquinas and the Second Person in the Formation of Virtues." In *Aquinas, Education, and the East*, edited by T. Brian Mooney and Mark Nowacki, 47–72. New York: Springer, 2013.

———. *The Second-Person Perspective in Aquinas's Ethics: Virtues and Gifts*. New York: Routledge, 2011.

Poinsot, John (Joannes a Sancto Thoma). *Cursus Philosophicus Thomisticus*. 3 vols. Edited by P. Beato Reiser, OSB. Turin: Marietti, 1930.

———. *Cursus Theologici*. 5 vols. Sarthe, France: Abbaye Saint-Pierre de Solesmes, 1931.

———. *Cursus Theologici In Primam Secundae Divi Thomae*. 2 vols. Edited by Didacus Ramirez. Alcala, Spain: apud Mariam de Quiñones, 1965.

Pollard, Bill. "Can Virtuous Actions Be Both Habitual and Rational?" *Ethical Theory and Moral Practice* 6, no. 4 (2003): 411–25.

Porter, Jean. *Moral Action and Christian Ethics*. Cambridge, UK: Cambridge University Press, 1999.

———. *Nature as Reason: A Thomistic Theory of the Natural Law*. Grand Rapids, MI: Eerdmans, 2005.

———. "Perennial and Timely Virtues." In *Changing Values and Virtues*, edited by Dietmar Mieth and Jacques Marie Pohier, 60–68. Edinburgh: T&T Clark, 1987.

———. *The Recovery of Virtue: The Relevance of Aquinas for Christian Ethics*. Louisville, KY: Westminster John Knox, 1990.

Rahner, Karl. *Hominisation: The Evolutionary Origin of Man as a Theological Problem*. London: Burns & Oates, 1965.

Ramírez, Jacobus M. *De Fide Divina: In II–II Summae Theologiae Divi Thomae Expositio (QQ. I–VII)*. Madrid: Luis Vives, 1972.

———. *De Habitibus in Communi: In I-II Summae Theologiae Divi Thomae Expositio (QQ. XLIX–LIV)*. 2 vols. Edited by Victorinus Rodriguez. Madrid: Luis Vives, 1973.

———. *De Hominis Beatitudine: In I-II Summae Theologiae Divi Thomae Commentaria (QQ. I–V)*. 5 vols. Madrid: Luis Vives, 1972.

Ray, A. Chadwick. "A Fact about the Virtues." *The Thomist* 54, no. 3 (1990): 429–51.

Rhonheimer, Martin. *The Perspective of Morality: Philosophical Foundations of Thomistic Virtue Ethics*. Washington, DC: Catholic University of America Press, 2011.

Roberts, Robert C. "Temperance." In *Virtues and Their Vices*, edited by Kevin Timpe and Craig A. Boyd, 93–111. Oxford: Oxford University Press, 2014.

———. "Thomas Aquinas on the Morality of the Emotions." *History of Philosophy Quarterly* 9, no. 3 (July 1992): 287–305.

Rogers, Eugene F. "How the Virtues of an Interpreter Presuppose and Perfect Hermeneutics: The Case of Thomas Aquinas." *The Journal of Religion* 76, no. 1 (January 1996): 64–81.

Ross, Lee, and Richard E. Nisbett. *The Person and the Situation: Perspectives of Social Psychology*. London: Pinter & Martin, 2011.

Rota, Michael. "Causation." In *The Oxford Handbook of Aquinas*, edited by Brian Davies and Eleonore Stump, 105–14. Oxford: Oxford University Press, 2012.

Roy, Louis. "Does Christian Faith Rule Out Human Autonomy?" *The Heythrop Journal* 53, no. 4 (2012): 606–23.

Russell, Daniel C. *Practical Intelligence and the Virtues*. Oxford: Oxford University Press, 2009.

Rziha, John Michael. *Perfecting Human Actions: St. Thomas Aquinas on Human Participation in Eternal Law*. Washington, DC: Catholic University of America Press, 2009.

Shanley, Brian J. "Aquinas on Pagan Virtue." *The Thomist* 63, no. 4 (1999): 553–77.

———. "Aquinas's Exemplar Ethics." *The Thomist* 72, no. 3 (2008): 345–69.

Sherwin, Michael S. *By Knowledge and By Love: Charity and Knowledge in the Moral Theology of St. Thomas Aquinas*. Washington, DC: Catholic University of America Press, 2005.

———. "Infused Virtue and the Effects of Acquired Vice: A Test Case for the Thomistic Theory of Infused Cardinal Virtues." *The Thomist*, 73, no. 1 (2009): 29–52.

Simon, Yves R. M. *The Definition of Moral Virtue*. New York: Fordham University Press, 1986.

Spaemann, Robert. "The Unrelinquishability of Teleology." In *Contemporary Perspectives on Natural Law: Natural Law as a Limiting Concept*, edited by Ana Marta González, 281–96. Aldershot, UK: Ashgate, 2008.

Stump, Eleonore. *Aquinas*. London: Routledge, 2003.

———. "The Non-Aristotelian Character of Aquinas's Ethics: Aquinas on the Passions." In *Faith, Rationality, and the Passions*, edited by Sarah Coakley, 91–106. Oxford: Wiley-Blackwell, 2012.

Suárez, Francisco. *Disputationes Metaphysicae*. Vol. 26, *Opera Omnia*. Edited by Carolus Berton. Paris: Vives, 1886.

———. *On Efficient Causality: Metaphysical Disputations 17, 18, and 19*. Translated by Alfred J. Freddoso. New Haven, CT: Yale University Press, 1994.

Swanton, Christine. *Virtue Ethics: A Pluralistic View*. New York: Oxford University Press, 2003.

Tangney, June P., Roy F. Baumeister, and Angie Luzio Boone. "High Self-Control Predicts Good Adjustment, Less Pathology, Better Grades, and Interpersonal Success." *Journal of Personality* 72, no. 2 (2004): 271–324.

te Velde, Rudi A. *Aquinas on God*. Aldershot, UK: Ashgate, 2006.

Thompson, Christopher. "Perennial Wisdom: Notes Toward a Green Thomism." *Nova et Vetera* 10, no. 1 (Winter 2012): 67–80. English edition.

Trianosky, Gregory W. "Virtue, Action, and the Good Life: Toward a Theory of the Virtues." *Pacific Philosophical Quarterly* 68, no. 2 (June 1987): 124–47.

Turkle, Sherry. *Alone Together: Why We Expect More from Technology and Less from Each Other*. New York: Basic, 2011.

Upton, Candace L. "Virtue Ethics and Moral Psychology: The Situationism Debate." *Journal of Ethics* 13, no. 2/3 (2009): 103–15.

Urmson, J. O. "Aristotle's Doctrine of the Mean." *American Philosophical Quarterly* 10, no. 3 (July 1, 1973): 223–30.

Van Tongeren, Paul. "Temperance and Environmental Concerns." *Ethical Perspectives* 10, no. 2 (2005): 118–28.

Van Wensveen, Louke. "Attunement: An Ecological Spin on the Virtue of Temperance." *Philosophy in the Contemporary World* 8, no. 2 (2001): 67–78.

Velleman, J. David. "What Happens When Someone Acts?" *Mind* 101, no. 403 (1992): 461–81.

Vlastos, Gregory. "Reasons and Causes in the Phaedo." *The Philosophical Review* 78, no. 3 (July 1, 1969): 291–325.

Wenz, Peter. "Synergistic Environmental Virtues: Consumerism and Human Flourishing." In *Environmental Virtue Ethics*, edited by Ronald D. Sandler and Philip Cafaro, 197–213. Oxford: Rowman and Littlefield, 2005.

Williamson, Jon. "Probabilistic Theories." In *The Oxford Handbook of Causation*, edited by Helen Beebee, Christopher Hitchcock, and Peter Menzies, 185–212. Oxford: Oxford University Press, 2009.

Wood, W. Jay. "Prudence." In *Virtues and Their Vices*, edited by Kevin Timpe and Craig A. Boyd, 37–58. Oxford: Oxford University Press, 2014.

Wood, Wendy, and David T. Neal. "A New Look at Habits and the Habit-Goal Interface." *Psychological Review* 114, no. 4 (2007): 843–63.

Zagzebski, Linda T. *Divine Motivation Theory*. Cambridge, UK: Cambridge University Press, 2004.

———. "Exemplarist Virtue Theory." *Metaphilosophy* 41, no. 1–2 (January 1, 2010): 41–57.

———. *Virtues of the Mind: An Inquiry into the Nature of Virtue and the Ethical Foundations of Knowledge*. Cambridge, UK: Cambridge University Press, 1996.

INDEX

Abbot Moses, 150–51

abstinence, 9

action: agency and, 99–100, 102; of animals, 100–1; automaticity and, 24–25; becoming virtuous through, 169–71; *duplex regula* and, 44–45; end of, 99; God and, 174, 203; habit and, 24–25, 27, 33; object and, 85–86; in Poinsot, 26–27; prudence and, 46–47, 52; reason and, 43–44; virtue and, 63–64, 135, 136–37, 138–40. *See also* human action

actional virtues, 160–61

Adam, 141–42

Adams, Robert, 63–64, 201–2

addiction, 3–4

agency: in animals vs. humans, 100–101; grace and, 198–99; habit and, 25–27; telic, 99–102

agent, of virtue, 16–18, 168

agonistic facility, 193–94

analytical Thomism, xxi

anger, 111–12

Annas, Julia, xvi

Anscombe, Elizabeth, 87

antecedent passion, 142–44

appetites, bodily, 9–10

Aquinas, Thomas (works): *Commentary on the Ethics,* 15, 48; *Commentary on the Sentences,* 16, 60–61, 63, 143, 185, 193, 199; *On the Power of God,* 65–66; *Summa Theologiae,* xvi, xviii,

xx, 16, 26, 42–43, 52, 59, 61, 63, 77–78, 194, 200; *Treatise on Habits,* 25–26; *Treatise on Morals,* xvi–xvii, 26, 77–78, 151; *Treatise on Temperance,* 16; *Treatise on the Passions,* 134–35; *Treatise on Virtue in General,* xviii, 68, 87, 135; *On Truth,* 76–77, 94, 144; *On the Virtues,* 13, 43, 48, 51, 59, 80, 114–15, 116, 119, 120, 122, 138, 139, 143–44, 169, 171, 174, 175, 176, 177, 181, 183, 192, 194, 195, 203

Aristotelian Thomism, xix–xx, 60

Aristotle, xviii–xix; causes in, 64–65, 77; deliberation in, 101; emotion in, 113; gifts in, 206; "good use" thesis and, 154; habit in, 27, 28–29, 38, 41–42; magnanimity in, 191–92; mode of virtue in, 115; nature in, 38, 94, 180; perfect in, 169; power in, 79; prudence in, 47; temperance in, 8, 17; virtue in, 24, 51, 61, 111, 113, 118, 123, 126n27

art, 151–58

artful errors, 157

atomism, 101–2

Augustine, xvi, xviii–xix, 59–61, 122, 131, 154, 191, 198

authority: despotic vs. political, 140–42; in Poinsot, 141–42; reason and, 141–42; temperance and, 12–13

automaticity, 24–25; facility vs., 33

autonomy, 45–46, 49–50

ABOUT THE AUTHOR

Nicholas Austin, SJ, teaches theological ethics at Heythrop College, University of London. He is the author of several book chapters, essays, and articles.

CPSIA information can be obtained
at www.ICGtesting.com
Printed in the USA
BVHW03s1601130318
510259BV00001B/28/P

9 781626 164734